FINANCIAL MANAGEMENT
FOR
SMALL AND
MEDIUM-SIZED
LIBRARIES

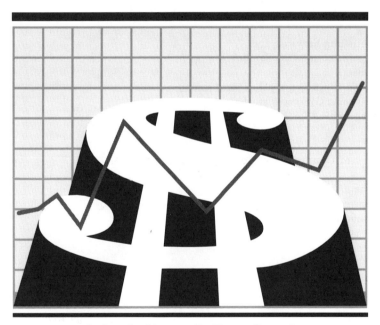

Madeline J. Daubert

AMERICAN LIBRARY ASSOCIATION
CHICAGO AND LONDON 1993

The paper used in this publication meets the minimum requirements of American National Standard for Information Sciences—Permanence of Paper for Printed Library Materials, ANSI Z39.48-1984. ∞

Managing Editor: Joan A. Grygel
Cover designed by Richmond Jones

Composed by Publishing Services, Inc.
  in Century Schoolbook and ITC Symbol
  on Xyvision/Cg8600
Printed on 50-pound Glatfelter, a pH-neutral stock,
  and bound in 10-point C1S cover stock
  by Malloy Lithographing, Inc.

Library of Congress Cataloging-in-Publication Data

Daubert, Madeline J.
   Financial management for small and medium-sized libraries by Madeline J. Daubert.
      p.   cm.
   Includes index.
   ISBN 0-8389-0618-4
   1. Library finance—United States.   2. Small libraries—United States.
I. Title.
Z683.5.U38   1993
025.1′1′0973—dc20   93-1076

Printed in the United States of America.

97 96 95 94 93   5 4 3 2 1

Contents

Scope and Purpose
of the Book

At a time when an ever-broadening range of information services is being provided to an increasingly complex clientele, librarians often are required to fulfill dual roles as information managers and financial managers. Economic realities increasingly require fiscal accountability to a cost-conscious public and corporate world, and the ability to communicate in financial terms is becoming a necessity. Providing the best possible services at the lowest cost requires knowledge of planning, budgeting, and cost control; it is also vitally important to maintain adequate records for financial reporting to internal and external groups.

While most organizations have one or more specialists devoted to financial and accounting responsibilities, libraries traditionally have left many of these responsibilities to the librarian. Because few libraries are independent legal entities, library statistics and accounting data are usually obscured within reports encompassing the organizations of which they are a part. Librarians often have had little control over the limited resources they have been allocated. This situation, combined with the professional librarian's primary dedication to service, has contributed to the fairly low level of financial accountability for libraries in the past. Because economic and financial pressures on libraries have greatly increased during the past few years, librarians who have little understanding or control over their financial resources are at great risk of losing a disproportionate amount of them, while those who earn the respect and confidence of management by demonstrating financial competence are more likely to be entrusted with responsibility for a fair share of an organization's funds. When money is scarce, detailed justification becomes even more critical.

Libraries are being held increasingly accountable by businesses, government offices, auditing teams, and other internal and external agencies. If professional librarians cannot provide accurate and reliable financial information to these agencies, it is likely to be gathered and provided by others whose interpretations and recommendations may not be in the best interest of the libraries and their patrons.

Librarians must understand the financial management cycle of planning, budgeting, controlling, reporting, and evaluating. They must engage in planning and setting attainable goals, including the raising of sufficient money to attain those goals. The librarian and information manager must understand the long-term planning process and the need to carefully define long-term goals and objectives. These objectives need to be further defined and prioritized as short-term goals, to produce budgets that accurately reflect the needs of the organization. The budgeting process must be used as a financial planning tool to allocate resources among programs and to control spending. Revenues and expenses must be continually monitored to ensure that legal and financial obligations are met. Control of spending through proper authorization of purchases, careful recording of items received, and supervision of inventory and disposals are all important factors in successful financial management. Librarians purchase and control relatively large and expensive assets and must be familiar with the processes necessary to track these assets from the purchase order to the financial statements. Equally important, the librarian must be able to communicate the necessary financial information to the accounting staff, comprehend the resulting financial reports, and understand the financial position of the library and its relationship to the parent organization.

This book will address topics in library cost accounting, such as analysis of various types of costs, measurement of unit costs, and allocation of overhead. On many occasions the librarian must be able to acquire or provide specific cost information in order to make an informed decision. The total cost of a product or service is made up of many components in addition to the direct cost; for budgeting and reimbursement purposes it is often important to be able to provide full cost information. It may be necessary to accurately measure the cost of the resources used to provide the information and services that are the output of the library and to produce reports that accurately reflect its performance.

Large-capital projects requiring the use of funds over a long period of time may require additional planning and budgeting skills. It is often necessary to evaluate alternative purchasing and financing techniques in order to arrive at informed decisions concerning the library's future. Knowledge of lease-purchase agreements, bond issues, and other long-term financing arrangements will prove helpful in making informed decisions concerning the capital budget and the long-term goals of the library. The librarian may be called upon to make important investment decisions in order to maximize the use of available funds. While it is doubtful that it will be necessary to learn the intricate details of investing, it is important to have sufficient knowledge to weigh the alternatives and select those that are best for the situation.

Librarians must be aware that they are competing with others for scarce resources. They may be competing for donations and allocations of funds from outside the organization, making it necessary to understand the sources and restrictions on these types of revenues, including possible tax and legal implications. With more and more areas in competition for the resources of the public and private sectors, it is often necessary to explore new and innovative methods to raise funds for expansion, or even for maintenance of existing programs. A knowledge of fund-raising techniques, an understanding of the rules that may govern the use of some of these funds, and the ability to manage large amounts of donated money are skills that often prove beneficial. Some funds have legal restrictions governing their use; it is important that these restrictions be clearly understood so that funds are spent as intended by the donor.

In an age of increasing automation, the contemporary librarian needs to be familiar with the potential of computerized spreadsheet software and integrated accounting systems that can track budgeted and actual expenditures and increase the accuracy and speed of the information process. Often these systems can be used to produce informative reports for use by the librarian or other interested parties inside or outside the organization. The financial impact of other automated library services and their effect on the changing roles of the library also must be recognized.

Because most librarians have limited training in accounting or financial management, this book is intended to provide a framework for understanding those principles necessary for management of the financial affairs of a library. It is hoped that the text will facilitate the reader's ability to function as a knowledgeable member of a larger management team. The book may be used as a complete text in a graduate course in library financial management, as supplemental reading in a library management course, or as a reference for a practicing librarian, board member, or trustee. It is intended to convey the basic principles of accounting, budgeting, and reporting that are common to most organizations, while relating these principles to the successful administration of a library. As financial managers, librarians must understand that, while the primary mission of a library *is not* to provide financial services, it *is* important to be able to finance the true mission of the library. In doing this, it is necessary to talk in terms of money and to measure performance in terms of money.

The information provided in this book is intended to provide librarians and library managers with the background necessary to manage the financial resources of the library, to communicate effectively with other managers concerning financial policies and procedures, and to make informed decisions concerning the use of available funds. This knowledge should enhance the librarian's professional status and will aid all librarians in achieving their ultimate goal of providing the best possible service to their clientele.

■1

The Financial Management Process

As a library manager, you have many opportunities to make decisions that affect the services provided by your library. Many of those decisions are affected by financial considerations, and an understanding of the financial management process is very valuable in obtaining and analyzing necessary information, making wise decisions, and communicating those decisions to others.

Several internal and external factors influence the financial management process of a library. Internally, the organization's structure and purpose and the unique qualities of its staff are reflected in the way its finances are managed to achieve specific goals. Needs of patrons; boundaries established by external funding sources; and current political, legal, economic, social, and technological constraints are all external factors that influence the financial decision-making process.

The form that financial management takes in any library depends on its relation to a parent body. Is the library fully independent and thus totally responsible for its own fund-raising, record keeping, and reporting? If so, the financial management of the library is completely under the governance of its board and its director, subject to its charter rules and to state and federal laws. Or is the library part of a larger organization that establishes its priorities and the means of accomplishing its goals, as well as the way in which funds are received, allocated, expended, recorded, and reported? If this is the case, the structure of the parent organization will determine many of the financial practices that will be followed by the library.

The financial responsibilities of library managers are as varied as the types of organizations of which the libraries are a part. Some libraries have total autonomy over their funds, with the authority to commit funds and to pay invoices. Others have all processing handled through a parent organization but nonetheless find it helpful to be able to track their own transactions in order to better manage the funds available to them. Although the organizational structure determines many of the detailed policies and procedures followed by any individual library, the basic fundamentals of good fiscal management may be learned and applied to all organizations.

The Library as an Independent Entity

Some independent libraries exist as a result of endowments or foundations established for philanthropic or research purposes. Most of those libraries that were established to serve the general public have been absorbed by public library systems; however, a few specialized libraries still remain to serve the needs of unique user groups. Those that remain independent are governed by the rules of their charters; funds are obtained and expended in accordance with the original restrictions of the founders and the laws of the state. The boards and directors of such libraries must recognize the importance of good financial management in the achievement of their library's mission of service.

The Library as Part of a Larger Organization

Economics has played an important role in the history of libraries, and many libraries that were once independent have had to relinquish their autonomy in order to survive. Some public and research libraries began as privately supported independent organizations. Large private collections have been donated to established libraries, while many libraries that previously survived on philanthropic support have been taken over by universities or tax-supported agencies. As a result most libraries today are part of larger organizations, and the financial activities of the library are part of the overall financial picture of the parent. The library must follow the budgeting, accounting, and reporting policies of the parent organization and must maintain sufficient records for later review and audit. A professional accounting staff is often responsible for financial functions such as establishing basic procedures, recording data, and creating reports. The establishment of priorities, the availability of funding, and the general financial procedures to be followed are heavily controlled by the parent organization.

A library that is part of a larger organization is governed by the rules of that organization in most of its financial affairs. Public libraries are part of city or county governments; school libraries are part of school systems; academic libraries are part of universities; law libraries are part of law firms or law schools; and medical libraries are part of medical schools and hospitals. These are only a few examples of libraries that exist as components of larger organizations. Purchasing and accounting practices extend throughout these organizations. Librarians must be knowledgeable about the procedures used and must adopt for the library policies that are compatible with the requirements of the parent organization, its financial staff, and any necessary external parties.

To achieve and maintain the optimum level of library service while dealing with the priorities and regulations established by others requires a great deal of knowledge and skill. By understanding the basic financial structure of your organization and recognizing your library's financial role, you can enhance working relationships and increase your chances of success in managing that part of the organization over which you have some control. Whether your library is a separate legal entity or part of a larger organization, it serves a unique function and therefore is likely to have some level of responsibility for its own financial management. The degree of success achieved in carrying out this responsibility may well depend on your skill as a financial manager.

Types of Organizations

There are two basic types of organizations: business organizations, which exist to make a profit for owners or stockholders, and nonbusiness organizations, which exist to provide services. Nonbusiness organizations include governmental units and nonprofit entities, which share many similarities in their accounting methods and financial procedures. Because of the great value of information in today's society, libraries exist in all types of organizations.

Business Organizations

Businesses are organized for the purpose of making a profit, that is, for revenues to exceed expenses. The success of a for-profit company is usually measured in terms of the profits earned. If revenues are less than expenses, eventually the business is likely to go bankrupt and close. Since expenses of a library may appear to decrease the profits of the business, it is often necessary for libraries in commercial enterprises to justify their existence and continually prove that they are providing cost-effective services. Although it is difficult to measure service in financial terms, it may be vital for the librarian in a for-profit organization to justify some services in terms of money. The cost of a librarian's time and services should be considered in the total cost of the product or service being sold. Information is recognized as a valuable commodity, and the costs of the retrieval and communication of information are acceptable costs to pass on to commercial users.

Libraries that are part of for-profit enterprises are expected to contribute to the earnings of their parent organizations. Such library services are likely to be analyzed in terms of their monetary value rather than their social value, whereas libraries that exist as part of governmental or nonprofit organizations are expected to provide less tangible social benefits to their communities.

There are three basic forms of organization for profit-oriented businesses. A *sole proprietorship* is a business entity in which one person has complete ownership and liability. A *partnership* consists of two or more persons who share ownership and liability as stated in a contractual agreement. A *corporation* is a separate legal entity that may be divided into shares of stock, with ownership and liability limited to the amount of each shareholder's investment.

The types of libraries that are part of for-profit organizations are as numerous as the types of businesses today. Law firms, accounting firms, insurance companies, and newspapers are only a few of the businesses with extensive libraries that play an important part in the operation of the enterprise.

Nonprofit Organizations

A nonprofit organization does not exist for the purpose of making a profit. Instead, it has some other mission, usually to provide service. While for-profit businesses may be organized in different ways, a nonprofit entity is a private organization that must apply for its nonprofit status and the accompanying exemptions by incorporating under the laws of the state. Although state laws may differ, most require that a tax-exempt organization must qualify under Section 501(c) of the U.S. Internal Revenue Code, which stipulates that no income or assets of the organization may be distributed to individuals and that if the organization is dissolved, its income and assets will be distributed either to a similar qualified organization or to the state. Unlike for-profit businesses, nonprofits have no owners, investors, or shareholders. In addition to exemption from federal taxes, these organizations may also be totally or partially exempt from state and local taxes, although certain types of transactions may be taxable.

Certain religious, charitable, educational, and scientific organizations may qualify under Section 501(c)(3) of the Internal Revenue Code, which provides that donations to these nonprofit organizations are tax-deductible. Because the ability to raise funds is often affected by the deductibility of the donations, this distinction may be critical to the existence of the organization. This type of organization is also eligible for preferred postal rates and may be exempt from payment of federal unemployment taxes.

In addition to the legal and tax differences between for-profit and nonprofit organizations, there are many conceptual differences. The performance of a nonprofit organization is not usually measured in financial terms but instead is measured by the extent to which the organization actually provides the services for which it was established. For example, the services of a library may be evaluated in terms of the number of books borrowed or the number of patrons using the library. Resources for nonprofits are likely to come from external sources that do not expect to receive benefits proportional to the assets provided; therefore, the concept of providing services equal to value received does not apply. Because of their concentration on service rather than financial matters, nonprofits have a tendency to have rather poor management controls where finances are concerned. Along with differences in purpose, libraries in for-profit and nonprofit organizations have many differences in their funding sources, budgeting and accounting practices, financial regulations, record keeping, and reporting. The lack of a profit motive is displayed in the accounting records and financial statements. These are designed to show the sources of funding and the purposes for which the funds are used rather than to show profits or losses of the organizations.

Those few libraries with wholly independent status, such as the Huntington Library in San Marino, California, are nonprofit organizations. They follow the accounting rules for nonprofit organizations and provide full financial reporting to the governing board and any interested external parties. Many libraries are part of larger nonprofit organizations, such as churches, private schools, charitable and community associations, and hospitals and universities. These libraries are affected by the rules and regulations that govern the larger parent organizations. A nonprofit organization is part of the private sector and may go bankrupt and close in the same manner as a for-profit business. Nonprofits do not have the taxing powers of a governmental agency to assure continuation of funding.

Government Agencies

Although government agencies do not exist to make a profit, they do not ordinarily close down or go bankrupt. Because of their taxing powers, they may increase taxes to cover debts, and may also default or postpone payments of interest. Government agencies are especially subject to external influences and political pressures, increasing the difficulty of internal management control. However, pressures on the tax base and rising public dissatisfaction with poor government management have made it increasingly important for libraries to do their part in the responsible financial management of public funds.

Today many libraries are part of some governmental unit. Hundreds of libraries serve the numerous agencies of the federal government. Public library systems are operated under the authority of city, county, or state governments; public school libraries operate under whatever agency governs the school system (city, county, or state). Even the libraries of public universities are part of the governmental system.

In most cases, public libraries are governed under state statutes. These statutes grant local governments power to establish public libraries, permit the authorization of tax levies for library purposes, and define the powers and duties of library boards. A public library is usually a division of some other governmental agency and as such is subject to that agency's guidelines for budgeting, purchasing, and controlling assets. School and academic libraries, whether public or private, likewise are governed by regulations that are shared with other divisions of their respective schools and universities.

Common Characteristics of Organizations

While there are many differences among organizations, there are also many common areas. All organizations have some purpose, whether that purpose is to make a profit or to provide a service. A library should develop a clear awareness of the needs of its clientele and the specific mission to which the library is dedicated. The board or governing body may wish to develop a formal mission statement that clearly outlines the purpose of the library. This mission statement then serves as a basis from which to begin the planning process.

All organizations must do some type of planning in order to accomplish their purpose, and the plans usually are converted into monetary terms, or budgets. All organizations should control operations to avoid waste, dishonesty, mismanagement, and error. Finally, organizations must produce reports that illustrate their financial status. They also periodically must evaluate results to assess the accomplishment of the goals and the fiscal solidarity of the operation.

By obtaining, recording, and analyzing significant financial information, and by applying the principles of sound financial management to library operations, it is possible to make informed decisions concerning the planned services in relation to the resources available. Fortunately, many of these principles of financial management are common to all organizations, and knowledge of them is readily transferable from one type of organization to another.

Within any organization it is important to clearly identify areas of responsibility. In large organizations it may be necessary for lower-level supervisors to work through their superiors. It is important, however, that managers who work directly with specific areas be consulted so that their input may contribute to final decisions. Managers should be held responsible only for those areas over which they have a reasonable amount of control and should participate in the processes of planning, budgeting, and supervision of operations. They also should receive reports and participate in the evaluation process. By encouraging the participation of those individuals who are most directly involved with the achievement of objectives, better results may be obtained and staff morale may be increased.

The Financial Management Cycle

The financial management process in any organization follows a pattern that may be called the financial management cycle. The cycle includes four basic steps.

1. Planning and programming
2. Budgeting
3. Operating and measurement
4. Reporting and evaluation

While planning and programming may be sporadic, the remainder of the process tends to be rhythmic and follows a similar sequence month after month, year after year. Plans, however vague, crystallize into budgets that form the financial plan for the operating period to follow. During and after the operating period, reports are produced that assist in evaluating the success of the programs. The evaluation process usually results in some modifications to the organization's plans that, in turn, are reflected in the new budgets to support the operations to follow. Budgets are usually prepared annually, while reports are likely to be produced on a monthly and annual schedule; this repetitive nature of the financial management cycle makes it possible to organize and simplify the process of preparing for future

Figure 1 ▪ *The Financial Management Cycle*

important dates and events. Because these events are fairly predictable, librarians will find it helpful to collect in advance the information that will be relevant to each critical point in the cycle.

Planning and Programming

The first step in the financial management cycle is the planning and programming process during which a library decides on its long-term goals and the broad methods by which it will achieve these goals to carry out its mission. This process is often described as strategic planning. Much of the strategic planning process is very informal, consisting of notes, memoranda, and conversations; the process may be formalized in meetings that result in specific decisions and the identification of specific goals. During the planning and programming phase, the library may begin to estimate some of the costs and benefits that may be expected. Although numerous factors are involved in the planning process, this book is primarily concerned with those factors that affect the financial management of the library. Goals are general statements that need to have specific objectives defined in order to be accomplished. These goals are usually affected by numerous external and internal factors, particularly the availability of funding and the needs and desires of both the funding agency and the library clientele. Political, technological, and economic factors are other important considerations in the strategic planning process.

A key aspect of establishing a library's goals and objectives is identification of the clientele. Public libraries may obtain this information from census data, while school and academic libraries should be in contact with administrators and teachers responsible for program development. Business and special libraries need to identify clearly their patrons and to keep abreast of changes in the business or industry that may affect their clientele. If service is to be provided to users outside the immediate area, those users must also be identified—Is a special library open to the public for research? Does a university library provide materials for local high school or community college students? Do nonresidents use the public library while on lunch breaks from work? What other resources are available in the service area of the library, and what guidelines are to be used in providing service to an expanded clientele? These are all factors to be considered when analyzing costs and establishing priorities.

Various methods can be used to gather data to analyze the services the library is providing (as well as any additional services that may be needed). Daily circulation records indicating numbers and types of materials checked out, attendance counts at various programs, and sample counts of users in specific areas of the library at different times of the day may supply useful data for an analysis of current services. A record of unfilled requests is also helpful in providing information concerning services that are needed or desired but are not being furnished.

In addition to analyzing the current needs of library patrons, changes must be anticipated in order to adequately prepare for the future. A public library in a stable area populated by young families will eventually see a decreasing demand for children's services and more demand for services for the elderly; an urban area in transition from single-family homes to apartments may need an increase in educational and recreational services. A new academic program in a school or university or a new business contract requiring innovative material may indicate a need for expanded or changing services in the libraries that serve these groups. It is important for the librarian to maintain continuous contact with those members of the organization who can provide information on new directions within the organization. Advance planning for these changes can help the library to use its resources to provide the services that are most beneficial to its patrons at any given time.

When the goals of the library have been identified clearly, it is helpful to designate specific programs to accomplish these goals. Programs may be functional, client-oriented, or service-oriented. Functional programs include administration, acquisitions, technical services, circulation, and reference. Client-oriented programs cover children's, young adult, or adult services in a public library; or tax, audit, or legal services in a public accounting firm. Service-oriented programs include branches, main library, bookmobile, or any other type of clearly defined program that fits the library's role. A business, medical, or academic library may choose to define its programs in terms of the departments it serves. Because each library is unique, careful thought should be given to clearly identifying and grouping programs that will be relevant to the planning process for the library concerned. There should be a direct correlation between programs and areas of responsibility so that individuals may be identified to manage and assume responsibility for each program.

After the library's programs have been identified, specific goals and objectives can be developed for each program and decisions may be made concerning the short-term objectives needed to accomplish the goals. For example, a children's services department might have a goal of providing programs appropriate for local children with specific objectives of providing a weekly story hour for preschoolers and a monthly film program for children ages six through ten.

Through an evaluation of its capabilities and an assessment of the external environment, the library can establish definite objectives and select the techniques to achieve them. Current resources are evaluated, and areas needing change are determined. Alternatives are considered carefully, priorities set, and a final list of goals and objectives established. By clearly identifying current and future needs, decisions can be made on whether present levels of service should be maintained, expanded, or diminished. If it is clear that priorities and services are in need of change, new objectives may be established, and a study of specific activities may begin.

Objectives must be stated in measurable terms so that it is clear exactly what is to be accomplished and how, and the means by which the accomplishment may be quantified. Statements should include the specific results to be achieved and the specified time by which these results will be attained. By sufficiently analyzing objectives to determine precise results and dates for accomplishment, it becomes possible to determine the costs of achieving these objectives. For example, a library may decide to increase its book stock from the current 1.5 books per capita to 1.75 books per capita during the next budget year. Because the time period is defined and both books and population may be measured, it is possible to estimate the cost of such an objective and to measure its success at the end of the time period. Obviously some margin of error is needed here, since it is not likely that the library will have an *exact* measure of its population at the beginning and end of the budget year.

The process of identifying specific objectives to accomplish the desired goals requires careful analysis of the library's operations. By stating objectives in measurable terms and by identifying standards of performance, it is possible to evaluate later whether or not the objectives have been met.

Budgeting

The planning phase of the financial management cycle moves from identifying long-term goals to stating the short-term goals and the specific objectives needed to accomplish them. To carry out the goals and objectives formulated during the planning phase, money usually is required. Through the preparation of a budget, the plan of the organization for a specific period is stated in monetary terms. It is important to reemphasize that the budget should be divided into segments corresponding with programs and areas of responsibility. By adhering to this standard, the manager responsible for a given function has input in budget preparation and control of funds assigned to that function.

The budget process also follows a cyclical pattern, usually repeating itself each year, since most budgets are prepared for a period of one fiscal year. A *fiscal year* is a twelve-month accounting period, which ordinarily is chosen to correspond to a natural cycle of business activity. It may be the calendar year, ending December 31, or it may be any other twelve-month period. Most governmental units use a fiscal year that runs from July 1 through June 30, and many companies who do business with these agencies select the same fiscal year. The federal government, however, uses a fiscal year that runs from October 1 through September 30, and it is often necessary to provide information to federal agencies based on the federal fiscal year rather than that of the library. Although this may increase the record keeping needed for budgeting and reporting, it is important in maintaining proper control over federal funds.

The budget is usually a negotiated process and, once completed, becomes a bilateral commitment between the librarian and upper management. The librarian is responsible for providing the planned services with the resources available, and management becomes responsible (perhaps through a higher agency) for providing those resources.

During the budget process, the various programs must be analyzed in terms of their goals and objectives, and funding needed to accomplish each objective must be specified. (Methods of analyzing the costs of these objectives will be discussed in detail in the remainder of this book.) Some objectives may be accomplished without additional costs; others may require further resources. Often there are alternative methods of achieving the desired objectives. It is important to analyze each of these methods and their corresponding costs, since the number of objectives to be accomplished often depends on the funds available. It usually is not possible to obtain funding for all requests; therefore, priorities must be established, taking care to consider both long-term and short-term goals. Activities for subsequent years must be considered during the budgeting process so that those objectives critical to the long-range plan are accomplished as necessary. Through analysis of historical information and future needs, the budget process provides a significant opportunity to obtain valuable information about the financial operation of the library and the services it provides.

Operating and Measurement

Following approval of a budget, the librarian must supervise the operations and assure that records are kept of the resources used, purchases made, and services provided. It is during this period that the principle of financial control becomes important; it is necessary to ensure that funds are being spent in accordance with the approved budget as well as with proper authorization and record keeping.

Specific operational procedures, such as determining how the library handles purchase requisitions, receives materials, and completes payments, may be dictated by other departments of the organization. Regardless of whether some of these processes are handled by other departments or within the library, it is important for the library manager to be able to ensure that all transactions that pass through the library are properly authorized and in accordance with sound accounting practices.

If the governing body has approved a budget for certain purchases and activities, the librarian has an obligation to use the funds for those purposes. The budget functions as a valuable management tool; it serves as a reference point to compare actual activity with planned activity. Because the library and its environment are not stagnant, it is highly unlikely that revenues and expenses will work out exactly as planned—in fact, such an occurrence probably indicates a need for some investigation. The reasons for differences should be understood clearly and procedures should be in place to revise the plan or budget if conditions warrant.

During the operating period many of the library's activities may be measured to determine the success of the library's programs in relation to the plan and to begin the process of evaluating areas in need of change. The operating period is the "action period" in the financial management cycle; although plans, budgets, and reports are only words and numbers written on paper, the activities that take place during the operating and measurement phase determine the final success or failure of the endeavor. Careful attention may be given to the plan and the budget, but if planned activities are not carried out, purchases are not properly made, assets are lost, or services are not provided, an accurate after-the-fact report of the situation will do little to recoup the time lost or to salvage the injury to a library's reputation. Records should be kept of

circulation
reference questions answered
on-line searches completed
attendance at programs
numbers of books purchased
money spent to purchase materials
money spent to provide services

These records provide the statistics with which the library can later evaluate its success in achieving its objectives. (Chapters 3, 8, and 9 of this book will emphasize the financial activities that must be recorded and the manner in which these records should be kept.)

Reporting and Evaluation

Reporting and evaluation should be an ongoing process, although procedures may be in place to provide a formal report and evaluation at the end of a specific time period. Library boards and upper management should be advised on a regular basis of how operations are proceeding in accordance with plans so that corrective action can be taken as soon as possible. Regular reports provide both the librarian and management with information on the success of planned activities and provide a means for evaluating both the library manager and the library program.

Reports should be available at each level of responsibility that has control of operations so that the manager responsible for an area receives information specific to his or her area. If reports include areas outside a manager's responsibility or authority, the manager may find it difficult to act upon the information. The library's reporting system should be compatible with other units of the organization so that items in the library report can readily be viewed as a part of the whole. Following a consistent reporting pattern also simplifies the design and analysis of various levels of reports. Since the report serves as a tool for evaluation, it should be designed so that critical information may be located and understood easily.

In addition to reports that compare budgeted and actual financial information, it is useful to analyze each funded objective in terms of its success. By careful analysis of reports that provide comparative information on the plan and the results of operations, managers may observe areas of strength and weakness. Following evaluation of the long-term plans, short-term budgets and daily operating procedures may be subject to change. Thus, a new cycle begins.

Accounting Standards

Accounting is the method by which financial and economic information is recorded, processed, and communicated to users so that they may make informed financial decisions. Although there are many different types of organizations, certain guidelines allow users outside an organization to understand and interpret the financial information presented. The standards used by business organizations to compile and report financial information are called *generally accepted accounting principles* (commonly known as *GAAP*). These standards allow accountants and financial managers to follow consistent practices leading to broader understanding of information provided, and allow individuals in different organizations to communicate and transfer knowledge effectively. The use of generally accepted accounting principles is particularly important in business organizations, since potential investors or lenders must be able to carefully and accurately analyze the financial position of any companies with which they intend to become involved. Because nonprofit organizations do not have investors and are not likely to seek large loans, the need for generally accepted accounting principles may not be as critical, but their existence provides a useful level of standardization for all accounting information.

Although accountants often refer to *generally accepted accounting principles*, there is actually no official list of such principles and no specific definition exists. The accounting profession has attempted to regulate itself and to improve accounting practice; for several years a number of accounting organizations have had input into the development of accounting standards. Most guidelines are provided by the Financial Accounting Standards Board (FASB), an organization made up of seven full-time members and supported by the business community. These standards serve to provide direction for the establishment of accounting systems and procedures used in a wide variety of organizations. The FASB has stated that nonprofit organizations should use the same accounting standards applicable to all organizations *unless some other treatment is required.* Special situations arise because some activities that occur in nonprofit and governmental organizations do not occur in for-profit enterprises. There also are some topics unique to nonprofit organizations that the FASB has not yet fully addressed.

A primary basis for the differences in financial record keeping between business and nonbusiness organizations is the existence of restrictions that external sources often place on funding for nonprofit or governmental organizations. For example, voters must approve the sale of bonds to finance a new public library building; these voters must later pay the taxes needed to pay off the bonds—and that tax money *must* be used for that purpose. A foundation may contribute funds to provide service to a target group, or an individual may specify that a donation is to be used only for large-print books or children's films. Because of these restrictions nonprofit and governmental organizations are required to keep additional accounting records to separate and monitor the distinct sources and uses of funds. This is not a problem business organizations face and has not been addressed by FASB.

Until the Financial Accounting Standards Board adopts specific guidelines for nonprofit and governmental accounting, it has designated four audit guides issued by the American Institute of Certified Public Accountants (AICPA) as sources of standards for various types of nonprofit organizations. These guides apply to health and welfare organizations, colleges and universities, hospitals, and other nonprofit organizations, including independent nonprofit libraries. Government entities follow similar guidelines provided by the Governmental Accounting Standards Board (GASB), while standards for federal agencies are set by the Comptroller General of the United States. Rules established by the Securities and Exchange Commission (SEC) and the Internal Revenue Service (IRS) also have a significant impact on U.S. accounting practices.

Accounting principles have been developed over a period of many years and are continually changing in response to social and economic conditions. Although there are differences in the accounting procedures used by for-profit, nonprofit, and governmental bodies, an understanding of the basic concepts of accounting will provide the background needed to understand the particular methods used by any organization. In the chapters to follow, this book will provide an overview of the various accounting concepts encountered in libraries and will explain how you can use these concepts to better manage and expand the financial resources available for library services.

System Integration

Information throughout the financial management system should be coordinated so that data collected for some purposes may be reconciled with data collected for other purposes. In some cases it may be possible to have an integrated system that contains complete information for planning, budgeting, operating, and reporting. Such a system would have a common database, which means that all information (data) would come from the same basic source. Because information used in a plan usually is not as detailed as that used in budgeting, operating, or reporting, the plan often is not included in the database. In order to compare operations with budgets and to report on activity, it is usually necessary to include budgeted and actual operating information in the same system, which then can be used for reporting and evaluation.

Information may be contained in a large computerized system or in several small systems that can obtain data from one another. In some cases information may be manually maintained. Whatever system is used, everyone should be working with the same plan, the same budget, and the same reported information so that there are no serious and confusing discrepancies when managers attempt to work together. One helpful way to ensure this is to confirm that all information is dated and clearly labeled and that a consistent list of recipients is maintained to receive specific updated information.

The long-range plan should be expressed in terms that relate to the budget categories used. The same categories should be used for recording the revenues and expenses during the operating period and should be carried through to the reporting process so that information does not have to be continually reanalyzed and reformatted. If possible, the same categories required for reporting should be used for planning, budgeting, and tracking operations. This greatly simplifies reporting and analysis, since information does not have to be categorized more than once. It is not usually difficult to design new reports as long as the required information is contained in the system. As ideas for new programs arise, they should be incorporated in or added to the current reporting structure.

You will often have choices as to the methods you will use to accomplish your library's planning, budgeting, operations, and reporting. As much as possible, you will find it beneficial to integrate the information systems of your library with those of the rest of your organization.

Summary

There are many factors, both internal and external, that affect the financial management process in a library. Among these are the organizational structure of the library and the library's role as an independent entity or a part of a larger organization. Legal restrictions, availability and continuity of funding, management structure, budgeting procedures, purchasing regulations, accounting rules, and reporting requirements all are dependent on the library's organizational status.

An understanding of the continuous flow of information through the financial management cycle provides librarians and administrators with an awareness of the importance of each phase of the operation and its relationship to the whole. The predictable and repetitive nature of the cycle affords the library manager the opportunity to gather information before it is required. Information that might otherwise be missing or difficult to obtain can be pursued as time allows throughout the fiscal year. Through attention to the goals and objectives of the library, analysis of historical information, collection of current operating data, and evaluation of financial and management reports, each segment of the financial management cycle can be used to improve the financial well-being of the library and enhance service to its patrons. It is important to identify areas of responsibility within the library so that each manager has input into the planning and budgeting process and receives regular information on those areas under his or her control. During the operating phase of the cycle, it is necessary to monitor the use of resources to ensure that funds are expended as intended to fulfill the goals and objectives of the library. Review of reports provides the opportunity to evaluate programs and revise plans if needed.

Accounting, which is a system for processing and communicating financial information, has certain standards that are continually being revised to meet the economic needs of a changing society. Accounting systems provide records of the operations phase of the financial management cycle to be used in reports for evaluation by internal and external users. With an integrated system that contains information on planning, budgeting, operating, and reporting, it is possible to understand the relationships between planned and actual activities and to determine the degree of success in meeting financial objectives.

Additional Reading

American Institute of Certified Public Accountants, Subcommittee on Nonprofit Organizations. *Audits of Certain Nonprofit Organizations*. 2d ed. New York: AICPA, 1988.

Anthony, Robert N., and David W. Young. *Management Control in Nonprofit Organizations*. 4th ed. Homewood, Ill.: Irwin, 1988.

Bryce, Herrington J. *Financial & Strategic Management for Nonprofit Organizations*. Englewood Cliffs, N.J.: Prentice-Hall, 1987.

Hendrickson, Kent, ed. *Creative Planning for Library Administration*. Binghamton, N.Y.: Haworth Press, 1991.

Jacob, M. E. L. *Strategic Planning: A How-to-Do-It Manual for Librarians*. New York: Neal-Schuman, 1990.

Lynch, Beverly P., ed. *Management Strategies for Libraries: A Basic Reader*. New York: Neal-Schuman, 1985.

McClure, Charles, et al. *Planning and Role Setting for Public Libraries*. Chicago: American Library Association, 1987.

Prentice, Ann E. *Financial Planning for Libraries*. Metuchen, N.J.: Scarecrow Press, 1983.

Ramsey, Inez L., and Jackson E. Ramsey. *Library Planning and Budgeting*. New York: Franklin Watts, 1986.

Razek, Joseph R., and Gordon A. Hosch. *Introduction to Governmental and Not-for-Profit Accounting*. Englewood Cliffs, N.J.: Prentice-Hall, 1985.

Schauer, Bruce. *The Economics of Managing Library Services*. Chicago: American Library Association, 1986.

Unterman, Israel, and Richard H. Davis. *Strategic Management of Not-for-Profit Organizations*. New York: Praeger, 1984.

■2

Understanding the Budget Process

After identifying the library's mission, programs, goals, and objectives, it soon becomes clear that achieving these goals and objectives requires a financial plan, or budget. A *budget* is a summary of planned expenditures and income for a given time period, usually one year. It is a very important management tool that expresses the plan of the organization in financial terms. When the final budget has been prepared and approved, it provides a guideline for activities to follow. In governmental units the budget is actually a legal document. During the budgeting period, alternatives must be evaluated and choices made concerning the library's activities for the future. Both long-term and short-term objectives must be considered, since each new year builds the framework for future years.

A completed budget answers two questions: "Where is the money coming from?" and "How is the money going to be used?" The first question is answered by planning for sources of support, which includes all sources of funding for planned activities. Support may consist of *revenues,* which are income earned through operations or other types of contributions that may or may not have restrictions on their use. The second question is answered by planning for *expenditures*, which are the specific ways in which the funds will be used to carry out the planned activities. Expenditures include *expenses*, which are the costs of operations, and also include other uses of the organization's resources. The terms *support* and *expenditures* are primarily used in governmental and nonprofit accounting, but because the terms are broader and more inclusive than *revenues* and *expenses*, they will be used in this chapter to explain many of the concepts of budgeting.

A business organization, which exists to make a profit, anticipates its profits during the budgeting period. The difference between budgeted revenues and budgeted expenses is the organization's anticipated *net income*, or profit. In most nonprofit and governmental organizations, the final budget usually stipulates that support and expenditures be equal so that the organization can provide the maximum service possible with available funds. Since the budget is only an *estimate* of revenues and expenditures, changes throughout the fiscal year may necessitate spending more or less than was actually budgeted. If your organization has less revenue than originally anticipated, you will probably be asked to spend less than your original budget may have allowed, and you will have to adjust your plans accordingly.

Occasionally an organization may choose to budget for a surplus to provide a measure of safety or to carry forward money for future years. As the difference between total support and total expenditures, a *surplus* in a nonbusiness organization is comparable to a profit in a business organization. In some cases an organization may choose to draw upon prior surpluses to provide funding for the current year, or it may choose to operate with a deficit, borrowing money to pay for current expenditures. Such deficit spending is rarely considered good financial management. For example, the federal government for years has issued bonds to cover operating expenses that exceeded the amount of other revenues so that the U.S. national debt is now in the trillions of dollars. Even this debt is limited by congressional action so that the federal government may be forced to plan for sufficient revenues to cover most of its expenditures. State and local governments, which cannot print money and whose credit would be jeopardized by the continual issuance of bonds to finance current expenditures, are much more concerned with balancing their budgets and avoiding deficit spending. Businesses sometimes choose to operate with a deficit in the hope that future profits over time will make the venture worthwhile. To do so, however, they must usually persuade lenders that the money borrowed will eventually be repaid.

The budget of any parent organization represents a composite of its smaller agencies. For example, a city budget may include revenues from a variety of taxes, investment income, fines, fees, and service charges and plans for expenditures for programs such as administration, libraries, cultural and recreational services, public safety, and public works. If revenues fall short, a decision must be made to reduce authorized expenditures or to finance them from the surplus that has been reserved for emergencies. Because these reserve funds provide an important safety net, it may occasionally be necessary to budget for expenditures below estimated revenues in order to create a needed surplus.

If expenditures continually exceed the amount of support available, any organization will eventually face severe problems. Because planning for the library's support is often done separately from planning for the expenditures needed to carry out the library's programs, negotiation and compromise usually are required before final budgets are reached.

Methods of Budgeting

There are many different budgeting methods that can be used in the preparation of an expenditure budget for a library. These are not necessarily mutually exclusive, and a combination of methods may best serve the needs of your library. The final budget will usually be submitted to a higher authority, which often determines the final format required. As a librarian, you can design and use the internal budget structure that best suits the needs of your library; the information can later be translated into the budget format needed for the entire organization.

When working with budgets, you will find that a spreadsheet format is very helpful. A *spreadsheet* is an arrangement of columns and rows that allows you to display information vertically and horizontally and to perform calculations on numerical data. Spreadsheets can be purchased in paper form as analysis pads, available in any business supply store, or you may have access to a computerized spreadsheet program. The spreadsheet format lends itself well to arranging the numerous items of information needed in preparing a budget and will help you organize your material in a workable form. Many of the budgeting examples in this book use a spreadsheet format, and you should find it very helpful in the budget process. The columns and rows may be used for either words or numbers, and a great deal of information may be displayed on a single sheet of paper.

Example 2.1 shows how a spreadsheet can be useful in combining the budgets of three separate areas in a library. Each row is totaled horizontally, and each column is totaled vertically. Observe that the total in the lower right is the same whether you add the bottom row horizontally or the right-hand column vertically; this is an important technique for checking the mathematical correctness of a spreadsheet.

Example 2.1 ▪ *Budget Spreadsheet*

Item	*Administration*	*User Services*	*Technical Services*	*Total*
Salaries	$100,000	$ 80,000	$45,000	$225,000
Benefits	25,000	20,000	11,250	56,250
Operations	20,000	40,000	20,000	80,000
Capital	10,000	100,000	5,000	115,000
Total	$155,000	$240,000	$81,250	$476,250

In a spreadsheet like the one shown in Example 2.1, any changes in any column or row would alter the totals; because of the numerous changes often made during the budget process, computerized spreadsheet programs that automatically update totals are very helpful.

Line-Item Budget

The most common budget format used is traditionally known as the line-item budget. This kind of budget is arranged primarily by expenditure lines, such as personnel, travel, supplies, and other items; for this reason it is also known as the *object-of-expenditure* budget. A line-item budget is often required by the parent organization, particularly in the for-profit sector, making it necessary for many libraries to produce their final budgets in this format.

Line-item budgets generally begin with information from the current or previous year and incrementally increase or decrease specific items by projecting cost increases, program changes, and other modifications. Budgets of this type are relatively simple to prepare. The format is easily incorporated into the accounting system, provides readily understood information, and furnishes the framework for financial reports that comply with legal requirements. Because actual revenues and expenditures are usually charged to line-item accounts, this type of budget also makes it easy to compare budgeted and actual revenues and expenditures.

The objects, or line items, used in the budgets of the whole organization generally encompass fairly broad areas. This also allows for some flexibility in the specific items that will be included each year. Once the budget is approved by the governing body, funds may be allocated for each individual object of expenditure. Usually the line items are assigned numerical codes that are consistent with those used in the accounting system. Groups of line items then "roll up" to larger groups that are frequently identified with a numerical prefix followed by Xs. For example, the major personnel codes will probably include separate lines for professional, technical, clerical, student, and temporary employees, all of which are added together in the category Personnel or Personal Services shown as 1xxx in Example 2.2. Fringe benefits also may be included in the Personnel budget, as illustrated in Example 2.2.

Example 2.2 ▪ *Personnel Budget*

Code	*Name*	*Budget*
1100	Professional	$ 50,000
1200	Technical	35,000
1300	Clerical	25,000
1400	Student	6,000
1500	Temporary Help	5,000
1600	Overtime	1,500
1900	Fringe Benefits	26,000
1xxx	Total personnel	$148,500

When line items are budgeted as shown in Example 2.2, it usually is permissible to spend more on one line if less is to be spent on another within the same category—for example, more might be spent on temporary salaries if less is to be spent on regular clerical staff. It usually is *not* acceptable to spend excess personnel funds on such items as supplies or travel, however.

Example 2.3 shows a summary budget worksheet in simplified line-item format. Categories such as personnel, supplies, travel, and books have been budgeted in detail as partially illustrated in Example 2.2, and the totals for each category have been transferred to a summary worksheet.

Example 2.3 ▪ *Line-Item Budget Summary*

Line item	Amount
Personnel	$148,500
Supplies	5,000
Travel	3,000
Books	49,500
Total	$206,000

Line-item budgets tend to allow for incremental increases; because all governing bodies are aware of the effects of inflation, it usually is not difficult to justify increases in most areas. Unfortunately, many areas of library expenditures have recently risen faster than the normal inflation rate. With many agencies making concerted efforts to decrease library funding, increases that may be justified nonetheless might prove unacceptable to funding agencies.

A line-item budget does not associate expenditures with the different functions of the library and has little relationship to the services actually provided. Because the same format usually is used for reporting, information provided to managers and governing bodies focuses on individual line items and may not demonstrate the success or failure of the library's programs or the achievement of the overall goals of the organization. For these reasons a line-item budget may be most effective when used in combination with a program budget.

Program Budget

A program budget focuses on the activities for which funds are to be spent and links the goals and objectives to the budget requests. Program budgeting emphasizes the long-range goals of the library and must begin by identifying the programs that require support. For example, the library's goal of providing materials to patrons in a timely manner might relate to the activities (program) of Technical Services, which would then budget for the specific objectives required to accomplish this goal. After the programs have been identified, it is necessary to define each program's objectives for the budget period and ascertain which activities are necessary to accomplish these objectives. The process concludes by identifying and determining the cost of the resources needed to support these activities.

The first step in preparing a program budget is to identify the services the library intends to provide and to group them into program areas that can correlate with management responsibilities. This should be closely related to the planning process and serves to provide the framework for the budgeting process. The programs can be separated by departments, activities, functions, or whatever structure is most appropriate for the library's particular situation. (Because of these differences, the terminology may also vary, and the budget may be described as a departmental budget, activity budget, or functional budget. Similar principles are applied in preparing each of these budgets.)

Allowing the managers to participate in budgeting provides valuable input and encourages better adherence to the budget after it has been approved. This process is sometimes known as *responsibility budgeting*. Each manager should identify the goals and objectives for his or her program, and alternative methods for achieving each objective should be developed. The cost of accomplishing each alternative must be detailed along with the anticipated effectiveness of each. The alternatives must then be evaluated in relation to the costs identified with each in order to identify the most cost-effective option. This procedure often requires a good deal of information, thought, and good judgment, but it can be very rewarding in beginning the actual process of accomplishing specific objectives for each program. When each alternative has been evaluated, the most cost-effective ways of achieving the objectives of each program should be included in the budget.

Within a large program, such as Library Extension Services, it may be appropriate to create smaller program budgets for services to specific populations of the community, such as the elderly or the blind. These individual program budgets eventually will be consolidated with others to create a budget for the organization as a whole.

Because the program budget requires deeper analysis of the specific goals and objectives of the library, its preparation is likely to be a more complex process than the creation of a line-item budget. However, the information gained during the program budgeting process may be very useful in analyzing historic trends in the library's service and in providing data needed to analyze the cost of specific programs or services. The analysis required to define program objectives and determine needed activities may prove very beneficial in preparation for achieving the goals and objectives of the next fiscal year.

Example 2.4 illustrates a summary program budget prepared for three functional areas—Administration, User Services, and Technical Services. The example briefly states the goals and objectives of each program area and the expenses budgeted to support the program during the new budget year.

Planning-Programming-Budgeting System

Although not widely used, the planning-programming-budgeting system (PPB) is a type of formal programming system widely known in nonprofit organizations. It was first discussed in the 1950s, practiced in government agencies in the 1960s, and officially abandoned by the federal government in 1971. Because the terminology still is used in many organizations, it is helpful to know the characteristics of this budgeting system. Since it is unlikely that you will ever use the PPB system, however, its discussion in this text will be limited, and no specific illustration will be provided.

The PPB system emphasizes programs and activities rather than evaluation and control. It also emphasizes the relationship of benefits to costs. This approach forces its users to practice long-range planning and to review and update programs and objectives frequently. Because PPB system budgets are organized by programs of service tailored to

Example 2.4 ▪ *Program Budget Summary*

Program: **Administration**

Program goal: To ensure the delivery of quality library service to patrons through careful planning, implementation and monitoring of programs, effective management training, and efficient business operations

Program objectives for budget year 1994–95:
- To increase patron awareness of library services through monthly news releases
- To provide each manager with monthly reports concerning budgeted and actual expenses

Program expenses:	Salaries	$100,000	
	Benefits	25,000	
	Operations	20,000	
	Capital	10,000	
	Total		$155,000

Program: **User Services**

Program goal: To provide timely reference services and appropriate materials for circulation

Program objectives for budget year 1994–95:
- To conduct two surveys to measure library usage and quality of service
- To determine the percentage of searches that result in the user locating the desired information

Program expenses:	Salaries	$ 80,000	
	Benefits	20,000	
	Operations	40,000	
	Capital	100,000	
	Total		$240,000

Program: **Technical Services**

Program goal: To provide cost-efficient and timely user access to library materials

Program objectives for budget year 1994–95:
- To analyze cost of cataloging new acquisitions to select the most effective means of cataloging
- To achieve and maintain an average of 28 days to catalog and process new materials

Program expenses:	Salaries	$ 45,000	
	Benefits	11,250	
	Operations	20,000	
	Capital	5,000	
	Total		$ 81,250

Total budget			$476,250

objectives rather than to programs identical with the units of administration, separate units of an organization are forced to coordinate their efforts and resources. Since it is often difficult to formulate goals acceptable to all parties, and because extensive analytical ability on the part of preparers and users is required, the PPB system has not gained widespread acceptance. While the concepts of PPB have been broadly recognized as sound, few organizations have taken the time to provide their staffs with the educational programs necessary to implement the system successfully.

Performance Budget

A performance budget emphasizes the work performed to provide services and may break down services into functional measures of work (input) and service (output). Each part of the organization must closely examine and justify each activity, which is then presented to the governing body as part of the overall picture. The interrelationship of various activities, as well as any duplication or conflict, can be recognized easily. Because the budget focuses on tasks and activities, the narrative description of each project may be very informative for the board, a legislative body, or the officers of the organization. Both input and output are measured, and the results and costs incurred must be carefully monitored, since these results will be used to measure and evaluate performance.

The performance budget allows for the calculation of *unit costs*, which are the total costs associated with one item or unit of service. Example 2.5 shows a simple performance budget for a reference department that expects to answer 80,000 questions (output) at a cost of $100,000 (input). Dividing the input by the output provides the cost of answering one question: $100,000/80,000 or $1.25.

Example 2.5 ▪ *Performance Budget for Reference Department*

Input Cost	Service Provided	Objective	Output	Unit Cost
$100,000	Reference	Provide responses to user questions by phone or in person	80,000	$1.25

Since it is difficult to measure service in terms of dollars, the risk is that the unit of measurement selected may not be the most meaningful one for meeting the true objectives of the library. Performance budgets are more difficult to prepare and understand than line-item or program budgets and are often considered too complex and time-consuming to be of value in the budget process. Elements of this budget concept may be useful in establishing objectives, evaluating alternatives, and identifying and comparing various costs associated with a program or service.

Zero-Base Budget

The zero-base budget system (also known as ZBB) was publicized during the 1970s when its use was attempted in several branches of the federal government. In zero-base budgeting the entire budget must be justified "from scratch"; it is possible that the very existence of the library or one of its departments may need to be justified. Through a complex series of decisions, the budget is then formulated.

The first step in zero-base budgeting is to identify each decision unit whose activities must be budgeted. One decision unit might be the entire library, or it might be smaller departments or service areas. These units should have a direct relationship with the budgetary decision making of the organization, so that costs can be directly identified with each unit. In a worst-case scenario, a local government struggling to balance a budget may require justification for continued funding of each department, such as library, police, fire, and public works; each of these would become a decision unit for purposes of zero-base budgeting. If programs have already been identified for budgeting purposes, these programs may be appropriate decision units for applying zero-base budgeting techniques.

After the decision units have been identified, the activities of each unit are defined and documented in a decision package for comparison with other units competing for resources. Appropriate items for inclusion in the decision package are the overall purpose of the unit, a description of its activities, the benefits provided by the unit, and the consequences of eliminating it. Various levels of performance and effort are considered so that a bare minimum, a status quo, and an increased level of service may all be considered. The first package is a basic one that requires the minimum funding for the unit to exist and states the benefits of the package, the effect of not funding it, alternative ways of providing the services, and the pros and cons of each alternative. Each succeeding package provides information concerning higher levels of service than the previous package and the increased costs and benefits that would result.

A public library might identify a decision unit for each service area, such as Adult, Young Adult, Children's, Reference, and Technical Services. The decision package for Children's Services might include the activities of collection development, preschool story hours, summer reading programs, and Saturday film programs. Each would be ranked according to importance and possible level of service to be provided. The lowest level of service might provide for small additions to the collection, one preschool story hour, a summer reading program, and the elimination of Saturday film programs; the next level of service might provide for more additions to the collection, two preschool story hours, a summer reading program, and one Saturday film program each month. The highest level might request more additions to the collection, two preschool story hours, two summer reading programs, and a biweekly film program. Costs for each level of service must be provided, along with the benefits of providing the service.

The decision packages are ranked by evaluating the cost of each versus its importance in reaching the objectives of the organization. After each department ranks its priorities, one list of prioritized packages is produced for further ranking; those packages deemed worthy of funding are included in the final budget. Each new budget period requires new evaluation and justification of all proposals and all areas.

Ordinarily, however, the decision units would remain essentially the same, and the decision packages would not change a great deal.

One of the primary advantages of zero-base budgeting is that it discourages the continuance of obsolete programs just because they have been previously funded. Zero-base budgeting may also be helpful when funding levels are changed, since the specific costs of various services have already been analyzed. If more funds than anticipated are available, a decision package may be added; conversely, if funding is diminished, the clear identification of the costs associated with each package provides a basis for eliminating certain packages.

Zero-base budgeting requires so much time and paperwork that it is rarely used as a total budgeting technique. While the method may have value because of the amount of in-depth analysis required, it is difficult to identify and justify each activity. There is also a natural tendency for a manager to resist the idea of reduced activity in his or her unit. Elements of this budget method may be useful in prioritizing and budgeting for new programs or equipment, or where no historical data are available. The principles of zero-base budgeting may also be useful in evaluating one-time expenditures and long-term projects.

Formula Budget

Formula budgets are often used in academic libraries where requirements for funds are decided by some predetermined standards of adequacy. These formulas may be used to determine total amounts to be budgeted for books and other library materials or to determine the total funding for the library. Such formulas usually provide specified quantities of materials per student, with possible variations for students enrolled in different programs. The number of units allowed is determined by the number of students enrolled; by multiplying the number of units by the allowable cost of each item, budget allowances may be determined.

Example 2.6 illustrates a simple method of formula budgeting in a state university. The amount of resources allocated to a specific area

Example 2.6 ▪ *Formula Budget for a University*

Academic Level	Dollars per Student Credit Hour	Number of Students	Average Credit Hours per Student	Total Funding
Doctoral—sciences	$1,050	20	9	$ 189,000
Doctoral—liberal arts	530	40	12	254,400
Master's—sciences	650	75	12	585,000
Master's—liberal arts	350	150	12	630,000
Upper undergraduate—sciences	400	600	15	3,600,000
Upper undergraduate—liberal arts	200	950	15	2,850,000
Lower undergraduate	100	3,000	15	4,500,000
Total formula funding				$12,608,400

is determined by the number of students in each program and the average number of credit hours taken by each type of student, using the following formula.

Dollars per student credit hour × Number of students
× Average credit hours per student = Total funding

The same method is often used in academic libraries to determine the amount to be budgeted for books and materials. For example, a public school library may be required to have library holdings of ten books per student. If the projected enrollment is 2,000, and the library currently has 19,000 books, funding would be needed for 1,000 additional books. (If 100 books are to be discarded, funding would be needed for 1,100 additional books.) Using an average cost per book (available from *Bowker Annual*), you could calculate the book budget.

Types of Budgets

Budgets are used for various types of financial plans. The plan for the financing of daily operations is outlined in an operating budget, while a separate capital budget may be required for financing long-term improvements. In preparing these budgets, you may choose to use features from many of the budgeting methods previously described, and the final format probably will be determined by the management of your organization.

Since the operating and capital budgets often plan only for the *total* amount of funding required, a cash budget may also be necessary to determine exactly when funds will be received and when specific disbursements must be made.

Operating Budget

The operating budget, or current budget, is the general-purpose budget used to plan for the activities of a given period, usually one fiscal year. Because the operating budget actually provides for the continued existence of an organization and its activities, it is the basic budgeting document and is a legal requirement of most governmental units and many other organizations. In some cases a *balanced budget* is required by law, meaning that combined revenues and available surplus must be adequate to cover operating expenditures.

Through careful analysis of available financial and nonfinancial information, those activities that will best serve the library's clientele can be selected for funding, and the groundwork can be laid for later expansion or improvement of services. Because the operating budget reflects the priorities of the library, its governing board, and funding body, it can provide a great deal of information on the purpose of the library and the services provided.

In preparing your operating budget, you may use aspects of many of the budgeting methods previously discussed. Prior-year budget and accounting information obtained from your accounting system probably will be arranged by line item, and your final budget may need to be in this format. Your library is likely to have some distinctions among services or functions that will lend themselves to program budgeting techniques. You can use some of the strategies of PPB and performance budgeting to analyze costs and benefits and to evaluate alternatives in view of the associated costs. Perhaps you will be required to prepare a formula budget, or you may use a formula to provide a comparison between your library and some recognized standard. Even though a zero-base budget may not be mandated, some type of zero-base review is desirable to ensure that each alternative is worthy of funding and that the most valuable ones are selected.

It may be useful for each program manager to develop a line-item budget detailing the specific personnel and other operating expenses needed to carry out the desired program. By providing each manager with the same instructions for developing the budget, all budgets may later be consolidated into the final format. For example, if the final budget must be in a line-item format, the specific line-item amounts needed to accomplish each program's objectives must be identified. This can be done through the use of a spreadsheet showing both programs and line items as in Example 2.7.

Example 2.7 ▪ *Program Budget in Line-Item Format*

Line Item	*Technical Services*	*Reference*	*Circulation*	*Administration*	*Total*
		Program			
Personnel	$8,000	$5,000	$6,000	$12,000	$31,000
Supplies	1,000	500	750	900	3,150
Travel	500	300	150	800	1,750
Books	—	2,500	3,000	—	5,500
Total	$9,500	$8,300	$9,900	$13,700	$41,400

Example 2.7 shows a simple budget originally formulated for four separate departments (programs) that has been converted to the line-item format required by the governing body. The totals budgeted for each program are shown by adding the columns, while the totals for each line item are shown by adding the rows. Note that the total in the lower right corner is the sum of the far right columns (added vertically) and is equal to the sum of the bottom rows (added horizontally). This is important in checking the accuracy of the addition.

Capital Budget

The capital budget is a plan for expenditures for long-lived assets, such as land, buildings, and equipment. It is also a plan for the financing of these expenditures, whether from current revenues or through long-term financing. These budgets usually cover a four- to six-year period and can be revised on a regular basis. The capital budget is an important part of the library's long-term plan since it establishes priorities and determines the methods to accomplish the goals and objectives that cannot be financed through current funds. A library's plans for expansion, for example, may be presented in a capital budget requesting a building addition to be financed through the sale of bonds. The initial bond sale would provide funds that would be used to pay contractors as work progressed, and the bonds would be repaid over a period of several years. A plan for improved patron services may be presented through the request for an automated system to be financed through a one-time community fund-raising project. Example 2.8 provides a brief example of a capital budget. This budget shows the item requested, a justification for the request, the amount of funding needed, and the source of financing. The preferred source of financing would usually be determined by the funding agency at the time the capital-budget request is being considered for approval.

Example 2.8 ▪ *Capital Budget*

Library
Capital Budget
1994–95

Project Description	Justification	Amount Requested	Source of Financing
Library building addition	To provide additional space for a growing collection, and to allow for separate facilities for children's programming	$200,000	Sale of bonds
Security system	To reduce numbers of missing materials and related costs of replacement	$ 10,000	Fund-raising project

Items that have significant value (usually more than $500) and a useful life longer than one year are known as *capital assets*, or fixed assets. Examples of these are books, equipment, land, buildings, furniture, and large computer systems. Library books, audiovisual equipment, furniture, and many other long-term assets are usually included in the operating budget because they can be acquired with current funds. Items such as new library buildings, major additions, parking lots, large computer systems, bookmobiles, or other major purchases may need to be funded over a period of several years and are usually included in a separate capital budget.

Whether an item is classified as a capital asset depends on its value and useful life, not the method by which it is purchased. The decision to record an item as a capital asset rather than an operating expense varies among organizations; what is considered a capital asset in one organization may very well be considered too small to be counted in another. Library books, for example, are likely to be considered an ordinary expense in many businesses but would be capital assets in a school, university, or governmental unit. What is of significant value in one organization may not be in another, and books that may have a long useful life in a public or academic library may be virtually useless after one year in a business library. Although a single book is not likely to be of sufficient value to meet the criteria of a capital asset, the aggregate value of a library's collection is significant. Where library service is an important function of an organization, the library's collection as a whole may be considered a capital asset.

Cash Budget

A cash budget is needed to plan for the actual inflow and outflow of cash in an organization. Although an operating budget may summarize activity for an entire year, it does not reflect the time periods when income and expenditures are likely to vary. For example, while personnel costs may be fairly even throughout the year, equipment ordered for the beginning of the fiscal year or interest payments on bonds may create a cash flow problem if not adequately planned for. Also, the release of funds from a governing body or funding agency may not correspond with the actual cash requirements of the library. In a governmental unit tax money may be received late in the fiscal year, although funds may be appropriated to libraries at the beginning of the year or on a quarterly or semiannual basis. Most organizations, whether for-profit or nonprofit, usually have periods in which revenues are higher or lower than others. In instances where the librarian is responsible for actual payment of bills, it is important to determine in advance that the cash will be available at the time it is needed. This can be accomplished by listing expenditures by month and analyzing available funds to determine whether money should be borrowed or expenditures shifted to pay bills as required.

A sample cash budget is shown in Example 2.9. Through careful analysis of the timing of expected support and expenditures, the library is able to meet all of its expenses while investing surplus funds for a short period of time to generate extra investment income. In the example shown, surplus funds in July, September, and October are invested in six-month certificates of deposit, which produce additional investment income when they are cashed in January, March, and April. The numbers in parentheses show that these amounts are being deducted from the surplus. By planning for the receipt of the library's allocation and grant funds and planning the timing of all expenditures, the library is able to meet all its expenses, maintain a small cash reserve, and increase its income through careful management.

Governmental Budgeting

In governmental agencies, the budget provides estimates of expenditures and the sources of financing for the upcoming fiscal year. As much as possible, governmental agencies budget for only those items that may be financed by current estimated revenues. This ensures that estimated revenues and estimated expenditures are equal. Since it is impossible to be totally accurate in these predictions, government agencies carefully monitor their incoming revenues so that authorized

Example 2.9 ▪ Cash Budget

	7/94	8/94	9/94	10/94	11/94	12/94	1/95	2/95	3/95	4/95	5/95	6/95	TOTAL 1994–95
Opening Cash Balance	$25,000	$24,625	$11,550	$29,175	$31,500	$21,425	$10,250	$26,675	$22,200	$14,825	$37,950	$25,675	
Source of cash													
Allocation	20,000			20,000			22,000			22,000			$84,000
Used book sales	100	500	100	100	500	100	100	500	100	100	100	100	2,400
Book fines	125	125	125	125	125	125	125	125	125	125	125	125	1,500
Nonresident user fees	100	100	100	100	100	100	1,000	600	200	100	100	100	2,700
Photocopying	300	300	300	300	300	300	200	200	300	300	300	300	3,400
Annual fund-raiser				6,000	1,000								7,000
Investment income	1,400	400	400	1,400	400	400	1,900	400	1,000	2,100	400	400	10,600
Grants and bequests			35,000					10,000				11,000	56,000
Total cash from operations	22,025	1,425	36,025	28,025	2,425	1,025	25,325	11,825	1,725	24,725	1,025	12,025	167,600
Total cash available	47,025	26,050	47,575	57,200	33,925	22,450	35,575	38,500	23,925	39,550	38,975	37,700	
Uses of cash													
Salaries/benefits	10,000	10,000	10,000	10,000	10,000	10,000	11,000	11,000	11,000	11,000	11,000	11,000	126,000
Utilities & maintenance	500	600	500	600	700	900	1,000	1,000	800	700	500	500	8,300
Travel	300	300	300	1,500	200	200	800	200	300	300	300	200	4,900
Other operating	600	600	600	600	600	600	600	600	1,000	600	600	600	7,600
Library materials	3,000	3,000	2,000	1,000	1,000	500	1,000	2,000	1,000	1,000	900	400	16,800
Equipment							2,500	1,500					4,000
Total cash used in operations	14,400	14,500	13,400	13,700	12,500	12,200	16,900	16,300	14,100	13,600	13,300	12,700	167,600
Net cash available	32,625	11,550	34,175	43,500	21,425	10,250	18,675	22,200	9,825	25,950	25,675	25,000	
Surplus for short-term investment	8,000		5,000	12,000			(8,000)		(5,000)	(12,000)			
Closing cash balance	$24,625	$11,550	$29,175	$31,500	$21,425	$10,250	$26,675	$22,200	$14,825	$37,950	$25,675	$25,000	

expenditures can be reduced if revenues are insufficient. In some cases a balanced budget is required by law. This means that combined revenues and available surplus must be adequate to cover operating expenditures.

It is helpful to understand some of the terminology involved in governmental budgeting since it is used in most public libraries and many academic libraries as well. *Estimated revenues* include investment income, fines, fees, and taxes; expenditures are budgeted as *appropriations*. Operating activities are financed by annual appropriations, which provide the authority to obligate funds during the fiscal year. This authority is also known as *budget authority* and provides the library with permission to purchase the products and services included in the approved budget. Buildings and major items of equipment are funded by continuing appropriations, with spending authority granted for a particular project rather than a particular year. Because the budget of a governmental agency is a legal document, it is very important that budgeted amounts not be exceeded without authorization for budget revision.

The Budget Process

Budget Preparation

The fact that most budgets are prepared annually means that a predictable schedule can be followed. The time and advance preparation required depend on the size and complexity of the organization. It is important to allow sufficient time to do a good job, since some research and analysis is usually required before final decisions can be made. Because price increases, personnel changes, patron needs and requests, and amount of available support are critical items that are continually changing, a budget prepared too far in advance will not make use of the most current information. Time must be allowed to incorporate as many of these factors as possible into the budget process.

One of the first steps in budget preparation is for the governing body or funding agency to formulate budget guidelines and to prepare and distribute budget instructions, including a budget calendar. Expenditure requests are then prepared by individual managers, and estimates of support are prepared by the funding agency. Expenditure requests and estimates of support are consolidated, reviewed, and revised as needed. A budget document is completed and presented to the governing body for approval. Following approval (with further review and revision if necessary), the approved budget is entered in the accounting records. If permitted, budget revisions are made as needed throughout the fiscal year.

Budget Guidelines and Instructions

Prior to the preparation of any budget, certain policy guidelines should be formulated and distributed to the individuals responsible for the actual budget preparation. These policies should be determined by the board or governing body that later will be responsible for budget approval; it is helpful to have a budget committee on the board to provide guidance and review services with the staff. In preparing budget guidelines, consideration must be given to current economic conditions and to the possibility of changes in revenue, taxes, fees, and capital projects, as well as inflationary adjustments and desired program changes. If information concerning general increases or decreases in funding for the following year is available, it should be included in the guidelines.

Guidelines should indicate planned changes in activities, assumptions about salary increases and related personnel policies, general inflation factors to be used in budget preparation, and changes in capital spending. An overall statement may be appropriate, such as a 5 percent increase in salaries and an inflation factor of 4 percent for other items. These guidelines will later be included in the instructions that are given to the managers responsible for budget preparation.

The budget calendar provides information on deadlines and critical dates in the budget process. By allotting a reasonable amount of time to each task and by providing each person involved with a copy of the calendar, the budget process can flow smoothly with minimal risk of misunderstandings. The calendar may be a complex flowchart or a simple listing of dates for various tasks to be completed. It is helpful to identify the individual or department responsible for the completion of each task as well as information that must be provided by one area to another.

The budget calendar should include dates for distribution of instructions, return of initial expenditure requests, preliminary reviews, final revisions, approval, data entry, printing, and distribution of the final budget. It is important to allow adequate time for each of these items so that the budget will be completed and approved prior to the beginning of the new fiscal year. While sufficient time should be allowed for departments to obtain necessary information, it is not practical to begin the formal budget process before realistic projections are made; four to six months should be adequate. Because daily operations should provide frequent feedback in the form of reports, departments should be continually gathering information that might be useful in preparing the next budget.

When the guidelines and budget calendar are complete, specific instructions should be prepared and distributed to all individuals responsible for budget preparation. Instructions should include copies of guidelines, along with required format, worksheets, due dates, and any other potentially helpful details. A copy of the current year's budget should be included with these instructions.

Preparation of a good instruction packet for managers is an important part of the budget process. Basic information that will be needed by everyone should be included in the packet. If instructions are not clear, much time will be wasted in asking unnecessary questions or correcting erroneous or missing information, and there will be duplicated effort in many areas. Depending on the size of the organization, it may be most efficient to communicate instructions for managers at a certain level and assign them the responsibility of compiling the budgets for the managers below them.

Expense or Expenditure Requests

Preparation of a detailed expense or expenditure request requires analysis of historical information and current trends, as well as the assignment of priorities to certain activities. This is likely to be the most time-consuming part of the budget process, requiring much discussion and decision making. The manager who has responsibility and authorization for the expenditures in a certain area should have significant input in the preparation of the budget for that area. This participatory budgeting process has proven to be much more effective than the former practice of imposed budgeting, where upper management prepared the budget and expected lower-level managers to carry out their decisions.

It is important to begin work on expenditure requests long before estimates of support are finalized so that information may be gathered and analyzed and needs may be prioritized well in advance of the final due date. Most budgets involve a series of compromises; expenditure requests are analyzed and decreased while sources of support are carefully examined so that necessary funds may be obtained.

A for-profit company usually prepares a companywide budget that projects anticipated revenues and expenses for the coming fiscal year. Most business libraries simply prepare an expense budget, with the necessary support provided by the earnings of the business. A business is concerned with providing good service to its customers while still maintaining a profit margin, and the changing conditions that affect the business are also likely to affect the library's budget. The library may be provided with more or less resources depending on what is needed to support the company's revenue-producing activities.

In a nonprofit organization that exists primarily to provide services, it is important to budget for the expenditure of all expected support. Not doing so implies that the highest level of service is not being offered. Balancing the expected level of support with the desired level of expenditures is a difficult task in today's economy, and compromises are often needed.

Since many areas of an organization usually are competing for limited funds, the total budget process requires a great deal of research, analysis, and cooperation. Although you will probably be directly concerned only with preparing a budget for your library, you will need to understand and respect the value of other units in your organization and to demonstrate the value of your library's services. Each area has legitimate needs and must select and justify requests so that the budget that finally is approved will include the most beneficial requests. An atmosphere of understanding and trust can greatly strengthen the process of negotiation; by demonstrating a thorough knowledge of the budgeting process as well as the financial affairs of the library and the organization, the librarian may contribute significantly to achieving this atmosphere.

Budget Revision

Changing circumstances may dictate that approved budgets be revised prior to the end of the budget period. One of the most common reasons for budget revision is the organization's failure to collect the anticipated revenues, which requires immediate budget reduction to prevent serious deficits. If such a situation arises, previous budget worksheets providing detailed cost information can be very useful in reevaluating alternatives and selecting areas for reduction that will least harm the library's ability to achieve its long-term goals and objectives.

In today's economy, it is far less common that budgets are revised upward. Increased revenues can simply be added to the organization's surplus or equity and carried forward with budget increases allowed in the new year. In a business enterprise that can correlate increased library activity with increased revenues, it is likely to be more acceptable to increase the current year's budget to correspond with this increase and to immediately provide the additional services required.

Summary

Many different budgeting techniques can be used in libraries, and some combination of these will be appropriate for almost any individual situation. Line-item, program, performance, formula, variable, and zero-base budgets all have features that may prove beneficial in the preparation of a budget. Budgets also serve a variety of functions, providing for short-term and long-term financial planning as well as for cash management over a period of time. Short-term plans are reflected in the operating budget, while long-term plans are reflected in the capital budget. Since the time when cash is available to an organization does not usually coincide with the time that disbursements must be made, it is also important to carefully plan for the inflow and outflow of funds by means of a cash budget.

During the budget process an organization selects its programs and activities by providing the necessary funding; the library, along with others in the organization, must justify its requests. Because of the cyclical nature of the budget process, it is possible continually to gather information and evaluate alternatives for the next budget period so that the library may achieve its maximum potential for service to its patrons.

Additional Reading

Anthony, Robert N., and David W. Young. *Management Control in Nonprofit Organizations*. 4th ed. Homewood, Ill.: Irwin, 1988.

Prentice, Ann E. *Financial Planning for Libraries*. Metuchen, N.J.: Scarecrow Press, 1983.

Ramsey, Inez, and Jackson E. Ramsey. *Library Planning and Budgeting*. New York: Watts, 1986.

Razek, Joseph R., and Gordon A. Hosch. *Introduction to Governmental and Not-for-Profit Accounting*. Englewood Cliffs, N.J.: Prentice-Hall, 1985.

Trumpeter, Margo C., and Richard S. Rounds. *Basic Budgeting Practices for Librarians*. Chicago: American Library Association, 1985.

Turock, Betty J., and Andrea Pedolsky. *Creating a Financial Plan: A How-to-Do-It Manual for Librarians*. New York: Neal-Schuman, 1991.

Van Deusen, Richard E. *Practical AV/Video Budgeting*. White Plains, N.Y.: Knowledge Industry Publications, 1984.

Vinter, Robert D., and Rhea K. Kish. *Budgeting for Not-for-Profit Organizations*. New York: The Free Press, 1984.

∎3

Fundamentals of Accounting

Accounting is the means by which financial information is recorded and processed so that it may be communicated to users. Accounting practices have developed over a period of hundreds of years, and standards are still changing to keep up with a changing world. To understand the many financial responsibilities involved in managing a library as well as to communicate effectively with others involved in financial decisions, you need to have a basic understanding of the accounting process, the underlying principles of accounting, and some of the jargon used by professionals in the financial field.

The concepts discussed in this chapter are intended to give you a basic understanding of accounting and bookkeeping terminology and procedures. If you have sole responsibility for maintaining the accounting records of your library, you should obtain a textbook that provides more in-depth information.

There are several types of accounting, which serve the needs of many different people. *Financial accounting* provides information for external users, such as trustees, investors or contributors, creditors and potential creditors, and any other groups who may be interested in the financial well-being of an organization. It is primarily concerned with the recording of financial information and the periodic preparation of various reports from such records. For example, at the end of the quarterly and annual reporting periods the accounting department reports what is owned (assets), what is owed (liabilities), what revenue has been earned, and what expenses have been incurred. *Management accounting* uses financial information, along with future estimates, to deal with specific problems, identify alternative courses of action, and select the best alternatives. Management accounting systems are designed to supplement the information obtained from financial accounting so that internal users have the information needed to make wise and informed management decisions. While financial accounting is primarily concerned with recording and reporting historical information, management accounting is concerned with communicating this information to users and providing supplementary information and analyses to assist in making decisions for the future.

Because management accounting information is derived from financial accounting, it is useful for library managers to have a fundamental knowledge of the way in which financial information is recorded and reported. At various times you will probably need to keep records and provide accurate financial accounting information; understanding the basic record-keeping procedures and the types of information likely to be needed can prevent a great deal of frustration and miscommunication. This chapter will discuss the fundamentals of accounting, while record-keeping procedures and reporting requirements will be discussed in Chapters 8 and 9.

The Accounting Entity

For financial purposes every organization is treated as a separate economic unit, and the financial affairs of the organization are kept separate from those of its owners and trustees (and from other organizations). This is known as the *entity concept* and is one of the basic concepts of accounting. For example, your library's funds or books should be kept separate from your personal funds or books, a trustee's personal funds or books, or another library's funds or books. This is one of the many reasons why, if you borrow materials from another library, you must ensure that the other library's property is clearly labeled and recorded.

An organization may be divided into several subentities, each with its own accounting records. It is then possible to obtain reports for individual units or for the whole organization. For example, a university may keep its records separate from its hospital, or a public library may keep its financial records separate from those of the police department. To do this successfully it is important that similar budgeting and accounting systems are used in all areas of the organization and that the systems be integrated as much as possible.

Money Measurement

All changes in the financial condition of the organization are measured in terms of money, and each recorded event that causes a financial change is called a *transaction*. Donations of money, interest received on investments, or money spent for salaries or supplies are all examples of monetary transactions that affect the financial situation of a library. Donations of books, buildings, artworks, or other nonmonetary items are valued in terms of money before they are entered in the accounting records. It can be said that money is the common denominator of accounting.

The Account

Because of the many financial transactions that take place in any organization, a method of sorting and filing these transactions is needed. The basic storage unit for accounting data is the *account*, and all transactions that affect a specific account are stored together. Just as librarians classify books and library materials, accountants classify accounts. Similar accounts usually are arranged together. Separate accounts are used for each type of asset, liability, equity, revenue, and expense.

Assets are resources owned by an organization that are expected to be of benefit in the future. Assets may be monetary items such as cash or receivables (money owed to the organization, such as library fines or book-return credits) or nonmonetary items such as land, buildings, books, and equipment. Assets may also include intangible items such as patents or copyrights. Assets likely to be realized in cash or consumed within one year are called *current assets*, while assets intended to last longer than one year are called *long-term assets* and include long-term investments as well as land, buildings, books, and equipment.

Liabilities are the debts of the organization; they may include amounts owed for credit purchases, mortgages, taxes owed to the government, or wages owed to employees. The difference between the assets and the liabilities of an organization is called *equity*; in the form of an equation this may be stated as

$$\text{Assets} - \text{Liabilities} = \text{Equity}$$

In nonprofit organizations the term *fund balance* is used instead of *equity*, and for individuals the difference between assets and liabilities is commonly known as *net worth*. The basic meaning of each of these terms is the same: assets minus liabilities. If your assets are greater than your liabilities, you have a positive net worth or equity and are in reasonably safe financial condition; however, if your liabilities are greater than your assets, you may be in financial trouble. This is true for an individual, a nonprofit organization, or a for-profit business.

Much accounting theory is derived from a simple equation known as the *accounting equation*, or *balance sheet equation*, so named because an important financial statement, the *balance sheet*, takes its format from this equation. Restating in different form the previous rule that assets minus liabilities equals equity, this equation states that

$$\text{Assets} = \text{Liabilities} + \text{Equity}$$

The importance of the balance sheet equation can be illustrated in the example of property with a mortgage. If the property (the asset) is worth $100,000 and the mortgage (the liability) is $80,000, the owner's equity in the property is $20,000. If the property can be sold for $100,000, the $80,000 mortgage could be paid off and there would be $20,000 remaining. If the property is worth only $70,000 but the mortgage is $80,000, the equity would be −$10,000, which would indicate a serious problem. The balance sheet is an important indication of the financial health of any type of organization.

Generally accepted accounting procedures require assets to be recorded at cost; most are not adjusted for changes in market value. If an asset is actually worth less than its recorded value, it may not be sufficient to pay off existing liabilities. This problem is one of many topics currently under discussion in the accounting profession.

In addition to assets, liabilities, and equity, accounts are used to record specific types of accounting activity such as revenues and expenses. *Revenues* are increases in assets an organization earns through its operations. For-profit businesses usually earn revenues through the sale of their products or services as well as through investments. Nonbusiness organizations have these same revenue sources but may also receive restricted-use contributions and grants. Governmental units have access to all of these revenue sources, but they may also assess and collect taxes, which are usually their primary source of revenues.

Expenses, the cost of goods and services used in operations, decrease assets or increase liabilities; as you can see from the accounting equation, the end result is a decrease in equity (or fund balance or net worth). The difference between total revenues and total expenses is called *net income*, or *profit* (or *loss*, if the expenses are greater than the revenues). The expenses of nonprofit and governmental organizations are recorded in the same way as in businesses, except for a difference in timing. To understand this difference, certain accounting terminology must be explained.

When goods or services are received, the organization either pays cash or incurs a liability for the amount of the order. This is called an *expenditure*, and this is the method used by most governmental and nonprofit organizations to record their decreases in fund balance due to operations. Expenditures also include any other payments of cash or incurrence of liabilities to obtain assets or services or to compensate for losses. The actual cash payment (or check) is called a *disbursement*. When speaking in accounting terms, the term *cash payment* usually means the same as a check, since it is not usually good business practice to make payments in cash.

At the time that resources are consumed or benefits are received, an expense is recorded. Because generally accepted accounting principles require that businesses record expenses during the time period that resources are consumed, this is the method used by for-profit enterprises. Since a single purchase may be easily consumed over a long time period, the exact measurement of expenses in a business can involve complex accounting and record keeping. Even in business, reasonable judgment is expected in the amount of record keeping required in relation to the size of the expense.

If you receive $300 in supplies in April, use them in May, and pay for them in June, the expenditure is incurred in April, the expense is incurred in May, and the disbursement is made in June. If you used the supplies evenly over the three-month period, you would allocate $100 of expense to each of the three months. (The expenditure would still be recorded in April and the disbursement would still be recorded in June.) Most nonprofit and governmental organizations record expenditures and disbursements only and make little effort to allocate expenses in great detail unless large amounts of money are involved.

Double Entry

All transactions are analyzed in terms of their effect on the accounting equation, which must always be kept in balance. To ensure that this equation is always in balance, accounting transactions must be recorded in a systematic manner. This is done by use of the *double-entry system,* which means that for every entry recorded in an account, there must be a corresponding entry in at least one other account. (This system has been in use for hundreds of years; the first known description of this system of record keeping was published in Italy in 1494. The author was a Franciscan monk named Luca Pacioli, a mathematician and friend of Leonardo da Vinci.)

The words *debit* and *credit*, derived from the Latin words for *left* and *right*, refer to how an account is affected by a particular transaction. If one account is debited, at least one other account must be credited, and total debits must equal total credits. This is the underlying principle of double-entry bookkeeping and accounting.

The *T account* is often used by accountants to analyze changes in an account. In simple terms, an account may be said to have three parts, one of which is its name. A second part is the left side, called the debit side, and the third part is the right side, called the credit side. This form creates a *T,* which appears as follows:

Name of Account	
Left or debit side	Right or credit side

To understand how a transaction can affect an account, let's look at some very simple transactions in a checking account. The checking account is a simple way to store a variety of transactions; as an analogy, you might think of its balance as a type of equity or fund balance, while the cash in the bank may be considered an asset.

1. You receive a $100 check, which you deposit in your checking account. You are familiar with the phrase "credit your account," but in accounting terms, here is what actually happens.

Cash in Bank	Checking Account
$100	$100

You have credited your checking account for $100, and at the same time you have increased your asset, cash in the bank, with a debit of $100. Notice that the debit entry is on the left side of the T account for Cash in Bank, while the credit entry is on the right side of the T account for Checking Account.

2. Next you write a check for $40 to buy supplies. This has the effect of debiting the account as follows:

Cash in Bank	Checking Account
$100			$100
	$40	$40	

You have decreased your checking account with a $40 debit and have also decreased the cash in the bank with the $40 credit. The difference in dollars between the total debits and total credits is the account balance. As you can see, you will have $60 left in your checking account, represented by the $60 in cash that the bank holds for you. Since there are no liabilities at this time, the accounting equation for this example would be

$$\text{Assets} = \text{Liabilities} + \text{Equity}$$
$$\$60 = 0 + \$60$$

The rules can be summarized as follows:

Assets		=	Liabilities		+	Equity	
Debit for increases	Credit for decreases		Debit for decreases	Credit for increases		Debit for decreases	Credit for increases

Because revenues increase assets, an increase in revenues is recorded with a credit to a revenue account and a matching debit to an asset account. An increase in expenses is recorded with a debit to an expense account and a corresponding credit to either an asset or liability account.

A checking account is a simplified example of accounting. You have probably gone through your checkbook occasionally to locate your expenses for tax-deductible items or to learn how much you spent on your electric bill last year. When you are keeping accounting records, whether for yourself or for your library, you will break down the basic checking account or library account into several smaller and more detailed accounts, such as interest revenue, gift revenue, supply expense, electricity expense, telephone expense, and so forth; and you would use several T accounts instead of one summary account. The principle of the T account and double-entry accounting remains the same.

The Chart of Accounts

Just as libraries keep their books and materials in a certain order, organizations keep their accounts in order by arranging them in a *chart of accounts*. The concept of the chart of accounts is very similar to the classification of books in a library, where books are sorted by the Library of Congress system, the Dewey decimal system, or some other method. Small libraries use less-complex classification systems than large libraries do; this same logic is true for accounting systems. Small organizations may have only a few accounts, while multinational corporations often have thousands. A small organization may use verbal descriptions of accounts, while larger organizations usually identify accounts with numeric codes.

When you are managing funds for a library, you will need to be familiar with the accounts for which you are responsible. The library may have one or more summary accounts, with numerous detailed accounts included in each. Most accounting systems today use some type of numeric codes with one or more sets of numbers to designate the base accounts. Another set of numbers is used to designate the specific types of revenues or expenditures within this base account. For example, the library's base account number might be 25000, with the detail code 100 used for personnel, 200 for supplies, and 300 for books. Items are charged to the detailed accounts 25000–100 for library personnel, 25000–200 for library supplies, and 25000–300 for library books. If other units in the organization also use the same detail codes 100, 200, and 300 (combined with their unique base account codes), it is fairly easy to determine your organization's total costs for personnel, supplies, and books.

The terminology used for these specific accounts varies from one organization to another. The base account may be known as the department, budget center, cost center, or one of many other terms. The detail account may be called a line item, an object code, expenditure code, subcode, or some other name.

To apply the concept of account codes, let's use an example similar to the one we used for the checking account.

1. You receive a $100 check, which you deposit in your library base account 25000. The detail code used for cash is 001, and the detail code used for revenue is 010.

25000–001 Library Cash	25000–010 Library Revenue
$100			$100

You have credited your library revenue account for $100, and at the same time you have increased your asset, library cash, with a debit of $100.

2. Next you write a check for $40 to buy supplies. The detail code used for supplies is 200.

25000–001 Library Cash	25000–200 Library Supplies Expense
$100		$40	
	$40		

You have decreased your supplies account with a $40 debit and have also decreased the library cash with the $40 credit.

3. Combining the two transactions we have the following result.

25000–001 Library Cash	25000–010 Library Revenue	25000–200 Library Supplies Expense
$100			$100	$40	
	$40				

Just as in the previous example, you will have $60 left in your library account, represented by the $60 in Library Cash.

4. Now let's assume that you receive an order for supplies that have not been paid for. The bill for this order is $25, and it will be paid in the next few days. Since you have received the supplies, you now have a liability, or an obligation to pay for them. We will use another detail code, 006, to represent this liability, which is commonly called *Accounts Payable*.

25000–006	25000–200
Library Accounts Payable	Library Supplies Expense
$25	$25

We will assume that you consume these supplies immediately, so that our balance sheet equation looks like this.

(Cash)	=	(Accounts Payable)	+	Equity
Assets	=	Liabilities	+	Equity
$60	=	$25	+	$35

5. Soon the check for $25 is written to pay for the supplies, and the transaction is recorded as follows:

25000–001	25000–006
Library Cash	Library Accounts Payable
$25	$25

6. Combining all the transactions, our T accounts are now:

25000–001	25000–010
Library Cash	Library Revenue
$100	$100
$40	
25	

25000–200	25000–006
Library Supplies Expense	Library Accounts Payable
$40	$25
25	$25

Summarizing the debits and credits in each account, we have a $35 debit balance in the cash account, $100 credit balance in the revenue account, $65 debit balance in the supplies expenditure account, and a zero balance in the accounts payable account. The balance sheet equation looks like this.

(Cash)	=	(Accounts Payable)	+	Equity
Assets	=	Liabilities	+	Equity
$35	=	$0	+	$35

Notice that your equity, or fund balance, did not change, since you used an asset (cash) to reduce a liability (accounts payable).

T accounts are helpful in understanding how the double-entry process works and are often used to simplify problems so that they may be analyzed. For everyday purposes, however, transactions are recorded in journals and ledgers, and it is unlikely that you will actually see T accounts very often.

The Ledger and the Journal

The system used for filing information concerning all the accounts is the *ledger*, which may be either a book containing a page for each account or a computerized accounting system that stores the information on tapes or disks. Originally, ledgers were books containing complete accounting information, usually with one page for each account, such as cash, supplies expense, and the numerous other accounts that might be needed by an organization. These ledgers were referred to as *the books*, and that term is still used today to describe the accounting records of an organization.

It can be very confusing to locate both sides of a transaction in a ledger; for this reason a journal may be maintained to provide a chronological listing of all transactions. The *journal entry* includes the date of the transaction, a description, the accounts that are debited and credited, and the dollar amount. (The relationship between the ledger and the journal is similar to the relationship between a shelflist and an accession list—the ledger is in account order while the journal is in chronological order.) Just as all entries in an accession book must eventually find their way to the shelflist, so must all journal entries be transferred to the ledger.

After information is recorded in the journal, it is transferred to the ledger through a process called *posting*, which may be a manual process or one of the processes in a computerized accounting system. Each amount from the debit column in the journal must be transferred to the debit column of the appropriate account in the ledger; the same must be done with each credit amount. Since every transaction must always have equal debits and credits, the total of all debits in the ledger must equal the total of all credits in the ledger.

Because errors may be made in entering amounts in the ledger, it is necessary to periodically check that debit and credit balances in the ledger are equal. This is done by preparing a trial balance by which the balances in every account are sorted into debit and credit balances, totaled, and compared. Total debit balances should equal total credit balances; if this is not the case, an error has been made in the ledger entries. The trial balance only proves that the debits and credits in the accounts are equal; it does not ensure that entries have been made to the correct accounts or that amounts entered are correct.

Manual bookkeeping systems provide many opportunities for human error and should be checked frequently. Just as automated systems have often replaced accession books and shelflist cards in libraries, modern accounting records are usually kept on computers instead of in paper journals and ledgers, and most accounts are now assigned numbers in addition to names. Computerized accounting systems have many controls that can detect or prevent certain types of errors and usually force the system to be in balance; however, it is still important to check reports on a regular basis to correct the many types of mistakes that the computer cannot detect.

Cash and Accrual Accounting

Initially, most individuals and organizations record revenues and expenses as cash is received or disbursed. This is called the *cash basis* of accounting. This system is simple and is adequate for some organizations, but it does not reflect unpaid bills or other commitments. When analyzing your personal financial situation you know that you need to consider factors such as a mortgage, credit card debts, or car payments. If a library has several outstanding invoices or payroll obligations, the cash basis of accounting may not reflect the library's true financial situation. To consider all of an organization's assets and liabilities and to obtain a complete financial picture, more complete accounting information must be obtained. This information is presented on an *accrual basis.*

The purpose of accrual accounting is to record revenue when it is earned and to record expenses when they are incurred. This is done by application of the *matching concept of accounting.*

Through the matching rule, revenues must be assigned to the accounting period in which they were earned, and expenses must be assigned to the period in which they were incurred. Because many organizations plan, budget, and report for specific time periods and because profits or losses must be determined for specific time periods, it is important that both revenues and expenses be correctly allocated. By adjusting the accounts to show unrecorded expenses and revenues and by allocating transactions that affect more than one accounting period, the cash basis of accounting is converted to an accrual basis.

To help you understand some of the differences between cash accounting and accrual accounting, think of the differences between a check and a credit card. When you write a check, the cash may be immediately deducted from your account; however, when you use your credit card, you have incurred an expense and a liability but have not yet disbursed the cash. With accrual accounting, it does not matter whether or not the cash has been received or paid for an item or service; if the legal commitment exists, the transaction must be recorded.

The cash basis of accounting is *not* in conformity with generally accepted accounting principles, but it is easier to understand and easier to implement than accrual accounting. Often the cash basis of accounting is used for daily operations, and adjustments are made at the end of the year to convert the cash basis to an accrual basis so that financial statements can be prepared.

In some small organizations there may be a need for very few adjustments, and the cash basis of accounting may provide a reasonably accurate picture of the organization's financial condition. Most large organizations, whether for-profit, nonprofit, or governmental, now prepare financial reports on an accrual basis in an attempt to comply with generally accepted accounting principles. The accrual basis of accounting and reporting provides a much more accurate picture of an organization's true financial condition than the cash basis.

Examples of library situations that commonly require adjustments to convert from cash to accrual accounting are books that have been received but not paid for (unrecorded expense), fines that have been charged but not received (unrecorded revenue), annual insurance premiums that were paid at midyear (prepaid expense to be allocated partially to the new fiscal year), or advance payments from patrons for future information-retrieval time (unearned revenue to be allocated partially to the new fiscal year). Entries for interest due or payable often need to be recorded as adjusting entries since the cash payments do not always coincide with the ending date of the fiscal year.

The Modified-Accrual Basis of Accounting

Many nonprofit and governmental organizations use a *modified-accrual* basis of accounting, which is a conservative compromise between the cash and accrual accounting methods. In this type of accounting revenues are recorded in the period in which they are measurable (meaning that the amount may be stated in terms of dollars) and available (meaning that they are collectible for use during the current accounting period). Therefore, the modified-accrual basis of accounting recognizes revenue when it is collectible as opposed to when it is earned. Tax revenues, which are reasonably assured of being collected, are recognized when due just as in the accrual method. Because of the uncertainty of collecting such revenues as membership dues and book fines, the modified-accrual basis of accounting does not record these as revenue until the cash is received.

The modified-accrual basis of accounting records expenditures as liabilities are incurred (usually when goods or services are received). For simplicity, prepaid expenses and the value of supplies on hand are often ignored when the modified-accrual method is used. If you have responsibility for providing the financial accounting staff with adjustments for revenues and expenses that have not already been recorded on the cash basis, it is important to clarify which accounting method is being used and what information is required.

Closing the Books

You probably summarize some of your library information on a monthly or yearly basis. Circulation records, reference assistance, and other services are often totaled on some regular basis for reporting or comparison purposes. Accounting information is also summarized at regular intervals. Most organizations do some monthly review in preparation for the official review that takes place once a year. By reviewing records periodically, errors may be found and problems dealt with before they become serious.

The primary accounting period used by most organizations is the fiscal year, which can be any twelve-month accounting period. At the end of each fiscal year, organizations usually review their financial status and prepare for a fresh start in the new fiscal year. Cumulative totals are prepared to show total revenues and expenses for the year being completed as well as the current financial condition of the organization. Then, revenue and expense accounts are cleared to begin the new year at zero, and net income (the difference between total revenues and total expenses) is added to the equity (or fund balance) of the organization. (If expenses exceed revenues so that a net loss is incurred, this is deducted from the equity or fund balance.) The process of completing adjusting entries and clearing the revenue and expense accounts is called the closing process or closing the books. (Most accounting departments also follow a monthly closing process that may or may not include making adjusting entries. This procedure encourages accounting information to be checked on a regular basis and assists in identifying the timing of many transactions.)

Assets, liabilities, and fund balances are considered permanent accounts because the balances are carried forward from one accounting period to the next. Revenue and expense accounts, however, are considered temporary because their balances are closed to fund balance at the end of the annual fiscal period. The new fiscal year begins with all year-to-date information at zero so that revenues and expenses are recorded for the new year and can be compared with budgeted and historical information.

Fund Accounting

If your library is part of a for-profit business, you probably have a library account that helps to keep your library expenses separate from the expenses of the rest of the organization. However, all revenues and expenses are eventually netted together to produce one total net profit or loss for the business. The balance sheet lists the assets and liabilities for the business as a whole, and the financial statements reflect the enterprise's success or failure in achieving its purpose: to make a profit.

A nonprofit or governmental organization exists to provide services and obtains money from various sources to provide those services. In some cases the source of funds (donors, taxpayers, or a governing body) may specify the purpose for which the funds are to be used. Voters may restrict use of some resources, such as money from the sale of bonds that have been approved for certain purposes. Bequests and donations to nonprofit and governmental organizations are often made with certain restrictions; the organization has a legal obligation to use these funds as specified by the donor.

Because of these characteristics, nonprofit and governmental organizations use *fund accounting*, in which money is separated according to its intended purpose. The resources of the organization are divided into distinct financial units, or funds, each of which functions as a separate entity. Each fund has a set of self-balancing accounts, which means that the assets must equal the sum of the liabilities and fund balance; each fund may have a complete set of financial statements and records. Although separate accounts are maintained for each fund, for reporting purposes funds with similar characteristics are usually grouped together. Because fund accounting allows an organization to keep track of money intended for different purposes, it is possible to evaluate the financial status of each individual area.

Restricted and Unrestricted Funds

Fund accounting also classifies funds as to whether they are restricted or unrestricted. Restricted funds reflect limitations placed on the use of resources by some party outside the organization. Donations made for a specific purpose, grants or contracts to support a specific activity, or bonds approved by voters to finance a specific project are all examples of restricted funds. These funds can be used only for the purposes specified by the donor or grantor at the time the funds were donated or the contract was signed. The donor may direct that the income from these funds also is to be restricted. Since there is a legal obligation to spend them only for the purposes the donor has designated, such funds must be kept separate. It is important to understand these restrictions prior to accepting the funds since some obligations may be impossible or undesirable to fulfill.

Unrestricted funds can be used for any purpose that furthers the organization's stated mission and is legally consistent with its terms of organization. Unrestricted funds may be obtained through earnings or contributions. In some cases unrestricted funds may have an advantage over restricted funds because the board or governing body is allowed greater discretion in using them.

To understand the principles of fund accounting, you might think of your personal finances in terms of funds. Perhaps you have a checking account for everyday needs, a savings account for long-term needs, and a retirement account. The checking account and savings account are unrestricted, and you may do as you wish with them. However, the retirement account has restrictions placed upon it by your employer and/or the federal government.

There are several variations in the fund names used among different nonprofit or governmental organizations. Funds can be categorized according to the characteristics and needs of the specific organization. Some of the most commonly used funds are current funds, plant funds, endowment funds, and agency funds.

Current Funds

Current funds usually are intended for current operating purposes during the present fiscal year. The various current funds are sometimes combined and called the operating fund, since this is the fund that finances daily operations. It may consist of both restricted and unrestricted funds. Current unrestricted funds have no external restrictions on their use, although by law they must be used to support the tax-exempt purpose of the organization. *Designated funds* are unrestricted funds that have been set aside by the governing body for a specific purpose; since these funds are not legally restricted, the governing body has the right to change this purpose at any time.

Current restricted funds must be used only in accordance with the specifications of the donor or grantor. They may be used for operating purposes as long as this use meets the legal requirements. Money received with such restrictions actually is not recorded as revenue until it has been spent as required by the donor. Instead, it is recorded as a direct addition to fund balance, with an equal liability stating the obligation to either perform the required services or return the funds.

Endowment Funds

Endowment funds may have been contributed to the library by a donor who has specified that the contribution is to be used for an endowment. The original amount of the endowment, called the *principal,* must generally be maintained and only the earnings from the principal may be used for operating purposes. Such a restriction is legally binding, and this type of contribution is called a *true endowment* or *permanent endowment.* In contrast, a *term endowment* provides that the principal will become available at some specified future time.

Quasi endowments are established by the board of directors; therefore, they may be changed at the board's discretion. Usually the purpose of establishing a quasi-endowment fund is to set aside the principal for the purpose of earning additional income; only the earnings are used for operating purposes. If necessary, however, it is legally permissible for the board to use quasi-endowment funds for operating purposes, although it would normally do so only in case of a financial emergency. Creating a quasi endowment for long-term use is comparable to designating funds for current use since the funds *may* be used at the board's discretion.

The income earned from endowment funds is usually available for operating expenses and may be used for general operations unless the donor's original gift stipulates a specific purpose. There may be restrictions on the type of investment that may be made by the fund as well as how the income is to be used. For example, income might be required to be used for purchasing books, maintaining a children's library, or enhancing a collection of nonprint media. Such restrictions should be considered when preparing the annual operating budget so that items that may be purchased with money from a restricted fund are not duplicated in the unrestricted budget.

Plant Funds

Plant funds are used to record transactions related to the acquisition, financing, and replacement of long-lived assets such as land, buildings, books, and equipment. The plant fund maintains records of the assets and any indebtedness incurred for their purchase. Assets are recorded at cost and remain on the records at their historical value until removed.

Because most libraries purchase books through the operating fund, librarians are sometimes surprised to learn that these books are listed on the financial statements as assets of the organization. Over a period of several years, the cost of these books is often significant. The cost of books and collections may be easily determined through the purchasing records, but it is also important that the library keep track of deaccessions and disposals so that the stated values may be reduced by the appropriate amount.

Plant funds are divided into as many as four subgroups.

1. *Unexpended plant funds* represent resources designated for the acquisition of long-lived assets. An example would be the proceeds of a bond issue to finance a new building; the money would remain in the unexpended plant fund and would be used as the building was being built. When assets are acquired, the costs are transferred to the investment-in-plant fund.

2. *Investment-in-plant* funds represent the capitalized value of long-lived assets. Donated assets are recorded at their fair market value at the time of donation, and other assets are recorded at cost. This fund is used to maintain a listing of all the organization's fixed assets, such as land, buildings, books, and equipment. Any liabilities associated with these assets also are recorded in this fund.

3. *Funds for renewals and replacements* are used to account for resources that will finance renewal or replacement of long-lived assets. An example would be money reserved to purchase a new heating system or to replace a roof. As these assets are replaced or repaired, costs are transferred to the investment-in-plant fund.

4. *Funds for retirement of indebtedness* are for payment of principal and interest charges on any loans used to purchase long-lived assets. In governmental agencies, this fund is called the *debt service fund*.

Just as new acquisitions of books and equipment are recorded as assets of the library, it is equally important to record the removal of any of these assets. Since these items are included on the financial reports of the organization, the accounting department must be notified of discards and losses before the financial statements are prepared each year. If original costs of equipment are recorded on an inventory list and the costs of books and audiovisual materials are recorded on the shelflist card, it is a fairly simple matter to determine the cost of materials that need to be eliminated from the library's assets. Shelflist cards for discarded materials may be removed during weeding and stored together until the information is needed by the accounting department at the end of each fiscal year. By totaling the original costs of the lost or discarded materials, the dollar amount of the adjustment can be determined. To maintain a computerized shelflist, a system for recording deaccessions for later removal from the accounting records needs to be in place.

Agency Funds

Agency or *fiduciary* funds involve a trust relationship in which the organization is entrusted with the management of funds that do not actually belong to it. Common examples are pension funds, trusts, and employee payroll withholding. Since the total amount of the assets is owed to the true owner of the funds, the assets and liabilities are equal and the fund balance in these funds is always zero. For example, if you hold $1,000 in cash that is owed to the IRS for tax withholding, you also have a liability to the IRS for $1,000. This results in a net fund balance of zero.

Perhaps your library keeps the accounting records for a library club or a local Friends of the Library group. Because these organizations are separate from your library, their financial affairs would be properly maintained in an agency fund.

Transfers Between Funds

In nonprofit or governmental organizations it is often necessary to transfer money from one fund to another. Even though the money remains within the same organization, transactions involving more than one fund must be recorded in the accounts. If there is a legal requirement to transfer funds (for example, if funds must be transferred to repay a bond), a mandatory transfer is made. If the transfer is made at the discretion of the governing body, it is a nonmandatory transfer.

If there are temporary borrowings between funds, the fund that makes the loan will record the amount as an asset, and the fund that receives the loan will record it as a liability. If transfers between funds have not been completed, the fund that owes the money shows a liability, while the fund to which the money is owed shows an asset on its financial records. This characteristic of recording transfers, assets, and liabilities between funds is unique to fund accounting.

Most of the basic accounting principles used in fund accounting are the same as those used in standard business accounting. Transactions are analyzed and recorded in accounts; adjustments are made as needed to close the accounting period; and financial statements are prepared. Fund accounting simply has an additional feature of separating each account into a group, or fund, according to its purpose. Because transactions must be recorded between funds, there is likely to be more accounting activity than is needed in similar business situations where these different fund groups do not exist.

Summary

Accounting is the process by which financial activity is recorded, analyzed, summarized, and reported. Librarians often record financial information and must provide accountants with important data. It is therefore important that librarians understand the language of accounting to communicate with financial managers and to interpret financial information provided to them.

The cash basis of accounting records transactions when money is received or disbursed. This type of accounting ignores money that may be owed to the organization or that the organization may owe to others. To show all of the assets and liabilities of the organization, adjustments are made to the accounts to convert them to the accrual basis before financial statements are prepared. The accrual basis of accounting uses the matching concept to assign revenues to the period in which they were earned and expenses to the period in which they were incurred. Nonprofit and governmental organizations usually use a modified-accrual basis of accounting that reflects revenues as they are collectible and expenditures as goods or services are received.

Nonprofit and governmental organizations receive their funding from outside sources that have the right to restrict the use of those funds. They use a method called fund accounting. In addition to the accounting methods used by business organizations, fund accounting separates accounts into groups, or funds, according to the ways in which the funds are to be used. Each fund functions as an individual entity and should be kept separate for purposes of budgeting, operating and measurement, and reporting.

Additional Reading

American Institute of Certified Public Accountants. Subcommittee on Nonprofit Organizations. *Audits of Certain Nonprofit Organizations.* 2d ed. New York: AICPA, 1988.

Bryce, Herrington J. *Financial & Strategic Management for Nonprofit Organizations.* Englewood Cliffs, N.J.: Prentice-Hall, 1987.

Gross, Malvern J., Jr., and William Warshauer, Jr. *Financial and Accounting Guide for Nonprofit Organizations.* Rev. ed. New York: John Wiley & Sons, 1983.

Hay, Leon B., and John H. Engstrom. *Essentials of Accounting in Governmental and Not-for-Profit Organizations.* Homewood, Ill.: Irwin, 1987.

Herbert, Leo, et al. *Accounting and Control for Governmental and Other Non-business Organizations.* New York: John Wiley & Sons, 1987.

Razek, Joseph R., and Gordon A. Hosch. *Introduction to Governmental and Not-for-Profit Accounting.* Englewood Cliffs, N.J.: Prentice-Hall, 1985.

Smith, G. Stevenson. *Accounting for Librarians and Other Not-for-Profit Managers.* Chicago: American Library Association, 1983.

———. *Managerial Accounting for Librarians and Other Not-for-Profit Managers.* Chicago: American Library Association, 1991.

■ 4

Analyzing Library Costs

How much does it cost?" All too often the answer to that question determines whether we can carry through those projects we most want or need. The branch of management accounting that deals specifically with costs is known as *cost accounting*. In long-term planning, budgeting, operating, reporting, and evaluating the programs and services of the library, an understanding of the principles that determine the real cost of specific products or services can assist you in making wise decisions. Obtaining detailed information on costs may be helpful in choosing budget alternatives, justifying additional funding because of hidden costs, or accurately identifying specific dollar amounts for situations in which some cost recovery is justified. When several similar libraries calculate the costs of similar activities, it becomes possible to compare costs and to discover areas in which efficiency can be improved. Such a comparison may provide ideas for attainable objectives for the new budget year as well as a means to measure performance at the end of the year.

The ability to provide accurate information concerning service costs may be extremely important if it becomes necessary to recover some of the costs from those using the services. A public library serving users outside the community may decide to charge these users a flat fee for a library card. It may charge a fee based on the number and type of services provided; it may even obtain some financial support from another funding agency. A city library that provides services to adjacent areas may obtain some funding from the county or nearby cities; the ability to provide specific data on the number, type, and cost of services provided will greatly enhance the possibility of obtaining such funds. Complete analysis of costs can be especially important in business libraries or other special libraries where the cost of library service is often billed to the department or client that uses the service. Hospitals and universities that obtain external funding for research may reasonably request reimbursement for some of the costs of operating their libraries; such requests should be supported with documentation.

There are several types of cost studies that are useful in libraries and information services. It is helpful to understand these, to be aware of their potential benefits and drawbacks, and to know which type of cost information is likely to be appropriate in a given situation.

Cost Analysis

Cost analysis provides basic information and data for other cost studies. It requires measurement of the resources used and understanding of the work completed. For example, analyzing the cost of cataloging library materials requires a basic understanding of the cataloging process and how time and resources are used in cataloging.

Cost analysis provides the data needed to complete a selected cost study. In particular, it deals with the question "What does it cost?" The first step is to define "it," the product or service being analyzed. "It" may be the process of cataloging a book, answering a reference question, creating a purchase order, or writing a check. Following this determination, the method of cost analysis must be selected.

Cost data may be obtained through fairly exact measurement techniques or through estimates. The more precise the cost study, the more expensive it is likely to be. Since it takes time and money to obtain information for cost analysis, only enough material necessary to make a decision should be gathered. It is important to make a judgment on the quantity of data required as well as the level of accuracy needed; these may vary with the purpose of the study. For example, if you have decided to provide a book-delivery service for the elderly, it takes very little analysis to determine whether the books may be delivered least expensively by a volunteer rather than by the library director or a library clerk. However, if you decide to charge for such a service, you would need much more-extensive information to decide on a reasonable fee. Similarly, information used internally to choose the cheapest alternative does not need to be as complete as information that must be presented to an outside agency in a request for funds.

A simple cost analysis often can be done using estimated information. Such a study can be completed within a short time and can provide sufficient information for internal decision making and comparison. A great deal of cost data is usually obtained during the budgeting process; this information can be used for cost studies with very little additional effort or expense. Other possible sources for dependable estimates are expense reports or brief surveys.

Fixed and Variable Costs

Costs that remain the same regardless of changes in the volume of services are called *fixed costs*. Examples of this are rent, building depreciation, and certain salaries. Costs that change in direct proportion to the amount of service are called *variable costs*. For example, the cost of supplies used in book processing would vary depending on the number of books purchased.

Some costs may change according to, but not in direct proportion to, changes in volume. Expenses for utilities might increase slightly if additional hours are added, but since there is usually a basic service charge and some utilities are in use even when the library is closed, the increase would not be in direct proportion to the increase in hours. This type of cost is called a *semivariable cost.*

To analyze costs and to make intelligent decisions, the librarian must be aware of which costs are fixed; without major changes in service (eliminating the library director or moving the library to smaller quarters, for example) these costs will not change. Therefore, they must be planned for, and no decisions concerning them need be made. Awareness of this fact can help simplify the budget process, since there is little value in scrutinizing costs that cannot be changed. However, variable and semivariable costs need to be carefully analyzed to determine the true costs of possible service alternatives, the total effect of possible changes, and the optimum level of service that can be offered with the funds available.

Direct and Indirect Costs

Many costs may be assigned to a specific activity; these costs are known as *direct costs.* In a library's reference area, for example, these would include salaries for the reference librarian and staff, purchases of reference materials, and furniture and equipment acquired for the reference area. In addition to these obvious costs, however, many indirect costs are also essential to the operation of the library. *Indirect costs* (also known as *overhead*) do not relate to specific activities; instead, they serve many areas and exist even if one or more activities are discontinued. Examples include a portion of the cost of the technical department that processes reference materials, administrative staff that handles the library's payroll and personnel functions, custodial services, utilities, and any other functions the reference department shares with the larger library or organizational unit. The full cost of a given program or activity is the total amount of resources used for that program or activity; to determine the full cost the indirect costs must be added to the direct costs.

Analyzing Personnel Costs

Personnel costs make up a major portion of the expenses of any organization. By carefully analyzing the time required to provide a service and the salaries and benefits of the individuals who provide it, reasonably accurate cost data can be obtained. To determine the personnel cost to be assigned to a certain function or activity it is often adequate to estimate the time spent on various activities and to multiply this time by the appropriate salary rate.

If precise information is required, time studies and work measurement may be appropriate; in this case, employees record time spent on specific activities. First, the activities must be carefully defined so that information is consistent and so that data obtained from each employee can be easily merged with data from the others. Although this procedure is necessary to provide accurate cost data, its application is often difficult and time-consuming.

If a time study is deemed necessary, it is important to obtain the cooperation and understanding of the staff. Requests for time studies are often met by staff resistance. Some employees may feel that time-keeping is demeaning to their professional status or that job performance is being measured. It is important to record both productive and nonproductive time and to keep the time-keeping system as simple as possible. Quarter-hour increments are adequate; half-hour increments may be preferable. If the data are to be converted to decimal form, this fact needs to be considered in deciding the time increments to be recorded. Because careless time-keeping will invalidate the study, accurate measurement must be stressed.

The period of measurement also must be carefully analyzed. Due to seasonal variations, it may be necessary to maintain time-keeping information for a long period or to provide a sample of data from different periods during the year. It is important to use a time period that is long enough to obtain a valid estimate.

Salary rates for clerical and nonexempt employees are usually provided on an hourly basis; hourly rates of salaried employees can be calculated by dividing the annual salary by the number of hours worked per year. To determine the cost of productive time, the annual salary should be divided by the number of hours actually worked.

For example, assume an employee with an annual salary of $20,000 is scheduled to work 40 hours per week for 12 months. The worker has 10 vacation days and 10 paid holidays; although each worker is entitled to 10 sick days, the average worker uses only 6 of these. In addition, each employee has two 15-minute breaks each day. Stated on an hourly basis, one year of work would be 2,080 hours (52 weeks times 40 hours) or 260 8-hour days. Simply dividing the annual salary of $20,000 by 2,080 hours would give an hourly wage of $9.62. However, several other factors must be considered to arrive at a more accurate hourly rate for productive time.

First, the fact that the employee does not actually *work* 2,080 hours must be considered. Although the worker is paid for 260 days, deductions must be taken for vacation (10 days), holidays (10 days), and sick time (6 days)—leaving 234 days of work. Since each employee takes two 15-minute breaks, the workday is actually only 7.5 hours long. This takes the number of hours worked during the year down to 1,755. If the $20,000 salary is divided by 1,755 hours, an hourly rate of $11.40 is obtained. Depending on the employee's function and the particular cost study desired, it may also be appropriate to deduct time spent in staff meetings or other time that does not contribute to the production of work.

Since fringe benefits are also provided by the organization, the salary cost for the worker is not the only cost incurred by the library. At the very least these will include some costs for FICA and Medicare taxes, worker's compensation, and unemployment insurance and will probably include costs for life and health insurance and retirement plans as well. In determining wage and salary rates to use for cost studies, it is important to include the cost of fringe benefits, since these are a significant expense of the organization.

Depending on how they are paid by the organization, fringe benefit costs can be determined through various acceptable methods. You might be able to calculate each individual's fringe benefits by calculating the exact amount of FICA and Medicare taxes, unemployment compensation, and other benefits. However, a fringe benefit rate for the whole organization often may be calculated by determining the total year-to-date expenditure for fringe benefits and dividing this amount by total year-to-date payroll costs. For example, if your organization has spent $50,000 on wages and salaries and $12,500 on fringe benefits, the fringe benefit rate is 12,500/50,000, or 25 percent. You should be able to obtain this information from your accounting or human resources department. Assuming that the fringe benefit rate for your organization is 25 percent, an employee with a salary of $20,000 receives a fringe benefit of $5,000, so the total cost for the employee's services to the organization is $25,000. Therefore, it is more appropriate to value the employee's time using the $25,000 figure rather than the previously mentioned salary of $20,000.

Using the total salary and benefit cost of $25,000 and the adjusted figure of 1,755 productive hours, the actual hourly rate for productive time is $25,000/1,755, or $14.25. As you can see, this is significantly different from the original estimate of $9.62!

An employee's hourly productive rate is only one of the factors needed to determine the cost of accomplishing a certain task. If you wish to know the average cost of one unit of service, you need to measure the units completed, such as books cataloged or reference questions answered. Perhaps you are trying to determine whether it is more cost effective to do in-house cataloging or to purchase this service from an outside vendor. To determine the in-house cost, you would need to know the number of items cataloged, the amount of time spent, and the employee's hourly rate, as well as any materials required to do the job. A more complete discussion of unit costs follows later in this chapter.

It may be important to know just how much time is spent on certain functions. You may want to assign an employee's time to specific tasks, such as administration, circulation, cataloging, or reference services. In this instance a time sheet such as the one shown in Example 4.1 might be helpful.

Analyzing Other Costs

In addition to measuring hours worked, it is important to record the cost of all other items directly related to the service or product being measured. For example, reference books are necessary to provide reference service, while book cards and pockets may be required for processing. These costs must be added to the personnel costs already identified to provide complete data for calculating the costs that may be attributed to a particular service or product.

Example 4.1 ▪ *Time Sheet for Cost Study*

Department _____ Name _____ Date _____

Show time spent on each task; enter time in tenths of hours.

Task number	1	2	3	4	5	6	7	8	9	10	Total
Time spent											

Task names and numbers

1	Administration	6	Reference
2	Training	7	Circulation
3	Cataloging	8	Processing
4	Purchasing	9	Inventory
5	Maintenance	10	Billing

Cost Allocation

Cost allocation studies identify supporting activities and determine reasonable methods of allocating their costs to the programs that they support. While direct costs usually are easily identified with their appropriate activities, indirect costs require careful analysis and must be distributed among their various purposes. To accomplish this the indirect costs must be identified and some acceptable basis of allocation determined. This may be a percentage of time, space, or whatever measure most accurately reflects the allocated product or service. Allocating costs with total precision may require much more-detailed analysis than is cost-effective; therefore, allocation of indirect costs, while providing increased accuracy of total cost, is not likely to be 100 percent accurate. Cost allocations and distributions are usually done using retrospective information, although budgeted data may also be used if it is more accurate.

When indirect costs are allocated among the library's programs so that the full cost of each service is determined, new approaches to budgeting and decision making may be developed. If outside funding is available, or if costs are being recovered from outside sources, it may be possible to justify recovery of full cost rather than direct cost of service. Understanding the full cost of a service can be important in selecting alternatives, such as deciding whether to purchase outside cataloging services or do in-house cataloging.

Identifying Cost Centers

To distribute costs among the appropriate areas, it is necessary to identify and collect these costs in cost centers. Frequently, these cost centers are identified as various departments, programs, or activities, and some costs are already being distributed to them. Examples of cost centers might be a reference department, a branch library, or a bookmobile. If data can be used in a form in which it has already been collected, cost allocation will be easier and less expensive than if a new cost study is required. In some cases, however, information may be desired on an area that is not already isolated; then, it is necessary to collect and assign the relevant costs to that area for the purposes of a study.

Some parts of an organization exist for the sole purpose of providing services to other parts. These may be described as *service centers*, and their associated expenses are a type of indirect cost. Those areas that provide service directly to the organization's clientele may be referred to as *program centers* or *mission centers*. To determine the full costs of the programs, those costs that may be identified with the service centers should be allocated to program centers. The service centers for a library might include Administration, Maintenance, and Technical Services, while the program centers might be Reference, Adult Services, Children's Services, and Circulation.

Direct Allocation of Costs

The simplest method of distributing service costs to programs is through *direct allocation*, where the direct costs of each service center are distributed among the various programs that use the services. For example, the cost of custodial services might be allocated to each program based on the number of square feet of building space each program uses.

The Step-Down Method of Allocation

Because service centers provide service to other service centers as well as to program centers, the direct allocation of service costs to program centers has serious weaknesses. These may be corrected by the use of the step-down method of allocation, where costs are first allocated to other service centers and later to the program centers. There is no reverse allocation of costs, which makes the sequence of steps in the allocation an important decision in spreading costs. There also is no allocation of costs across program centers, although in fact one center may provide service to another. The method provides a reasonable level of accuracy through fairly simple means and, therefore, is likely to be adequate but cost-effective. Example 4.2 illustrates the process of step-down allocation.

In Example 4.2, the $1,000 of Administration costs are allocated first, with $250 to Maintenance, $100 to Technical Services, $400 to Program 1, and $250 to Program 2. Total Maintenance costs are then $450, which are allocated next with $100 to Technical Services, $200 to Program 1, and $150 to Program 2. The Technical Services costs then total $500, which are allocated with $300 to Program 1 and $200 to Program 2. Each of these indirect costs is added to the direct costs of Program 1 and Program 2, showing the full cost for each program. Note that the total of the direct costs of the service centers and program centers in column (1) is $7,500, which is equal to the total costs of the two programs after allocation in column (5). The costs of Administra-

Example 4.2 ▪ *The Step-Down Allocation Process*

	(1) *Direct Costs*	(2) *Adminis- tration*	(3) *Main- tenance*	(4) *Technical Services*	(5) *Total Program Cost*
Administration	$1,000				
Maintenance	200	+ $250			
Technical Services	300	+ 100	+$100		
Program 1	4,000	+ 400	+ 200	+$300	= $4,900
Program 2	2,000	+ 250	+ 150	+ 200	= 2,600
Total	$7,500	$1,000	$450	$500	$7,500

tion, Maintenance, and Technical Services have been fully allocated to the two programs through the step-down process.

Example 4.2 shows the step-down process using a predetermined basis of allocation (which is not shown). The basis of allocation and the order in which allocations are made are very important in achieving a reasonable degree of accuracy in the step-down method. Service departments must be carefully analyzed to determine the bases and order of allocation. Example 4.3 illustrates a step-down allocation and shows the basis of allocation.

To analyze the departments to determine the bases and order of allocation, Administration is selected to allocate first because it serves everyone through personnel, payroll, and related functions. Total direct costs for Administration are calculated, and a basis of allocation is determined. In the case of Administration, the number of employees in each department is a reasonable basis. Ignoring the number of employees in Administration (since there is no purpose in allocating expenses to itself), costs then are allocated based on the remaining thirteen employees. The $50,000 of administrative costs are allocated as follows:

3/13 ($11,538) to Maintenance, which has 3 employees
2/13 ($7,693)　to Technical Services, which has 2 employees
3/13 ($11,538) to Reference, which has 3 employees
2/13 ($7,693)　to Children's Services, which has 2 employees
3/13 ($11,538) to Adult Services, which has 3 employees

Then, each of these costs is added to the direct costs of each area.

Maintenance costs, which now total $33,538, are then allocated based on the number of square feet in each department. Because there is no reverse allocation, the square footage used by Administration is ignored, and only 10,500 square feet are allocated. The $33,538 of Maintenance costs are allocated as follows:

30/105 ($9,582) to Technical Services
20/105 ($6,388) to Reference
25/105 ($7,985) to Children's Services
30/105 ($9,582) to Adult Services

These costs are also added to the previous costs.

Example 4.3 ■ Step-Down Allocation Showing Basis of Allocation

Cost Center	(1) Basis of Allocation	(2) Number of Employees	(3) Square Feet	(4) Processed Books	(5) Direct Costs	Allocated Service Center Costs			Total Program Center Costs
						Administration	Maintenance	Technical Services	
Administration	No. of Employees	4	2,000	—	$ 50,000				
Maintenance	Square Feet	3	—	—	22,000	$11,538			
Technical Services	Books Processed	2	3,000	—	42,000	7,693	$ 9,582		
Reference	—	3	2,000	2,000	30,000	11,538	6,388	$ 7,903	$ 55,829
Children's Services	—	2	2,500	5,000	20,000	7,693	7,985	19,758	55,436
Adult Services	—	3	3,000	8,000	25,000	11,538	9,582	31,613	77,733
Total		17	12,500	15,000	$189,000	$50,000	$33,537*	$59,274*	$188,998*

*Difference due to rounding.

Technical Services now has $42,000 in direct costs plus $7,693 allocated from Administration and $9,582 allocated from Maintenance for a total of $59,275. This cost is then allocated among Reference, Children's Services, and Adult Services, based on the number of books processed for each department.

2/15 ($7,903) to Reference
5/15 ($19,758) to Children's Services
8/15 ($31,613) to Adult Services

Thus, the full cost of each department may be calculated.

Reference = $30,000 + 11,538 + 6,388 + 7,903 = $55,829
Children's Services = $20,000 + 7,693 + 7,985 + 19,758 = $55,436
Adult Services = $25,000 + 11,538 + 9,582 + 31,613 = $77,733

Note that the full costs of the three programs are

$55,829 + 55,436 + 77,733 = $188,998.

This is approximately the total direct costs of the service centers plus the program centers. The difference is due to rounding.

Other bases of allocation might prove more accurate in other situations. Example 4.3 would probably be more accurate by using time expended for each department as a basis of allocation, but this would require detailed time-keeping for employees in Administration, Maintenance, and Technical Services. It is doubtful that the additional accuracy would be worth the time required.

Reciprocal Allocation

Because the step-down method of allocation does not permit reverse allocation, it is slightly inaccurate and may be significantly affected by the sequence of the step-down process. (For example, you might wish to repeat Example 4.3 allocating the Maintenance department first and Administration second and compare the results.)

A more accurate allocation method is the *reciprocal method*, which is performed by a set of simultaneous equations. Because there are as many equations as there are service centers and program centers, this method can become quite complex and ordinarily will be used only when a computer model is available.

Benefits of Cost Allocation

Cost allocation studies help show the relationship among various parts of an organization and the role of each in the larger environment. They show the importance of indirect costs and point out the risk of developing budget projections and cost saving measures without taking these into account. These studies can be extremely helpful in long-term planning, budgeting, and management review, as well as for purposes of analyzing and comparing the true costs of various programs. Valid comparisons can be made by considering the full costs of various programs compared with their relative values in fulfilling the mission of the library.

When the costs of service departments are recognized, the actual effect of changes in programs can be predicted and budgeted more accurately. Such information can be particularly useful in cases where some cost recovery may be involved. The ability to demonstrate the full cost of a program to a governing or funding agency may be instrumental in obtaining the increased funding needed to cover all or part of the indirect costs. When considering services where some reimbursement may be necessary, analysis and allocation of costs can provide excellent support data for determining the amount to be charged.

Unit Costs

Often it is desirable to know the unit cost of a particular function or process, such as the cost of processing one book or the cost of providing service to a patron. To calculate the unit cost of any function, the total cost must be divided by the number of units. Total cost information may be gathered from cost allocations as shown in Examples 4.2 and 4.3; or specific information concerning time and materials used for a particular project may be collected and analyzed.

By dividing total costs of an activity by some measure of output the average cost per unit (for example, the cost of cataloging one item) can be determined. In determining unit costs, the unit of measure must first be determined. In libraries, units are often defined in terms of services, such as technical processing, reference assistance, circulation, interlibrary loans, and instructional services. These also can be broken down to determine costs of services in various departments, such as Children's Services, Adult Services, branch libraries, and bookmobiles.

Examples 4.2 and 4.3 demonstrated a method of calculating the full cost of operating a program or department. These calculations may be carried further to determine the unit cost of a specific function within a department. In Example 4.3, Technical Services processed a total of 15,000 books, at a full cost of $59,274. The unit cost of processing one book can be calculated by dividing $59,274 by 15,000 books, or $3.95 per book. If Reference, which operated at a full cost of $55,829, served 60,000 patrons, the average cost (or unit cost) per patron served was $55,829/60,000, or $0.93.

Determining the unit costs of specific functions within Technical Services would require a further breakdown of departmental output, such as the percentage of time spent in acquisitions or cataloging. If Technical Services determines that 40 percent of its productive time is devoted to acquisitions and 30 percent to cataloging (with the remaining 30 percent involved with other processing functions), the unit cost of acquiring and cataloging a book may be determined. If the full cost of operating the department is $59,274, then 40 percent ($23,709) of that cost is due to the acquisition function. If 15,000 books are acquired, the unit cost per book acquisition is $23,709/15,000 = $1.58. If the unit cost of processing had already been calculated as shown in the previous paragraph, this same result could be achieved by multiplying the processing cost ($3.95) by 40 percent (the percentage of processing time devoted to the acquisition function). The result would still be $1.58 ($3.95 × .4). The same procedure could be followed to determine the unit cost of the cataloging function.

While it is interesting to have information that reflects the costs of individual activities, it must be remembered that the result usually provides only average costs. Because of this, the unit costs are not likely to be entirely accurate for any individual case. They do, however, provide helpful information for making financial decisions. For example, in deciding whether to do in-house cataloging or purchase outside services, unit cost information is very helpful. Such analysis might be further broken down to determine the individual costs of cataloging children's books, fiction, and nonfiction so that a combination of in-house and purchased services might be used. Because of the many variables in each cost study, it is important not to rely heavily on unit costs as performance indicators.

Determining an Indirect Cost Rate

Government contracts usually allow for the recovery of indirect costs as well as direct costs of completing a project. The amount of allowable indirect costs is determined by the use of an indirect cost rate, or *overhead rate*. The calculation of the overhead rate for federal purposes is subject to regulation and negotiation; unallowable items are not included as either direct or indirect costs. The indirect cost rate is determined by dividing total indirect costs by total direct costs.

$$\text{Indirect cost rate} = \frac{\text{Total indirect costs}}{\text{Total direct costs}}$$

For example, an organization with $50,000 in indirect costs and $100,000 in direct costs would have an indirect cost rate of $50,000/$100,000, or 50 percent.

Universities and research organizations often receive grant funding to accomplish certain tasks. These grants cover many types of direct costs, such as salaries, supplies, and equipment directly related to the research project. When an organization applies for grant funding, a request also may be made not only for recovery of direct costs associated with the project but also for recovery of indirect costs (overhead). Therefore, many agencies are able to recover some of their indirect costs associated with these grants. For example, if the direct costs of a project are determined to be $200,000 and the indirect cost rate is 50 percent, the amount of recoverable indirect costs is $100,000. As you can see, complete analysis of indirect costs can be very important to an organization!

The Library as Overhead

The previous discussion centered on the determination of various costs and their allocation within the library. As part of a larger organization, however, the library often becomes one of the many indirect cost centers, or service centers, of that organization. A business library exists to serve the business, a medical library exists to serve a medical school and hospital, and a university library exists to serve the university. The costs of operating these libraries are indirect costs of the larger organization, and a need may exist to determine these costs for the purpose of allocation or recovery.

If the library applies for a grant, in addition to the direct costs it anticipates, it may request recovery of a portion of the indirect costs that support the library, such as maintenance and utilities. In the case of an independent library, the costs of operating the service centers of the library are the indirect costs.

If the parent organization applies for a grant, it also may include a request for indirect cost recovery, including those costs incurred to provide library service. In this case, the library is a service center of the parent organization and all its expenses are part of the indirect costs. Occasionally a grantor requires that an organization provide services equal in value to a portion of the grant; the value of indirect costs may be used to fulfill all or part of such a requirement. Whether you are responsible for determining the indirect cost amounts or are simply providing information to others working on such requests, an understanding of the concepts and importance of cost accounting will prove worthwhile.

Cost-Effectiveness and Cost-Efficiency

Cost-effectiveness studies are used to determine which of several alternative methods performs best according to the given criteria at a given level of costs. Cost-effectiveness is usually consistent with cost-efficiency, which attempts to provide a given level of output at a minimum cost. The objective of cost-effectiveness is to minimize costs; the objective of cost-efficiency is to maximize service. Data must be obtained through cost analysis or cost estimation.

Cost-effectiveness focuses on achieving the highest level of service or performance at a given level of costs. This type of analysis may be helpful to the library in determining how well it is accomplishing its objectives in providing service to its clientele. Since the levels of library expenditures are usually determined by several outside factors, the ability to provide the highest level of service for the lowest cost is important. For example, changing a special program from Thursday to Saturday may increase the number of patrons served without any additional cost. Service may be measured in terms of numbers of users served, attendance at special programs, percentages of satisfied users, numbers of books acquired or circulated, processing time for new books, or other criteria that reflect the objectives of the library's programs.

Cost-efficiency focuses on achieving a given level of service at the lowest cost. Measurement of unit costs provides one measure of the efficiency of an operation; if unit costs can be lowered without reducing the level of service, the library is operating on a more efficient level. If you can reduce your processing costs by processing children's books in-house, for example, you have reduced your costs and thus achieved increased efficiency. By carefully analyzing data collected for the determination of program costs and unit costs, it may be possible to determine potential areas for cost reduction.

During the library's planning process, specific goals and objectives are identified along with the criteria for accomplishing these objectives and evaluating performance. Both cost-effectiveness and cost-efficiency may be used as performance indicators, but it is important to use a number of performance measures so that individuals will not concentrate on one area to the detriment of others.

Cost-Benefit Studies

Cost-benefit studies compare costs with benefits for the purpose of evaluating alternatives. They are more likely to be used to make long-term decisions than for short-term analysis and are particularly useful in making capital investment decisions, such as evaluating major investments or purchases of fixed assets.

Cost-benefit analyses are usually undertaken for the purpose of determining the value of an activity or an investment in relation to its cost. For service organizations such as libraries, benefits are usually measured in terms of service, which is difficult to compare with costs since service is often abstract and difficult to measure in monetary terms. If there is a direct relationship between costs expended and services provided, a subjective judgment must be made as to whether the services are worth the cost.

When both costs and benefits can be measured in monetary terms, a cost-benefit analysis may be very beneficial. For example, if the cost of mailing an overdue notice is sixty cents, it is not reasonable to mail notices for fines of thirty cents, since the cost would be greater than the benefit. Although this is an exceptionally simple illustration of cost-benefit analysis, it does portray the concept in monetary terms.

If two alternatives are available, the preferred choice is the one that provides more benefits for the same cost. If benefits are equal, the preferred choice is the one with the lower costs. To make a decision, there must be some way to relate the benefits to the costs. Care must be taken to ensure that there is a true connection between costs and benefits and that comparative proposals have similar objectives. (More detail on the topic of cost-benefit analysis is included in the discussion in Chapter 6.)

Cost-effectiveness, cost-efficiency, and cost-benefit studies all focus on the concept that the benefits of a program should merit its cost. By combining cost-benefit analysis with cost-efficiency and cost-effectiveness studies, intelligent decisions concerning the use of resources can be made. It often is not necessary or feasible to undertake a formal study to make a wise decision concerning the relationship of benefits to costs; common sense and good judgment may be adequate.

Summary

Cost studies can be used to determine the true costs of services provided and can be helpful in budgeting and controlling these costs. The ability to analyze costs and use cost data effectively can be very useful in planning for the library's future and in making good management decisions. With a thorough understanding of the various options available and the costs associated with each of those options, alternatives can be evaluated for long- and short-term planning, and short-term costs can be predicted with reasonable accuracy when creating the annual budget.

In addition to the direct costs of providing library services, there are many indirect costs that must be considered when analyzing full costs. The ability to analyze and allocate indirect costs can be valuable in determining the full cost of a product or service or when calculating unit costs for comparison purposes. The information can be used to recover some of these costs from clients or funding sources, to compare costs with associated benefits, or to aid in other decision making. Since in various situations library services may be considered either direct or indirect costs, librarians should understand how a careful and accurate analysis of library costs may be important to both the library and the parent organization.

Additional Reading

Anthony, Robert N., and David W. Young. *Management Control in Nonprofit Organizations.* 4th ed. Homewood, Ill.: Irwin, 1988.

Coffey, James R., ed. *Operational Costs in Acquisitions.* Binghamton, N.Y.: Haworth Press, 1991.

Cummins, Thompson R. *Planning, Measuring, and Evaluating Library Services and Facilities.* New York: Neal-Schuman, 1991.

Mitchell, Betty Jo, Norman E. Tanis, and Jack Jaffe. *Cost Analysis of Library Functions.* Greenwich, Conn.: Jai Press, 1978.

Pitkin, Gary M., ed. *Cost-Effective Technical Services: How to Track, Manage, and Justify Internal Operations.* New York: Neal-Schuman, 1989.

Plate, Kenneth H. *Cost Justification of Information Services.* Studio City, Calif.: Pacific Information, Inc., 1983.

Prentice, Ann E. *Financial Planning for Libraries.* Metuchen, N.J.: Scarecrow Press, 1983.

Roberts, Stephen A. *Cost Management for Library and Information Services.* London: Butterworths, 1985.

Rosenberg, Philip. *Cost Finding for Public Libraries.* Chicago: American Library Association, 1985.

Smith, G. Stevenson. *Accounting for Librarians and Other Not-for-Profit Managers.* Chicago: American Library Association, 1983.

_____. *Managerial Accounting for Librarians and Other Not-for-Profit Managers.* Chicago: American Library Association, 1991.

■5

Preparing the Operating Budget

The background in budgeting, accounting, and cost analysis that you have acquired in the past few chapters will help you in the actual process of budget preparation. Most often, you will be concerned with the operating budget, which most organizations prepare every year. The operating budget outlines in detail the plan of support and expenditures for each fiscal year and provides a framework for operations as well as a yardstick by which activities may later be measured and controlled. The preparation of the annual operating budget provides you with a unique opportunity to influence the direction of the library and to make important decisions to achieve its long-term goals and objectives. You will analyze details from the past, identify the needs and problems of the present, and evaluate alternatives for the future. It is a time-consuming but very important task, often providing an opportunity to meet with management, members of the governing body, funding agencies, and clientele and to present ideas and participate in decision making. By analyzing the library's goals and determining the means by which they may be achieved, you will establish the priorities for the upcoming budget period and lay the groundwork for the future.

Your board, governing body, or upper management should provide you with the guidelines and instructions to be followed in the preparation of your operating budget. These may include financial guidelines, changes in policies or programs requested by management, worksheets, prior-year budget and actual information, and a schedule for completion and approval of the final budget prior to the beginning of the new fiscal year. It is important that the individuals responsible for working with the final budget be active participants in its preparation. By communicating the guidelines for budget formulation to the appropriate areas and by permitting those library managers to prepare and negotiate their budgets, a collective agreement may provide for a commitment to uphold the budget as much as possible.

For a newly established library, with no historical information to use as a basis, some of the principles of zero-base budgeting may be helpful in preparing the first operating budget. It will be necessary to analyze each activity from scratch to determine the costs of service. The amount of service that can be provided with the revenues available will be a major factor in determining what services the library will provide during its first year.

Your initial budget is likely to be some type of program or functional budget detailing the expenses of each service area. The final budget should be prepared in the format used by the accounting and reporting systems so that both the library and the parent organization can readily prepare and understand regular informative reports. The final budget is usually a program budget, a line-item budget, or some combination of the two.

As mentioned earlier, spreadsheets are very useful in budget preparation, and computerized spreadsheet software greatly simplifies the process of library budgeting. Known data, such as current and prior-year budget and actual information, can be used as the basis for the spreadsheet. Using basic formulas and a variety of possibilities, it is possible to see the financial effect of different options. For example, the effect of increasing or decreasing a book budget by a given percent can be rapidly seen in the change in the totals. If you have access to even an inexpensive spreadsheet program, you will find it very helpful in preparing your budget.

Preparing the Expense or Expenditure Budget

Before preparing the expense or expenditure budget for the new year, it is beneficial to obtain information for the current and prior years. Information on prior-year expenditures is probably already on file in the library; if not, it should be readily obtainable from the accounting department. This provides a basis for comparison with current and future expenditure levels, displays trends, and serves as a reminder of unusual expenditures that may need to be included. Past budgets also reflect expenditures for services that have already been approved; using these records as a basis for the new budget eliminates the need to explain everything from scratch.

You will be preparing next year's expenditure budget before the current year is completed. While prior-year expenditure information will be very helpful, current-year information more accurately displays current trends. For this reason you may wish to prepare an estimate of what the total expenditures will be for the current year. As the end of the fiscal year approaches, this information is often required by upper management to ensure that revenues will be sufficient to cover estimated expenditures. If revenues are expected to be less than anticipated, you may be required to find ways to reduce this year's expenditures before the budget year ends.

Preparing a Current Estimate

A current estimate is prepared by adding projected estimates to already known year-to-date information. To obtain an estimate on salaries, for example, multiply the number of pay periods remaining by the total salary amount for one pay period and add this number to the year-to-date salary amount. Add the amount of outstanding book and equipment orders to year-to-date figures for those items, and so forth. This up-to-date information will provide a basis for beginning the new budget and will also supply valuable information when compared with prior year expenditures and future year requests. Preparing a current estimate should also assist you in controlling your budget for the remainder of the year since you still have time to act on areas that appear likely to have budget deficits or surpluses. Example 5.1 illustrates a spreadsheet used to prepare a current estimate for comparison with the current budget.

Example 5.1 ▪ *Current Estimate*

	Current Year Actual			Current Year Budget
	Year-to-Date	*Remaining*	*Total*	
Salaries	$150,000	$35,000	$185,000	$188,000
Fringe benefits	30,000	8,000	38,000	37,600
Total personnel	180,000	43,000	223,000	225,600
Supplies	2,500	500	3,000	2,900
Travel	1,700	100	1,800	2,000
Telephone	1,000	250	1,250	1,200
Utilities	3,000	600	3,600	3,800
Total operating	8,200	1,450	9,650	9,900
Books	35,000	5,000	40,000	40,000
Periodicals	8,000	1,000	9,000	9,200
Equipment	16,000	1,500	17,500	17,300
Total capital outlay	59,000	7,500	66,500	66,500
Total expenses	$247,200	$51,950	$299,150	$302,000

The Status Quo Budget

Using the information obtained from the prior year and the current estimate, you can prepare a status quo budget for each expenditure line. This will provide an estimate for a new budget with the current level of services and personnel. The maximum level of service attainable with the current level of funding should be determined. Examples later in the chapter will show in detail how you can prepare a status quo budget.

If you plan no changes in programs or activities during the next year, perhaps your completed status quo budget will be your final budget. However, changes in regulations, business conditions, or the library's patron base, as well as previously unfilled requests, are appropriate areas to review. This is the time to analyze and prioritize the objectives of each program and to identify any changes in costs related to each objective. Are additional services needed, or are some current services obsolete? Any activities that are to be added, changed, or discontinued need to be carefully considered, and the level of expenditure should be adjusted accordingly. By applying some of the principles of cost analysis and zero-base budgeting previously discussed, specific costs should be identified for each requested change or addition to the library's programs. All available information concerning the library's current and planned programs should be considered in preparing the operating budget.

If you have been given guidelines to follow concerning allowable levels of expenditures, it is important to determine how you can achieve your most important objectives within these guidelines. For example, you may have been told that there will be a 3 percent increase in salaries, that fringe benefit costs will increase by 4 percent, but that your overall budget must be 5 percent lower than last year. This is a difficult situation, but one that is all too common today. There are usually certain trade-offs in budgeting, and you must decide on your priorities at this time. Should you reduce your book budget? Can some subscriptions be canceled? Must a new program be postponed? Should a vacant position be left unfilled? Can the library open one hour later each day to reduce personnel costs? A decrease in costs in some areas may free up funds that then can be redistributed for new priorities.

Like most projects, budgeting can be simplified by breaking it down into smaller tasks. Operating budgets for libraries may be divided into three main categories: personnel, operating expenditures, and capital outlay, or equipment. Since the final library budget will need to be in the same general format as the budget for the remainder of the organization, there are likely to be many variations of this pattern. In order to carefully assess the priorities of each budgeted area, it is important to understand what each area of the budget comprises and how these expenditures are important to the library's operation.

Budgeting for Personnel Costs

Personnel costs make up a large portion of any operating budget. The personnel budget should begin with a *position classification plan* that lists all approved positions with titles and salaries. Positions that are currently filled should be identified with current salaries; increases need to be determined at this time so that positions may be accurately budgeted. Vacant positions that are expected to be filled during the budget year should be shown with an estimated salary on the personnel worksheet.

A salary increase factor is usually provided by the governing body as part of the budget guidelines. This provides a means to increase current salaries by a given percentage in order to arrive at a figure for budgeted salaries for the new year. For example, if salaries are to be raised by 4 percent, multiply the current salary levels by 1.04.

Completed personnel budgets are usually broken down into the various staff categories, such as professional, clerical, student, or temporary. It is important to budget for a reasonable amount of overtime and temporary help to cover vacations, vacancies, or emergencies, as well as to complete special projects. Prior-year information may be reviewed and compared with the current situation. An employee anticipating maternity leave, a midyear retirement, or the anticipated implementation of a new computer system may provide reasons for modifications in the personnel budget.

In preparing a status quo budget with no new programs or services, personnel should be budgeted at current levels. If new positions are requested to increase services or implement new programs, these should be itemized separately until they are approved. The budget request should include complete information on such positions, including title, salary range, qualifications, duties, and the way in which the additional personnel are expected to enhance the library's programs.

To prepare the personnel budget, begin by listing your present staff and their present salaries, along with any approved positions that may be vacant. Multiply current salaries by the allowed salary increase, and establish a hiring rate for any vacant or new positions. If your final budget needs to separate professional and clerical positions or positions in different departments, take this into account when you set up your personnel worksheets.

Because there are usually some vacant positions during a budget year, often it is customary to use a *salary vacancy factor* to reduce the total personnel budget slightly. This factor, usually around 3 to 5 percent, represents the portion of the personnel budget that is likely to remain unspent because of hiring delays or the hiring of new personnel at salaries lower than those of current personnel who may leave. For example, if the organization's total personnel budget for all areas is $200,000, using a salary vacancy factor of 4 percent would mean that only $192,000 actually would be budgeted. This budget practice allows an organization to budget more closely and to budget funds where they are most likely to be utilized.

The salary vacancy factor is used most effectively in larger organizations, since the likelihood of vacancies is spread over a larger group. An individual manager or librarian may not be allowed to reduce the personnel budget to this extent, but the salary vacancy factor may be used at a higher budget level to predict actual expenditures. Totals budgeted for fringe benefits would be reduced by the same percentage as the salary vacancy factor. Because some vacancies may have been anticipated long in advance to balance the original budget, most organizations do not allow unexpended funds in the personnel budget to be shifted to other areas.

Fringe Benefits

Fringe benefits are provided to employees in addition to their wages and salaries and may be an important factor in hiring and retaining competent employees. Fringe benefits include employer-provided retirement plans, Social Security, unemployment insurance, health and disability insurance, and other benefits that may vary with each organization. Vacation leave and sick time are important fringe benefits but are not usually included in the budget since they are not normally paid separately from regular salaries.

Fringe benefits are budgeted separately but are directly related to personnel and salary costs. They may be budgeted as individual line items or as a percentage of total payroll costs; this should be decided by the board or senior management prior to the distribution of budget instructions. If possible, fringe benefit rates to be used for the new budget year should be provided with the budget instructions so that they need not be calculated by individual managers.

Some organizations choose to budget and pay for fringe benefits at the organizational level. While this simplifies the budgeting process for individual managers, it does not provide an accurate indication of each department's costs.

Because personnel and fringe benefit costs make up such a large part of the operating budget, organizations seeking to reduce expenses must carefully analyze the benefits that they provide. By careful structuring, costs of these benefits may be controlled and employees may obtain some tax advantages. It is important to understand what these benefits are and how they affect your budget.

Social Security and unemployment insurance rates are determined by law, and it is necessary to determine the rates for the year being budgeted as well as the base salaries to which they will be applied. Both employees and employers contribute to the Social Security system through payment of FICA (Federal Insurance Contributions Act) taxes. The employee contribution is matched by a contribution by the employer, and the percentage and the base salary to which it is applied usually change annually.

The Federal Unemployment Tax Act (FUTA) provides for an assessment against employers for the purpose of financing programs to assist unemployed workers. Most states also have funds to provide for unemployment compensation benefits to workers who lose their jobs for various reasons. These funds are provided through the payment of a state unemployment insurance tax, which is a percentage of some base amount earned by each employee. Like FUTA, the state unemployment tax is paid by employers, and the rate and base amount may change each year.

Worker's compensation insurance protects both workers and employers from losses related to job-related injuries. Regulations differ among the various states but generally provide for some payment of expenses and damages when an employee is injured at work, regardless of fault. The insurance also provides the employer with protection against lawsuits, and the cost of the insurance is borne by the employer.

Life insurance is not a mandatory benefit, but many employers choose to make a group life insurance policy available to their employees because of the lower rates available. Usually a term policy, renewed each year, is selected because of its lower cost. These policies usually can be converted if or when the employee leaves the organization. Employers often provide some coverage for the employee, while the employee may be required to cover the cost of an optional policy for a dependent or spouse.

Health insurance costs have risen faster than the rate of inflation in recent years and have become a major concern for both employers and employees. Because employers may obtain group rates, they usually can obtain lower costs and less-restrictive coverage than might be obtained by individuals. Insurance companies offer several different alternatives for health insurance coverage. A basic plan may cover specified amounts for hospital charges and physician fees. Major medical policies are designed to protect against catastrophic illness and may be used to supplement a basic plan. To keep costs down, most plans require a deductible, which requires the employee to pay the first part of any claim. Usually the insurance company also requires that the employee pay a percentage of the remainder up to a certain dollar amount. After that dollar amount is reached, the insurance will pay 100 percent of the claim up to a maximum amount.

Health Maintenance Organizations (HMOs), unlike insurance companies, directly provide health and medical services for which they are paid a fixed amount in advance. Because the HMO must absorb all costs, it is less inclined to prescribe unnecessary treatment. Since enrollees have already paid for services, they often are more willing to use HMOs; therefore, problems may be detected and treated earlier, resulting in overall cost savings. Thus, the HMO may be able to offer a contract that lowers costs to both employer and employee. Many employers are required by law to provide their employees with the opportunity to select an HMO that qualifies for federal certification based on services provided.

Selection of an insurance plan or an HMO requires careful study and comparison of costs, benefits, and user-satisfaction levels. Cost and benefits information can be obtained from the insurance companies, while statistics on user satisfaction can be obtained from the companies or from other plan participants. All contracts should be read carefully before a final decision is made.

Flexible spending accounts are a government-approved method for employees to pay health-care and dependent-care expenses with tax-free dollars. Three plans are possible: one to pay premiums for medical or dental coverage, one for unreimbursed health-care expenses (such as deductibles, vision care, etc.), and one for dependent care, such as day care for children or dependent parents. Employees contribute to the plans with pretax dollars, which are then exempt from both income tax and FICA taxes. Contribution levels are decided annually by each employee, and any amounts not used are forfeited. It is important that each employee understand the benefits of participating in such a plan and be provided with complete instructions and worksheets in order to make an informed decision. Flexible benefit plans usually are administered by companies with expertise in the field but are worthy of consideration because they can save money for both employees and employers.

By offering your employees a flexible spending account, you may help to offset some of the costs of rising health insurance, since the cost of shifting some expenses to employees is minimized. The employee has more spendable income because medical and dependent-care expenses are paid with pretax dollars; an employee can pay a higher portion of the cost of medical benefits without a reduction in take-home pay. And, because the contributed funds are not subject to FICA tax, the employer also saves the amount of the matching FICA taxes. In any organization with several employees, this can amount to thousands of dollars that may be used elsewhere.

Many organizations provide some type of retirement plan for their employees and may pay all or part of the costs. If your organization contributes to the employees' retirement fund, this should be included in your fringe benefit estimates. The administrator of the pension fund should be able to supply the amount that will be needed in the following year. The amount is usually budgeted as a percentage of salaries.

In addition to plans funded by the organization, there are several retirement plans that provide tax advantages for the participants. Even if you cannot fund a pension plan for your staff, you may allow them to participate in their own tax-sheltered plans. Under Section 403(b) of the Internal Revenue Code, public schools, some hospitals, and 501(c)(3) organizations (those for which contributions are tax-deductible) may contribute to pension contracts for their employees; the employees' salaries are reduced by the amount of the contribution, and that amount is not taxed until funds are withdrawn. The earnings on these funds are also tax-deferred and provide a means for employees to save for retirement more rapidly than by saving after-tax earnings. Organizations that do not meet the requirements to use Section 403(b) plans may set up similar plans under Section 401(k) of the Internal Revenue Code. Amounts that may be contributed are controlled by law and are subject to annual revision. These plans, which may be administered by insurance companies or through other approved pension contracts, have little impact on budgets because they are paid for by the employees. However, by assisting employees in making the most of tax-exempt flexible spending accounts and tax-deferred retirement plans, you can help to provide benefits for your employees with little or no additional cost to your organization.

A cafeteria plan recognizes the fact that different employees need different benefits. Rather than increasing the total fringe benefit package, an organization may permit each employee to select the amount and combination of desired benefits that best fit his or her particular needs. Each employee is provided with a certain employer-paid benefit level and may select the mix that is most appropriate for his or her situation. In some cases the employee may choose to receive cash in lieu of benefits that are of little value to the individual or may choose to pay the cost of desired benefits that exceed the employer-paid amount. Although cash received under a cafeteria plan is taxable to the employee, many other qualified benefits are nontaxable. When funding is not available to meet the increased costs of current fringe benefits, offering a cafeteria plan to employees can allow the organization to control its costs while still providing employees with the benefits most worthwhile to them.

Each organization should carefully analyze which fringe benefits it can provide to its employees without incurring significant additional costs. Businesses may offer discounted services or products, while academic communities may provide free athletic facilities, discounted admissions to university events, or other benefits that are valuable to the employees but of minimal cost to the employer. As long as these benefits are not significant, they are not currently taxable. Flexible hours, or flex-time, may be attractive to some employees with little change in service or costs; other low-cost suggestions that fit individual situations may be obtained from employees.

Fringe benefits may be budgeted in detail by each department, or the process may be simplified by using one fringe benefit rate for the organization as discussed in Chapter 4. An estimated fringe benefit rate can be determined by dividing total fringe benefit costs by total salary costs. After verifying new Social Security and unemployment rates, obtaining health insurance estimates from the insurance carriers, and estimating an employer's retirement contribution at 2 percent of total salaries, an organization with twenty employees might estimate the fringe benefit costs for the coming year as shown in Example 5.2.

Example 5.2 ▪ *Fringe Benefit Cost Estimate*

Total current year salaries for all positions	$500,000
Total salaries for new budget year with 4% increase ($500,000 × 1.04)	$520,000
Total benefits for the new budget year	
Social Security* (.0765 × $520,000)	$ 39,780
Unemployment taxes (.062 × $7,000 × 20 employees)	8,680
Health plans	81,540
Retirement contribution (.02 × $520,000)	10,400
Total	$140,400

*All employees in the example are paid less than the annual Social Security base of $57,600.

The fringe benefit rate may be found by dividing $140,400 (total fringe benefits) by $520,000 (total salaries) or 140,400/520,000 = .27 or 27 percent. By using this rate throughout the organization, each department can be assigned a fairly accurate fringe benefit amount, and duplication of effort is avoided because each manager does not have to research the current-rate information.

Although budgeting and paying for fringe benefits at the organizational level may simplify the budgeting process for individual managers, omitting fringe benefit information from the departmental budget provides a less-accurate indication of each department's cost than if this information were shown. Even if each department is not required to budget in detail, an allocation of a portion of the fringe benefits to each department's budget and expenses is preferable to ignoring such costs at the departmental level.

Example 5.3 shows a personnel budget worksheet for a library with three departments: Administration, User Services, and Technical Support. Each position is listed with the appropriate individual's current salary in the first column. Because a 4 percent salary increase has been allowed for the new budget year, the second column shows current salaries times 1.04. One vacant position, for a clerk in Technical Support, is listed in the second column at the estimated hiring rate. Fringe benefits are to be budgeted at 27 percent of regular salaries, so total fringe benefits for the new budget year may be estimated by multiplying the new salary totals in the second column by .27.

Example 5.3 ▪ *Library Personnel Worksheet*

	Current Salary	New Salary (4% increase)	Fringe Benefits (27%)
Administration			
M. Doe, director	$ 33,000	$ 34,320	$ 9,266
P. Wade, secretary	15,000	15,600	4,212
Total	48,000	49,920	13,478
User Services			
K. Chu, librarian	30,000	31,200	8,424
P. Ray, librarian	30,000	31,200	8,424
L. Jones, clerk	15,000	15,600	4,212
Total	100,000	104,000	28,080
Technical Support			
R. Walsh, librarian	29,000	30,160	8,143
C. Sill, technical assistant	25,000	26,000	7,020
Clerk (vacant)	—	15,600	4,212
Total	54,000	71,760	19,375
Total library regular salaries	$202,000	$225,680	$60,933

Other Operating Expenditures

Many nonpersonnel costs are incurred in carrying out the normal operations of the library. Examples are travel, training programs, postage, supplies, printing, data services, utilities, rentals, and maintenance. These expenditures should be carefully analyzed and any possible efficiencies should be put in place to minimize waste and reduce costs.

Some budgeted items may be increased by the use of a simple inflation factor (that is, if 4 percent inflation is expected, the current estimate would be multiplied by 1.04). More precise information may be available for certain items—for example, if no postage increase has been announced, it may not be necessary to increase the postage budget at all, but if your supply vendor has announced an overall 6 percent increase, you need to plan accordingly. To make the budget as accurate as possible, exact information should be used wherever possible.

Travel should be budgeted separately by determining specific training programs and meetings to be attended, the personnel who will attend, and the estimated cost of each trip. (If temporary help will be needed to cover an absence, remember to include this in the personnel budget.)

Certain supplies (catalog cards, book pockets, etc.) may be purchased in quantity on an annual basis. By reviewing the current supply inventory and preparing a new supply order, it is possible to begin to budget some supply needs. If new catalogs are not yet available, vendors should be contacted to determine general price increases and changes in shipping costs.

Suppliers of maintenance agreements and rental items should be contacted if new price information has not yet been obtained. When equipment is needed on a regular basis over a long period, leasing or buying it is usually the best option. Occasionally, however, there may be special projects or circumstances when an item is only needed for a short period of time. In such an instance it may be wiser to rent the equipment, as long as the total anticipated rental cost is less than the cost of leasing or buying. If an item is budgeted for short-term rental, be sure to determine any costs for delivery, installation, and removal of the equipment, as well as any special supplies that will be needed.

Online data services may be purchased at fixed rates or per-minute rates. If recent trends show that your library is using increased services at per-minute rates, you should compare the cost of per-minute service with fixed rate service or CD-ROM subscriptions. In addition to being easier to budget, CD-ROMs may encourage users to do more of their own searching so that the overall usage increases at no extra cost. Another important factor to consider in analyzing costs of online services is the speed of your modem, which links your computer to these services. The cost of a new modem with a higher baud rate (transmission speed) may be recovered through decreased online time.

Professional fees, including legal, accounting, and consulting fees, should be budgeted as operating expenditures. These should be identified by the specific projects expected to incur the fees, such as an annual audit or fund-raising campaign. You may also be required to budget some overhead costs as part of your operating budget. If so, it is likely that you will be provided with this information and will have little control over the amount to be budgeted.

The normal trend in budgeting is to apply some inflation factors to the current budgets and ask for increases for all existing programs. While this is a simple technique and may be subject to the least controversy, it is not necessarily in keeping with the idea of providing the best services to a changing public. This year's world may be different, this year's patrons may be different, and this year's services may need to be different. Even though a zero-base budget technique may not be required and is probably not practical on a formal basis, some zero-base thinking is appropriate when preparing the operating budget. The budget preparation period is the optimum time to apply some of the cost-analysis techniques discussed in Chapter 4 to analyze current services and decide if each provides benefits worthy of the cost. Are maintenance contracts costing more than the maintenance required, or could good service be provided while cutting back on some of these contracts? Is rental equipment being used sufficiently to justify its continued rental; should it be discontinued, or could it be purchased at a lower overall cost? Do the full costs of programs and unit costs of services justify their continuation at current levels, or could some little-used programs and services be discontinued or shared with another nearby library? By careful analysis funds often can be freed up to provide more valuable programs and services to the patrons.

It is important to ensure that operating expenditures have been budgeted as needed to support any planned capital purchases. Special paper for new microfilm or computer printers, insurance on a new bookmobile, or an increased utilities budget for a building expansion are examples of items in the operating budget that may be affected by changes in capital spending.

Capital Outlay and Equipment Purchases

Capital outlays describe the cost of items that are expected to last more than one year. Some of these larger items, such as land, buildings, and major equipment, may be budgeted separately with a capital budget, which provides for long-term financing of such projects. Others, however, are included in the operating budget and are paid from current-year funds. Examples are books, office equipment, furniture, microforms, and some computer equipment and software.

Whether you classify books and small equipment items as capital expenditures or operating expenditures will depend on the accounting rules of your organization. The classification of an item as a capital asset depends on its useful life and its value; the cutoff point varies among organizations but is usually around $500. There are significant differences in the ways in which business and nonbusiness organizations budget and account for capital assets. (A discussion of some of these differences may be found in Chapter 6.)

There are numerous budgeting techniques for books, periodicals, and other library materials. Book budgets may be projected at current levels using inflation factors, or they may be increased or decreased to meet specific program objectives. The desired number of books may be budgeted at an average cost per book. The accuracy of such cost averages may be improved by estimating the numbers of children's books, adult books, reference books, etc., so that different averages are used for each category. The rules of formula budgeting (see Chapter 2) are often applied to book budgets.

The principles of zero-base budgeting are appropriate when planning for new equipment since there often is no logical relationship between the items purchased in one budget year and those needed the next year. A worksheet should list furniture, computer hardware and software, and other equipment; the cost of each item; and justification for the purchase. Quantity discounts or any other discounts available to the library should be sought. During the budgeting period a great deal of progress should be made on the actual selection of such items, since their cost and availability have a significant impact on the library's program. The effect of each purchase on other operating expenditures should also be determined at this time.

The Final Budget Worksheet

Example 5.4 shows a brief budget worksheet, which may be helpful in preparing and displaying your final budget. Current- and prior-year

Example 5.4 ▪ *Budget Worksheet*

	Prior Year Actual	Current Year Budget	Current Year Estimate	New Year Budget
Administration				
Salaries	$ 45,000	$ 48,000	$ 48,000	$ 49,920
Overtime/temp	500	600	550	600
Benefits	13,000	12,900	12,900	13,478
Supplies	2,000	2,500	2,450	2,600
Postage	1,500	1,500	1,450	1,500
Travel	2,300	2,400	2,500	2,500
Equipment	600	500	500	350
Overhead	7,000	7,200	7,250	7,500
Total	$ 71,900	$ 75,600	$ 75,600	$ 78,448
User services				
Salaries	$ 90,000	$100,000	$100,000	$104,000
Overtime/temp	1,000	1,000	1,100	1,100
Benefits	26,000	26,000	26,000	28,080
Supplies	5,000	6,000	5,800	6,000
Postage	2,000	2,200	2,200	2,200
Travel	1,500	1,800	1,700	1,800
Books	30,000	32,000	32,000	35,000
Periodicals	5,000	6,000	6,100	6,500
Data services	3,000	4,000	4,400	4,800
Equipment	1,900	1,500	1,500	1,500
Overhead	15,000	15,400	15,500	16,000
Total	$180,400	$195,900	$196,300	$206,280
Technical support				
Salaries	$ 37,000	$ 69,000	$ 59,000	$ 71,760
Overhead	400	400	450	400
Benefits	11,500	17,000	15,500	19,375
Supplies	5,000	6,000	6,100	6,100
Travel	2,300	2,400	2,500	2,500
Equipment	200	350	350	300
Overhead	10,000	10,250	10,300	10,600
Total	$ 68,400	$107,400	$ 96,100	$113,035
Library total	$320,700	$378,900	$368,000	$397,763

information is shown, with the far right column displaying the new budget request. Personnel and fringe benefit information has been transferred from the worksheet in Example 5.3, and other line items are added as appropriate. Your own final worksheet will need to use the line items specified in the budgeting and accounting system of your organization.

Example 5.5 illustrates how you may display your new budget in both program and line-item format, since this may be the final format required by your organization.

Example 5.5 ▪ *Program/Line-Item Worksheet*

	Adminis-tration	User Services	Technical Support	Total Library Budget
Salaries	$49,920	$104,000	$ 71,760	$225,680
Overtime/temp.	600	1,100	400	2,100
Benefits	13,478	28,080	19,375	60,933
Supplies	2,600	6,000	6,100	14,700
Postage	1,500	2,200	2,000	5,700
Travel	2,500	1,800	2,500	6,800
Books		35,000		35,000
Periodicals		6,500		6,500
Data services		4,800		4,800
Equipment	350	800	300	1,450
Overhead	7,500	16,000	10,600	34,100
Library total	$78,448	$206,280	$113,035	$397,763

It may be necessary to prepare more than one level of expenditure request to reflect a minimum level of service, the current level, and an improved level that includes some new or increased services. It is useful to compile information for a budget that maintains the status quo and to outline specific costs of desirable program changes. Perhaps you can document the need for additional services that would justify funding at a level above the guidelines you were given. An analysis of benefits (and the effect of *not* making the change) should be helpful in obtaining the necessary funding if any is available.

For illustrative purposes, assume that Examples 5.4 and 5.5 have been prepared to continue the current level of service, or status quo, with allowable salary increases and inflation factors applied for materials and services. User Services, however, would like to provide an additional service that would require hiring a part-time librarian and purchasing additional equipment and supplies. Unfortunately, this may not be possible. Instead, it may be necessary to decrease the budget so that the overall budget is actually 5 percent lower than the previous year; this would require reducing one full-time employee to part-time and cutting back on many other items. These two options are illustrated in the User Services budget shown in Example 5.6.

Example 5.6 ▪ Budget Worksheet for Various Levels of Service

	Current Year Budget	New Year Status Quo Budget	New Year Budget w/ New Program	New Year Budget w/ 5% Decrease
User services				
Salaries	$100,000	$104,000	$114,000	$ 94,000
Overtime/temp.	1,000	1,100	1,100	500
Benefits	26,000	28,080	30,780	25,380
Supplies	6,000	6,000	8,000	5,525
Postage	2,200	2,200	2,200	2,000
Travel	1,800	1,800	2,200	1,000
Books	32,000	35,000	36,000	30,500
Periodicals	6,000	6,500	6,800	5,800
Data services	4,000	4,800	5,000	4,400
Equipment	1,500	1,500	2,000	1,000
Overhead	15,400	16,000	16,000	16,000
Total	$195,900	$206,980	$224,080	$186,105

Reviewing Budget Requests

After preparing individual budgets for each program or area of responsibility, all budgets must be reviewed for accuracy and for the likelihood that each projected budget will allow the area to meet its objectives. Each area responsible for preparing a budget should be prepared to provide worksheets that show in detail the planned expenditures for the new budget year with backup information concerning the sources of the estimates. The initial worksheets should show prior-year expenditures, estimated expenditures for the current year, and the proposed level of expenditure for the new-budget year. These worksheets are used to justify new and continuing expenditures and to provide specific information for the board or governing body. They will assist in the review process, which usually must be completed shortly before the final budget is due.

Projecting Total Support

Because libraries ordinarily do not earn revenues for their services, they are subject to many outside financial constraints. Most organizations project total revenues based on current conditions, and the allocation of these revenues to fulfill the requirements of various programs is determined by the governing body. Final approval of total support will probably be provided by some higher level of authority—perhaps the library board, a state or local legislative body, your city or county manager, or one of the higher financial officers of your organization. Ability to persuade these higher authorities that expenditure requests are sound and worthwhile is likely to have some influence on the total level of support finally given to the library.

Any projections of direct library revenues, such as user fees or library fines, should be budgeted by the librarian. Fines and lost-book charges can best be budgeted by analyzing past trends; if a decision has been made to raise the amount of the fines, total estimated income can be increased accordingly. Income from the library's endowment or trust funds, if such funds exist, may be projected using the current rate of return for the investments. Some income is easy to determine, such as fixed amounts of dividends or interest. If your investment advisor determines that investment income is likely to decrease, it would be wise to use the lower projected amount in the budget. Revenues from donations and fund-raising activities may also be estimated based on past experience and current economic conditions—with a conservative approach being safest.

Some estimates of support should be available before expenditure budgets are prepared so that guidelines provide specific information about allowable increases or required decreases, such as an allowable 3 percent salary increase but a required decrease of 5 percent in total expenditures. A careful study of current economic trends should help to forecast whether support is likely to be increased or decreased in comparison to the previous year, although firm estimates of support usually are not available until late in the budget process. Exact information on business conditions, the size of the tax base, tax rates, tuition and fee increases, enrollment projections, and other items affecting funding often are not available until immediately before the beginning of the new fiscal year.

Ideally, support would be projected prior to preparing the expenditure budget so that those involved in the budget process could prepare a budget that would fully utilize all expected support. In actuality, however, this is rarely the case; those who wait until revenue projections are available to prepare a budget will find themselves with far too little time to do an adequate job. Instead, it is necessary to gather advance information to prepare the desired expenditure budget, knowing that not all preferred options will be available. Detailed budget information on all programs and line items must be compiled so that changes can be made when necessary.

Government agencies may have the taxing authority to raise revenues equal to the amounts budgeted by their various components, but it usually is not acceptable to raise taxes enough to cover all requests. There may be constitutional or legislative limits on the amount of allowable tax increases, or those in power may simply be voted out of office. Because of this, total expenditure requests are weighed against projected revenues, compromises are made, and often expenditure requests are decreased and taxes are increased. When taxes provide the library's primary source of support, you can use the previous year's appropriation as a reasonable starting point. An awareness of current economic conditions in the area should help you to be aware of whether your library is likely to receive increased or decreased funding during the next year.

In a nonprofit or government organization, the final budget should provide a plan for the expenditure of all projected support. If budgeted expenditures are less than projected support, the library probably is not providing its highest level of service. If expenditures are greater than expected support, funds must be obtained from other sources; this may not be a desirable option.

Consolidating Expenditure Requests and Estimates of Support

After all expenditure requests have been received, they must be consolidated. The library director usually is responsible for consolidating all requests of the library, which will then be added to the requests of the other units of the organization. If several departmental requests are included in the overall library budget, the director should be briefed by the staff to achieve a full understanding of all requests and their justification.

Because the final budget must be consolidated into the format required by the governing body, it is very important that each unit prepare its final request in the same format. A worksheet may be provided by your parent organization, or you may design your own for internal use. A separate budget should be displayed for each program, with a consolidated worksheet summarizing all programs. A consolidated line-item budget may be required, with the line items corresponding to the account codes used in the accounting system.

Prior to submission to the governing body, the library director should review all budget requests to ensure that the guidelines have been followed and that expenditure requests do not exceed the guidelines. If several program areas are involved, you may need to work with individual managers to make decisions concerning priorities and areas that may need to be increased or decreased. Through careful analysis the soundness of the budget, its adherence to the guidelines, and the likelihood of its acceptance can be determined. Depending on availability of funds and agreement on priorities, revisions are often necessary.

Estimates of support must be consolidated and compared with the total expenditure requests. If estimated support is not sufficient to fund all expenditures, either expenditure requests must be reduced or more support must be obtained. Both of these options present difficult challenges, but these challenges must be met to complete the budget process successfully.

In deciding which requests for funds have the highest priority, negotiation is often necessary. Within the library, various programs may compete for funds; within a larger organization, libraries may find themselves competing with many other departments and agencies. Often there may be two levels of review and negotiation, one negotiated within the library by the various library managers, the library director, and the library board; another within the organization, negotiated between library management and the governing body that has final authority to approve the budget.

The Budget Package

When the preliminary budget has been completed and reviewed, a comprehensive budget package should be prepared for presentation to upper management or the governing body. Since it may also need to be presented to the funding agency or a higher level of management, it is important that it be clear, complete, and attractively packaged. The following information should be included.

1. The budget message discusses the financial issues of the past year and those anticipated in the new fiscal year. It includes assumptions used in preparing the new budget; significant changes in programs, policies, and personnel; and the library's outlook for the future.

2. The budget summary lists any budgeted revenues by source and states budgeted expenditures. The budget summary should display the necessary information in the required financial format. It may also show goals and objectives for the new budget year and justification for changes and their cost. Prior-year comparisons are helpful in this summary.

3. Supporting schedules provide details that support revenue projections, departmental expenditure requests, and fixed charges. Where relevant, unit cost information should be included.

4. The schedule of equipment and/or capital projects, if appropriate, should include specific costs and justification for purchase.

5. A detailed justification of new budget recommendations should fully explain any requests for new or expanded services.

6. Supplementary material such as graphs, charts, worksheets, cost studies, or any other information may be helpful.

Presenting the Budget

There are many different ways in which the budget package can be presented to the administrative board and funding agency. The librarian may have the opportunity to present the budget directly to the funding agency and to answer questions in person. Alternatively, the librarian who prepares the budget may present it to the governing board or a supervisor, who in turn presents it to the funding agency or upper management. It is critical that the budget be presented clearly so that the important ideas will be transferred from one approval body to another; therefore, your written budget package is particularly important. Professional jargon should be kept to a minimum so that the information is clear and understandable to all those involved in the final decision.

The budget presentation offers a good opportunity to inform the funding agency of the library's accomplishments for the previous year, assuring the agency that previously budgeted funds have been well managed and were worthwhile. This information provides a transition to the presentation of the current-year request, possibly with explanations of areas in need of change.

If an oral presentation is necessary, be sure to rehearse for a critical audience in advance of the presentation. This will allow you to perfect your presentation and to change any unclear areas. Know your audience, setting, and the time allowed. Visual displays are very helpful, whether included in an oral presentation or in a written document. If audiovisual aids are to be used for an oral presentation, be sure that the room setting is appropriate and that necessary equipment is available and in good working order.

It is helpful to know the feeling of the audience before the final presentation is completed. If there are prejudices to be addressed or political games to be played, these factors must be considered. Although the needs of the library may be noble ones, individuals in upper management or in the funding agency often have power to change or delete areas that do not please them for unrelated reasons.

It is reasonable to expect that some questions will be asked during and after the presentation. With good preparation, it should be possible to answer many of these questions; those that cannot be answered should be noted, and a response should be returned to the questioner as soon as possible.

Review, Revision, and Approval

After the completed budget has been presented for approval, it may be necessary to revise the budget request as required by upper management, the board, or the funding agency. Budget reduction requires a careful analysis of programs and priorities to determine how costs may be reduced with the least negative effect on services. Each line item and each program should be carefully scrutinized to determine all possible cost reductions. Discontinuance of little-used subscriptions, closing facilities at off-peak periods, delays in purchasing desired equipment, or even staff cuts may be necessary to meet the required budget objectives.

At the end of the negotiation process, a final budget is agreed upon by the library managers, the library director, and the governing body. This agreement represents a commitment on the part of all parties to adhere as much as possible to the plans and activities encompassed in the budget. Unless circumstances require a change, the budget is the authorized plan of operation for the fiscal year to come.

Recording the Approved Budget

Following budget approval, the budget must be recorded in the accounting records. As soon as possible, managers should be informed of their approved budgets and reminded of their commitment to adhere to them in achieving the goals and objectives of their programs.

Summary

The process of preparing the annual operating budget provides an opportunity for various levels of management to negotiate and agree on the goals and objectives of the library and of the organization and to translate these objectives into specific financial terms for the coming year. The budget process allows you to explore in depth the services you provide and the costs of these services, to evaluate costs and benefits, and to select those services most worthy of funding for the next fiscal year. Prior-year information and current estimates, combined with guidelines on allowable increases or required decreases, provide a basis for preparing the new budget. This is supplemented by information on program changes and other factors so that the final budget reflects the library's financial plan to provide services for the new year. The ability to provide complete information on specific alternatives and program costs should enhance your prospects of obtaining support to provide the services needed and desired by your patrons.

While it is impossible to predict the future of either the library or its operating environment, the budget process offers the opportunity to analyze trends and carefully study the available alternatives. In this way, progress can be made to successfully begin the new fiscal year.

Additional Reading

Anthony, Robert N., and David W. Young. *Management Control in Nonprofit Organizations*. 4th ed. Homewood, Ill.: Irwin, 1988.

Basch, N. Bernard, and Judy McQueen. *Buying Serials: A How-to-Do-It Manual for Librarians*. New York: Neal-Schuman, 1990.

Bryce, Herrington J. *Financial & Strategic Management for Nonprofit Organizations*. Englewood Cliffs, N.J.: Prentice-Hall, 1987.

Gross, Malvern J., Jr., and William Warshauer, Jr. *Financial and Accounting Guide for Nonprofit Organizations*. Rev. ed. New York: John Wiley & Sons, 1983.

Lee, Sul, ed. *Budgets for Acquisitions*. Binghamton, N.Y.: Haworth Press, 1991.

Prentice, Ann E. *Financial Planning for Libraries*. Metuchen, N.J.: Scarecrow Press, 1983.

Razek, Joseph R., and Gordon A. Hosch. *Introduction to Governmental and Not-for-Profit Accounting*. Englewood Cliffs, N.J.: Prentice-Hall, 1985.

Shreeves, Edward, ed. *Guide to Budget Allocation for Information Resources*. Collection Management and Development Guides. Chicago: American Library Association, 1991.

Trumpeter, Margo C., and Richard S. Rounds. *Basic Budgeting Practices for Librarians*. Chicago: American Library Association, 1985.

Van Deusen, Richard E. *Practical AV/Video Budgeting*. White Plains, N.Y.: Knowledge Industry Publications, 1984.

Vinter, Robert D., and Rhea K. Kish. *Budgeting for Not-for-Profit Organizations*. New York: The Free Press, 1984.

6

Long-Term Planning and Capital Budgeting

It is important for every library to look to the future to determine not only its long-term goals and objectives but also the means by which they will be attained. These considerations must always be kept in view while preparing the operating budget for each new fiscal year, and special care must be taken to ensure that the long-term goals are not lost in budgeting for the short term. Without careful long-term planning, time will rapidly go by, and your library may fail to achieve its maximum level of service.

You will find it helpful to prepare a long-term plan even if only on an informal basis. What new services do you need to provide in the next few years? What changes in your patron base do you foresee? What are your current needs that cannot be met with current budget constraints? Is a new building or automation system needed to provide a higher level of service, or even to maintain the current level? Answers to questions such as these will help you to decide on the library's future goals and to analyze the methods by which you will achieve them.

Many of the library's goals and objectives may be accomplished through the annual operating budget, and many of the smaller capital items can be purchased with operating funds. Significant changes in materials and services provided to patrons may be made each year simply by establishing priorities and carefully allocating funds to those areas considered most important. Occasionally, however, most libraries face a situation where major changes cannot be made without a financial plan that covers a period greater than one year. New or expanded buildings and facilities, major repairs and renovations, automated systems, or added services such as branch libraries and bookmobiles all require funds not usually available and often not spent during a single budget year.

Just as you would purchase a house or a car with long-term financing, libraries often must obtain long-term financing for their major improvements. And just as you might save for years for a child's college education, so must a library plan in advance for the achievement of its long-term goals. Since the effects of these changes will usually last longer than one year, it is reasonable to plan for their financing over a longer period. Large projects or items that must be financed for a period of longer than one year are usually included in a separate capital budget that shows the planned acquisition, disposition, or reconstruction of such items. This budget is not limited to one fiscal year but instead covers the duration of the project. Capital projects are accounted for in the plant fund, as discussed in Chapter 3.

The capital budget is commonly used for major acquisitions such as land, buildings, automation, or large one-time equipment purchases. It also may be used for major renovations or repairs, such as a new roof or heating system. Because these items are too expensive to be fully funded from current-year revenues, they are likely to require long-term financing. Items included in the capital budget are often intended to create major program changes in the library and should be the result of serious long-range planning.

A capital budget may be prepared and approved separately from the operating budget, or capital requests may be included with the operating budget request. The preparation of a capital budget requires a great deal of advance planning, and many decisions must be made when considering the purchase of a capital asset. Each item needed must be thoroughly analyzed to determine both feasibility and cost. If an item is deemed necessary, various alternatives to acquire it and to pay for it must be considered.

In addition to the initial cost of a capital item, the long-term costs of maintenance and operation and their effect on the operating budget in current and future years must be determined, as well as the resulting impact on resources that will be available for other programs. For example, if a bookmobile is to be added, costs must be projected for insurance, fuel, and repairs, as well as any additional salary expense that may be incurred as a direct result of the purchase. Automated systems require maintenance of hardware and software and may also require additional personnel and supplies. All of these items will need to be funded from current and future operating budgets, and the money should be reasonably assured before the capital purchase is made. If funds will not be available to support the project in the future, it should be rejected.

Because procedures for capital budgeting vary widely among organizations, there are few standard formats for capital budgets (a brief example was shown in the discussion of capital budgeting in Chapter 2). The request for any capital project should provide information describing the project, its total cost, proposed sources of funding, the benefits it will provide to the library's patrons, and its relationship to the current and future goals of the library. A large project may require supplemental requests for related items, such as new furniture and equipment needed for a new library building.

Through long-term planning, the assets that need to be acquired over a period may be identified and prioritized. In some cases it may be possible to measure both costs and benefits in terms of money. If so, it is appropriate to evaluate alternatives based on economic information. When both costs and benefits cannot be measured in terms of money, the selection will be made based on subjective judgment.

Cost-Benefit Analysis

When decisions must be made involving the expenditure of large sums of money, it is helpful to be sure that these expenditures will be beneficial to the organization. Some benefits may be measured in monetary terms, particularly those projects that are undertaken to reduce costs or to increase efficiency. For example, money spent on new storm windows, building renovations, or new equipment may reduce the cost of operations (in savings of utilities, supplies, maintenance, etc.) and eventually save an amount equal to or greater than their cost.

One method of analyzing the cost versus the monetary benefit of a capital project is the *return-on-investment method*, in which the return is calculated by dividing the annual savings by the total investment. For example, if a $10,000 investment in storm windows would save $2,000 per year in heating and air-conditioning costs, the return on investment would be calculated as follows:

$$\text{Return on investment} = \frac{\text{Savings}}{\text{Investment}} = \frac{\$2,000}{\$10,000} = 0.2 = 20\%$$

If an annual return of 20 percent is higher than the library can obtain elsewhere, the storm windows may be considered a good investment. Taking into account such factors as added comfort and a desire to conserve natural resources, they might be judged to be a good investment even with a much lower return.

Another simple way to analyze costs is to determine the *payback period*, which is the inverse of the return on investment. Using this method, the length of time it would take to recover the investment cost in savings is determined by dividing the total investment by the annual savings as follows:

$$\text{Payback period} = \frac{\text{Investment}}{\text{Savings}} = \frac{\$10,000}{\$2,000} = 5 \text{ years}$$

The payback period may be compared with the expected life of the asset to be purchased—if the item will be worn out or become obsolete before the end of the payback period, it would not be a good investment.

The Time Value of Money

Both the return-on-investment method and the payback-period method of cost-benefit analysis ignore such factors as inflation, compound interest, and the time value of money. The *time value of money* concept means that one dollar received today can be invested so that it will be worth more than a dollar in the future. You are probably familiar with this concept from your own savings account, which probably earns compound interest. Through *compounding,* interest is paid on the principal and added to your account; at the next interest period, the interest is calculated on the new total of the principal plus the interest. Over time, the amount of interest gained is significant.

It also is possible to determine how much money will be needed today to produce a specific amount of money in the future. This *present-value* concept is based on the principle of compound interest. While tables are available to assist in such calculations, the basic concept works as shown in Examples 6.1 and 6.2.

Example 6.1 ▪ *Compound Interest*

Assume the investment of $200 at 5 percent for one year, compounded yearly.

After one year you will have 100 percent of your principal ($200), plus an additional 5 percent ($10).

$200 principal + $10 interest = $210 available one year from now

At the end of the second year you would have the $210 plus another 5 percent ($10.50).

$200 principal + ($10 [first year's interest] + $10.50 [second year's interest]) = $220.50 available two years from now

Example 6.2 ▪ *Present Value*

If you would have $210 one year from now by investing $200 at 5 percent, then the present value of $210 one year from now at 5 percent is $200. Or

$$\frac{\$210}{100\% + 5\%} = \frac{\$210}{1 + .05} = \frac{\$210}{1.05} = \$200$$

Using the same method, the present value of $200 one year from now at 5 percent is

$$\frac{\$200}{1 + .05} = \frac{\$200}{1.05} = \$190.48$$

If you know that you will need a certain amount of money in a few years for a major repair or replacement or for a special project, you may use present value tables and formulas to determine how much money you need today and what rate of return you need to produce the amount required in the future. The tables and a more complete explanation of their use may be found in most business mathematics textbooks.

Depreciation

The method of spreading the cost of a long-lived asset over its useful life is called *depreciation*. As previously discussed, generally accepted accounting principles require a reasonable matching of revenues and expenses with the appropriate time periods. When depreciation accounting is used, a portion of the total cost of an asset is charged as an operating expense even though there is no cash outlay. Depreciation is a means of reducing the value of an asset as it is used by an organization, and the amount by which the asset's value is reduced is recorded as an expense of the time period. Some assets, such as rare artworks or historical treasures, are considered to be inexhaustible and therefore are not depreciated. Although individual books usually fall below the dollar value that is depreciated, the collection as a whole is of significant value to the library and therefore may be subject to the rules of depreciation.

Depreciation almost always is recorded in for-profit businesses, but there are presently many differences in the methods of recording depreciation in different types of nonbusiness organizations, and the topic is a subject of current discussion among accounting boards. The FASB has ruled that privately operated nonprofit organizations *must* recognize depreciation. Public organizations governed by the rules of the GASB are not required to recognize depreciation but may choose to do so. Because most public libraries and many academic libraries are part of governmental units, depreciation currently is not recorded in most libraries. Whether or not your organization records depreciation in the accounting records, it is important to understand the concept.

Methods of Computing Depreciation

In determining the computation of depreciation for an accounting period, several factors are important. The first is *cost*, which includes not only the net purchase price but also any reasonable expenditures required to make the item ready for use. Freight, taxes, and installation charges are examples of expenditures that must be added to the purchase price to determine the amount to be depreciated. A second factor is the *residual value*, or anticipated salvage value at the time of disposal. The difference between the cost of the item and its residual value is the *depreciable cost*, which is the actual amount to be depreciated. Finally, the *estimated life* of the asset must be determined; this may be measured in terms of years or some other appropriate units, such as hours of use or units of production. Life estimates for depreciable assets are available from various sources, including the Internal Revenue Service.

At the time an asset is purchased, its *book value*, the value recorded on the financial records of the organization, is equal to its cost. (Remember, cost includes not only purchase price, but taxes, freight, and installation charges as well.) As depreciation is applied, the book value is reduced by the amount of *accumulated depreciation*, which is the total depreciation expense that has been used during the life of the asset.

One of the simplest methods of depreciation is the *straight-line method*, by which the depreciable cost of the item is divided by its estimated life.

$$\frac{\text{Cost} - \text{Residual value}}{\text{Estimated life}} = \text{Annual straight-line depreciation}$$

Example 6.3 demonstrates the use of straight-line depreciation.

Example 6.3 ▪ *Straight-Line Depreciation*

A desk is purchased for $500, plus $40 tax and $60 delivery charge. It is expected to last for 10 years and is estimated to have a residual value of $50.

Cost = $500 purchase price + $40 tax + $60 delivery charge = $600

Depreciable cost = $600 cost − $50 residual value = $550

$$\text{Annual depreciation} = \frac{\$550 \text{ depreciable cost}}{10 \text{ years estimated life}} = \$55 \text{ per year}$$

A similar method of depreciation is the *production method,* which substitutes another unit of measure for the years used in the straight-line method. This method is particularly appropriate for machinery, such as copy machines, as shown in Example 6.4.

Example 6.4 ▪ *Production Method of Depreciation*

A copy machine is purchased for $2,000 and is expected to have a residual value of $200. It is expected to produce 100,000 copies during its useful life.

$$\text{Per copy depreciation} = \frac{\$1,800 \text{ depreciable cost}}{100,000 \text{ copies}} = \$0.018 \text{ per copy}$$

If 5,000 copies are made during the year, the amount of depreciation expense to be recorded is $0.018 × 5,000 = $90.

The straight-line and production methods of depreciation allocate the cost of an asset *equally,* based on some predetermined unit of time or production. Because many items become outdated long before they are discarded, sometimes it may be more appropriate to use a method of depreciation that recognizes that a larger percentage of an asset's value is lost during the early years. Such depreciation methods are known as *accelerated depreciation,* and include the declining-balance method and the sum-of-the-years'-digits method, which are shown in Examples 6.5 and 6.6. Both of these methods result in higher depreciation charges during the early years of an asset's life. Because library materials may rapidly become out-of-date, accelerated depreciation methods may be especially appropriate for library collections.

The declining-balance method may have several variations, but the most common is the *double-declining-balance method*, where the asset is initially depreciated at double the straight-line rate.

Example 6.5 ▪ *Double-Declining-Balance Method of Depreciation*

An asset is purchased for $10,000, and is determined to have a residual value of $1,000 and a useful life of 5 years. The rate used for straight-line depreciation would be 20% (100%/5 years), and the rate used with the double-declining-balance method is then 40% (20% × 2). This fixed rate of 40% is applied to the remaining book value at the end of each year. Estimated residual value is not used in computing depreciation except in the last year, when the depreciation amount used is the amount required to reduce the book value to the residual value.

Time	Cost	Yearly Depreciation	Accumulated Depreciation	Book Value
Purchase date	$10,000			$10,000
End of year 1	10,000	40% × $10,000 = $4,000	$4,000	6,000
End of year 2	10,000	40% × 6,000 = 2,400	6,400	3,600
End of year 3	10,000	40% × 3,600 = 1,440	7,840	2,160
End of year 4	10,000	40% × 2,160 = 864	8,704	1,296
End of year 5	10,000		296*	9,000	1,000

*Depreciation amount allowed to reduce book value to residual value.

The *sum-of-the-years'-digits method* of depreciation is similar to the declining-balance method; however, the depreciable cost is used in the computation, and the depreciation amount is determined by use of a fraction rather than a percent. The denominator of the fraction, which remains constant, is the sum of the digits representing the years of life of the asset. The numerator of the fraction changes each year and represents the number of remaining years of useful life. For an asset with an estimated life of five years, the denominator is 5 + 4 + 3 + 2 + 1 = 15, and the numerators for each year in succession are 5, 4, 3, 2, and 1.

Example 6.6 ▪ *Sum-of-the-Years'-Digits Method*

As in Example 6.5, an asset is purchased for $10,000 and is determined to have a residual value of $1,000 and a useful life of five years. The sum-of-the-years'-digits method of depreciation would produce the following results.

Time	Cost	Yearly Depreciation	Accumulated Depreciation	Book Value
Purchase date	$10,000			$10,000
End of year 1	10,000	5/15 × $9,000 = $3,000	$3,000	7,000
End of year 2	10,000	4/15 × 9,000 = 2,400	5,400	4,600
End of year 3	10,000	3/15 × 9,000 = 1,800	7,200	2,800
End of year 4	10,000	2/15 × 9,000 = 1,200	8,400	1,600
End of year 5	10,000	1/15 × 9,000 = 600	9,000	1,000

Because the recording of depreciation requires additional accounting effort, most organizations determine some dollar value below which items are not depreciated. A calculator that costs $50 and has an estimated useful life of five years will not ordinarily be depreciated, since the effort of recording the depreciation amount for each of the five years is not worth the time it would take. If it is not to be depreciated, the total cost of the calculator would be considered part of the normal operating expenses.

Decisions concerning depreciation should be made when planning for the purchase of capital items since the method of depreciation to be used (if any) will affect the amount of expense to be charged to current and future budgets. If the full cost of any item is included as an operating expense, it is not appropriate to record depreciation expense on that item; to do so would be to count the total expense twice.

Operating Expense versus Capital Expense

To understand the difference between considering the cost of an item to be an operating expense that is totally charged against the current year's expenses or a capital expense to be depreciated over current and future years, we will consider a $500 equipment purchase on the first day of the new fiscal year so that the item is in use for the full year. Examples 6.7 and 6.8 show the difference in the accounting records when the cost of an item is considered an operating expense versus a capital expense.

In Example 6.7, the item is charged as an operating expense of the current year.

Example 6.7 ▪ *$500 Equipment Purchase as Operating Expense*

Operating expense recorded in year 1	$500	equipment purchase
Operating expense recorded in year 2	0	
Operating expense recorded in years 3,4,5	0	
Recorded value of asset (book value) at end of year 1	0	

Since the item has been charged as an operating expense of the current year, it is considered to have no long-term value, and no further record keeping is required.

In Example 6.8, the item is capitalized, listed as an asset on the books, and depreciated over its useful life of five years using straight-line depreciation.

Depreciation would continue to be recorded for five years, until the item is fully depreciated, and the book value and accumulated depreciation would remain on the records until the asset is disposed of. As you can see, recording a capital item requires significantly more record keeping, and the value of the item in relation to the business as a whole is an important consideration.

Example 6.8 ▪ *$500 Equipment Purchase as Capital Expense*

Operating expense recorded in year 1		$100 depreciation
Operating expense recorded in year 2		100 depreciation
Operating expense recorded in years 3, 4, 5		100 depreciation
Recorded value of asset (book value)		
at end of Year 1	$500	cost
minus	(100)	accumulated depreciation
=	$400	net book value
Recorded value of asset (book value)		
at end of year 2	$500	cost
minus	(200)	accumulated depreciation
=	$300	net book value

Leasing versus Purchasing

There may be times when a library needs a capital item but does not wish to pay for it all at once. Through a lease, the library (the lessee) may pay another party (the lessor) for the use of the asset for a certain period of time. Because many libraries are tax-exempt, they do not have the tax benefits from the depreciation of assets that may be advantageous to for-profit businesses. This is one of many reasons why it often may be possible to lease an item at a lower total cost than would be required to purchase it.

Because a lease does not require a substantial outlay of cash at the time of acquisition, it may be an attractive alternative when funds are not readily available. Even when funds are available, it may be beneficial for the library to invest or spend them elsewhere and enter into a leasing agreement for certain capital assets. The return-on-investment method is one appropriate way to analyze the costs of leasing versus purchasing the asset. When interest rates are high it may be possible to earn a greater amount in interest on invested money than would be spent to lease the desired asset.

An *operating lease* is similar to a rental agreement; the library does not take ownership of the asset, and the lessor is responsible for maintenance and insurance. In a *capital lease*, the lease payments effectively pay for the asset over the term of the lease, and the lessee usually is responsible for maintenance and insurance. Depending on the specific terms of a capital lease agreement, the library may take ownership of the property at the end of the lease period with little or no additional investment, since the payments already made approximate the fair-market value of the property.

There are specific accounting rules for handling capital leases, since the item may be included in the library's assets even though it has not been fully paid for. If you decide to enter into a lease agreement in which you will probably take ownership of the asset at the end of the period, be sure to discuss the lease with your accounting department so that they can record it properly.

Planning for Library Construction and Renovation

One of the largest capital projects confronting most librarians is the construction of a new library or a major renovation of the existing one. Building or renovating a library to bring patrons and library materials together in a satisfying atmosphere requires a team effort. This team consists of the librarian, the architect, and the chairman of the building committee. A consultant may be needed to assist in the development of a plan to estimate the costs of operating and financing a new library and to assist with a referendum and the marketing of bonds and notes. Although they are not formal members of the team, those individuals who eventually will be paying for and using the new or renovated facility must be considered throughout the design and construction process.

In planning for a new or renovated library, there are many factors to consider. Compliance with regulations concerning safety, access for disabled persons, and environmental considerations must be taken into account during the planning process; ignorance of these issues may have expensive consequences.

Along with initial construction costs, long-term costs of operation and maintenance must be considered. The design must allow for advancing technologies and provide the systems to support the sophisticated data distribution requirements of the future. Energy efficiency, durable furniture and floor coverings, practical location of service areas, and quality design of staff work space are some of the details that will affect operating budgets for years to come. Since a new facility usually is intended to offer more and better services, an increase in operating funds for more staff and materials, as well as for utilities and insurance, likely will be needed.

Financing Capital Projects

After a capital project is approved, funding must be sought and financing arrangements completed. A *capital campaign* may be organized to obtain the funds through gifts and contributions. If the project cannot be funded through internal funding sources, the capital budget should identify sources of outside borrowing and a schedule to repay such obligations.

One of the most common long-term financing methods used by public libraries is the sale of bonds, or a *bond issue*. A *bond* is a security that represents money borrowed from an investor. The bond must be repaid at a specific time and requires periodic payments of interest (usually twice a year).

If major capital improvements are agreed upon by the library director and the board, a request may be made to the local governmental unit for a bond issue to fund the project. If the request is approved, it is placed before the voters. Following voter approval, legal assistance is needed to draft the bond issue; when it is acceptable to the public, the project is approved and funded.

Bonds issued by governmental units are known as *municipal bonds*. Municipal bonds must be accompanied by a *bond counsel opinion* stating that the bonds are legal and binding obligations of the issuer and that the bond interest is exempt under applicable state and federal tax laws. The bonds are usually *general obligation bonds,* which are secured by the "full faith and credit" as well as the taxing power of the governmental unit. Another type of municipal bond is a *revenue bond*, which is secured by revenues from the project. Since libraries usually do not generate sufficient revenues to finance bonds, these are not commonly used for library purposes.

Municipal bonds are rated according to the community's ability and willingness to repay; a higher rating usually results in a lower interest rate, which lowers the total long-term cost of the bond issue to the library and the taxpayers. If a bond issue can be combined with local contributions, the demonstrated support of the public may result in a lower interest rate on the bonds. Interest earned on municipal bonds is not subject to federal income taxes and usually is also exempt from taxes in the locality in which they are sold. This makes them an attractive investment for individuals in high income tax brackets.

The initial bonds may be sold by negotiation or by competitive bidding to a group of *underwriters*, securities dealers who buy the bonds for the purpose of reselling them to other investors. Municipal bonds are usually sold in denominations of $5,000, which is the *par value* or *face value* of the bond and is the amount paid when the bond matures. They often are sold with staggered maturity dates, or *serial maturities*, allowing the issuer to spread out the debt and pay back the bonds at different times.

Contracting for Capital Projects

Some capital projects cannot be completed with the resources of the organization and outside contractors are needed. Great care must be taken in selecting a contractor to complete a capital project, particularly when public funds will be used. The purchasing department of your organization should have specific procedures that must be followed when items costing above a certain amount are purchased. These procedures may include requirements for advertising, bidding, and selecting vendors to provide the necessary products or services. While the purchasing agent must provide the expertise on bidding and awarding of final contracts, an understanding of the process and careful reading of documents may protect you from serious disappointments.

Invitation to Bid

The invitation to bid provides notice to potential suppliers that bids will be taken on certain items. The notice includes the place and time of the bid opening, the items involved, the name and address of the individual from whom bid documents may be obtained, information on the cost of bid documents and the deposit required, and notice of publication of bid information in the media.

Instructions to Bidders

Instructions to bidders inform potential suppliers about the legal aspects of the bid, required qualifications of bidders, procedures, and contract information.

General Conditions of the Contract

General conditions provide specific information concerning contract rights and responsibilities, legal requirements, and similar matters. Standard forms and agreements, including a performance bond, various releases and waivers, and any other required forms, complete the legal agreement between the supplier and purchaser. A *performance bond* provides insurance that the contract will be completed satisfactorily or that the contractor or his bonding agent will pay a penalty. If for some reason a contractor cannot complete the work satisfactorily, the library is provided with other means to complete the work.

Detailed Specifications

Before requesting bids or entering into a contract for a capital item, it is important to provide clear, detailed, and complete specifications for the product or services that are required. These may be broken into groups so that specifications for buildings, furniture, and equipment may be provided in detail within the appropriate group. Performance specifications should be included wherever possible. Because competitive bidding is encouraged, it is very important to ensure that the lowest acceptable bid will include all the necessary items for completion. If these are not specified in the request for bid, it is likely that the contract will be awarded to someone who will not provide exactly what is needed. While some compromises may be necessary, important specifications should be clearly defined, so that the product selected will meet the need for which it was purchased.

Requiring a specific brand is often not allowed, and the term *or equal* usually must be included in the specifications. In this case it usually is helpful to include more than one comparable item, and to specify the person or persons who will decide what is "equal." While a bidder may submit a bid that is qualified or limited to only those specifications that the bidder can meet, such a bid does not legally have to be considered.

It may be helpful to require that the bidder provide information on comparable contracts it has fulfilled in the area in the past few years. If this requirement is made, you should take the time to visit those locations to ensure that the product and service will be satisfactory to you.

The Contract

A written document usually is required before a contract is considered binding. The contract should describe the criteria for quality control, total cost of the project, methods of inspection, procedures for acceptance of the product or service, and possible penalties for delays. A guarantee also may be included in the contract.

As appropriate, contracts are issued for work to be done on the project, and payments are made as work is completed. It is customary to hold back a retained percentage of the total payment, which is not released until the project has been fully accepted. This amount is usually 10 percent of the total contract.

Repayment of Debt

If money has been borrowed for a project, it must be repaid with interest. Interest on bonds is paid on a semiannual or annual basis; the principal is usually paid at the end of the period when the bond becomes due. Sufficient funds must be set aside each year to pay the current interest and to establish a reserve to pay the principal when due. In governmental organizations, money used for the repayment of long-term debt is often kept in a separate debt service fund. If part of the project is financed with restricted resources, a separate capital projects fund may need to be established. If available funds are not immediately needed to pay for the project, they should be invested to increase the resources as much as possible.

Investment of Idle Funds

Libraries often have money available that will not be spent in the near future. Appropriations may be received at the beginning of each year, providing funds that must be allocated throughout a twelve-month period. Endowment funds not intended for current use must be invested wisely to achieve a reasonable income. Funds obtained for large capital projects usually are not spent as soon as they are received and may be temporarily invested while the project is under way. By obtaining some added revenue through investments, a smaller bond issue or capital campaign may be needed.

Although the initial funds for endowments, capital projects, and other purposes may carry legal restrictions governing the way in which they may be spent, investment earnings from these funds usually are unrestricted unless otherwise specified in the gift or funding agreement. Such earnings may be an excellent source of unrestricted income, since they may be used at the discretion of the board to carry out the mission and goals of the library. It is very important to ascertain from the original gift or agreement whether investment income from specific resources is restricted or unrestricted, since access to future income can have a significant effect on the library's long-term plans.

Before making a commitment to any specific investment, three characteristics of the investment should be analyzed. These are liquidity, safety, and total return. *Liquidity* defines the ease with which the investment may be immediately converted to cash. Money in a bank account or money market fund is highly liquid; a check or withdrawal slip provides immediate access to the money. Mutual funds, stocks, and bonds are less liquid, not only because a few days may pass before a redemption check is available but also because a loss may be suffered if the money is needed when the stock or bond market is low. Real estate and similar items have very low liquidity, since it may be months before any acceptable offer is obtained. When selecting an investment, the length of time the funds are to be invested is an important consideration.

Safety defines the level of risk associated with the investment, which usually increases with the potential for reward. There are two levels of risk to consider in long-term investments. One is *investment risk*: Will the money and expected gains be available when the investment matures? The other is *market risk*: Will inflation reduce the value of the investment, or will a loss be suffered if it must be sold at an inopportune time?

Total return, or *yield*, combines the income (dividends or interest) received from the investment while it is held and the gain or loss on the investment at the time it is sold. Some investments pay high dividends but have little potential for appreciation, while others may increase in value but provide little income. Investments may decrease in value and provide no income, which results in a net loss. Those investments that may offer the potential for the highest yield also may offer the potential for greatest loss; as such they are considered high-risk investments and are probably not suitable for libraries or nonprofit organizations.

It is important to invest unused funds for maximum return with minimum risk. While there are many opportunities for investment today, the governing body of a library has an obligation to invest idle funds in a conservative manner. Although most investments will be made through a securities broker, it is important to understand the many types of investments and the basic principles of investing and to convey to the broker the investment objectives of the library.

Money Market Funds

Money market funds are completely liquid and can be redeemed for cash at any time. Shares have a fixed value of $1, and interest usually is compounded daily. These funds usually pay higher interest rates than bank savings accounts and may be purchased through large brokerage houses or through banks. There are differences in interest rates among funds; their performance is rated on a regular basis in most major newspapers. Not all money market funds are insured, but they usually are considered very safe and conservative investments.

Certificates of Deposit

A certificate of deposit (CD) is a money market instrument issued either by a bank or a savings and loan and should be insured by one of the federal deposit insurance corporations. A CD has a specific interest rate and date of maturity. There usually is a penalty if the CD is cashed in before its maturity date. If there is some doubt as to the length of time the money may be invested, it may be wise to purchase several CDs with varied maturity dates so that funds are likely to be available as needed. It also is possible to buy CDs through brokers who maintain a secondary market to sell these CDs without penalty.

Bonds

Bonds that are issued by an organization are liabilities of that organization. The purchase of bonds involves certain risks. One is the ability of the issuer to repay the principal and interest as stated. Bonds are rated through the evaluation of the financial integrity of the issuer and the issue. Moody's Investors Services and Standard & Poor's are two of the major rating services for bonds. The highest quality bond is rated Aaa by Moody's, or AAA by Standard & Poor's. Ratings range from AAA or Aaa to D, which signifies that the bond is in default and may not be repaid. Ratings are not recommendations or forecasts of the bonds' future performance but do offer a measure of assurance as to the financial stability of the issuer. It probably would be unwise, and possibly even illegal, for a library board to invest in any securities that have less than an A rating. Risk may be reduced by purchasing insured bonds; in this case it is important to know who is insuring the bonds, since it is possible for insurance to be provided by companies that do not have the ability to pay in the case of default.

If a bond is held to maturity, the full face value is received, and the yield is exactly the same as the stated interest rate. However, as interest rates increase, the market value of a bond decreases; as interest rates decrease, the market value of a bond increases. Bonds sold prior to maturity may result in a gain or a loss depending on the change in interest rates since the original purchase. Some bonds are sold with a *call* provision that allows the issuer to redeem the bonds early after a stated time. If interest rates fall, an issuer may choose to call in the old debt and issue new bonds at a lower interest rate, although it will pay the bondholders a premium to do so.

Municipal Bonds

Municipal bonds have been previously discussed as a means of funding long-term projects for libraries. Just as a community may sell municipal bonds, it may also buy them. Because the interest they pay is usually tax exempt, municipal bonds ordinarily pay a lower interest rate than taxable securities. Since most libraries are already tax exempt or part of tax-exempt organizations, there is usually little reason to purchase municipal bonds when higher rates of return are likely to be available on other securities.

Treasury Securities

Treasury securities are considered the safest investment available because they are backed by the "full faith and credit" of the U.S. government. These securities are considered to be above AAA in quality and therefore are not rated. They also are never "called," so the maturity date and rate are guaranteed.

There are three types of Treasury securities with varying maturities; although all are bonds, they are known by three names. The first, known as *Treasury bills* or *T-bills*, have maturities of 91 days (three months), six months, or a year. They have a minimum face value of $10,000 but are sold at a discount so that they are purchased for less than face value and redeemed for face value when they are due. The difference represents the yield. *Treasury notes* mature in one to five years and pay interest semiannually. Denominations of $5,000 are available for those with terms of less than four years, and $1,000 for four- to five-year terms. *Treasury bonds* are available in medium-term (five- to ten-year) and long-term (ten- to forty-year) maturities with semiannual interest payments and minimum denominations of $1,000.

GNMAs

Ginnie Maes (GNMAs), which are bonds backed by mortgages, provide high yields with U.S. government safety. Investors receive monthly payments based on the interest and principal from the underlying mortgages. The GNMA program is administered by the U.S. government–owned Government National Mortgage Association, and its bonds are fully guaranteed. For this reason GNMAs have a credit rating of AAA, the highest rating available to securities.

Ginnie Maes are bought and sold in increments of $5,000, with minimum face values of $25,000; monthly payments of interest and principal are paid to the investor. GNMAs usually mature in thirty years, at which time the final installment of principal and interest is due.

Investors who do not have sufficient money to purchase a GNMA bond may participate in a GNMA fund. The price per share of a GNMA fund will vary with changing interest rates; rising interest rates will cause the share price to drop and lowering rates will cause the price to rise. This characteristic has the tendency to even out the yield of the fund so that it is approximately equal to the current rate of return on a GNMA bond.

Corporate Bonds

Corporate bonds usually provide slightly higher yields than government bonds but may be accompanied by a slightly higher level of risk. However, bonds in some regulated industries, such as banking and utilities, may offer a reasonable combination of safety and high yields. Prior to investing in such bonds, it is advisable to check the bond ratings.

Zero-Coupon Bonds

A zero-coupon bond is a fixed-income security that is issued at a substantial discount and does not make regular interest payments. Instead, the interest that a normal bond would pay is figured into the original issue price to determine the amount of the discount. For example, a six-year-maturity zero-coupon bond might be purchased for $639 and redeemed at the end of six years for $1,000. The compounded rate of return on such an investment would be approximately 7.6 percent.

There are many types of zero-coupon bonds on the market, including government-backed Treasury bonds.

Zero-coupon bonds are based on the present-value concept (discussed earlier in this chapter), since one dollar invested today at compound interest will be worth more than one dollar in the future. A zero-coupon bond may offer an excellent means for a library to provide funds for a future obligation.

Stocks

A share of stock is evidence of an ownership interest in a corporation. Owners of *common stocks* participate in earnings after the claims of other securities are satisfied and have the lowest priority in the event of liquidation. *Preferred stocks* have high priority in receiving dividends and in settling claims if the business fails and so are slightly less risky. Both types of stock offer opportunities for appreciation but are considered risky investments in comparison to those mentioned previously.

Mutual Funds

Mutual funds invest in a variety of securities and thus spread the risk among a group of securities of similar types. Mutual funds may invest in stocks, bonds, or a combination of investments and often are targeted at a certain type of security, such as energy, gold, or government securities. Although these funds are professionally managed, they vary greatly in their performance and risk factors. Many publications regularly rank mutual funds with comparisons of risk and performance. A library should select a mutual fund with the same care that it would give to investing in an individual security. Many conservative mutual funds are available that may be suitable for the library's investment needs.

Some mutual funds charge a *load*, or fee, for sales and purchases of shares of the fund, while others are *no-load* funds that are subject only to a management fee on the assets of the fund. Since the sales charge reduces the amount of money available for investment, a fund that charges a sales load must earn a higher rate of return to match the performance of a no-load fund.

When selecting investments for library funds, many factors must be considered. One of the primary factors is the length of time for which the funds are likely to be invested. Endowment funds, which are to remain invested indefinitely, may be appropriately placed in investments that have little liquidity but that produce income to be used by the library. Funds that are to be used in the near future should be invested conservatively to provide as much guaranteed income as possible for the time in which they are not being used.

Example 6.9 provides a simple illustration of some of the ideas presented in this chapter. Suppose your community passes a referendum approving the sale of $1 million worth of ten-year bonds to finance a new public library building. The bonds will pay 3 percent interest, $30,000 per year or $15,000 two times per year, which will be tax-free

Example 6.9 ▪ Cash Budget for Library Building Construction

Quarter beginning:	3/94	6/94	9/94	12/94	3/95	6/95	9/95	12/95	3/96	6/96
Opening cash balance	$ 0	$1,013,000	$824,130	$719,221	$628,413	$520,547	$426,752	$315,870	$219,029	$105,069
Sale of bonds (3/1)	1,000,000	—	—	—	—	—	—	—	—	—
Payment to contractor	—	200,000	100,000	100,000	100,000	100,000	100,000	100,000	100,000	100,000
Interest to bondholders	—	—	15,000	—	15,000	—	15,000	—	15,000	—
Total cash used	—	200,000	115,000	100,000	115,000	100,000	115,000	100,000	115,000	100,000
Cash available for investment	1,000,000	813,000	709,130	619,221	513,413	420,547	311,752	215,870	104,029	5,069
Investment earnings:										
6% investments	9,000	9,000	9,000	9,000	6,000	6,000	3,000	3,000	0	0
4% investments	4,000	2,130	1,091	192	1,134	205	1,118	159	1,040	51
Closing cash balance	$1,013,000	$ 824,130	$719,221	$628,413	$520,547	$426,752	$315,870	$219,029	$105,069	$ 5,120

to the purchasers of the bonds. The bonds are sold on March 1 and you have $1 million. You have selected a contractor, and the building plan calls for the contractor to be paid $200,000 at the beginning of the project, followed by $100,000 every three months, with $100,000 to be retained until the building is completed and accepted. The building is scheduled to be completed in two years.

Because you are a tax-exempt organization, you can invest your unused funds in a taxable security that pays a higher rate than tax-free securities. Let's assume that you can invest money for a period of one year or more at 6 percent and that money invested for less than one year will pay 4 percent; each investment will pay quarterly interest. You invest $200,000 for two years, $200,000 for eighteen months, and $200,000 for one year—all in fixed-income securities paying 6 percent. The remaining funds plus the interest as it is paid are invested at 4 percent. Your first payment to the contractor will be on June 2. The building is to be completed two years from now in May, so the final payment to the contractor will be in June if all goes as planned.

Using a cash budget as shown in Example 6.9, you can plan exactly when you will need the funds. The example shows how the funds would earn interest and how they would be used to pay the contractor and to pay interest to the bondholders for the first two years.

The money remaining at the end of the two-year period would be applied to the later repayment of the bonds. A similar plan could calculate how much tax money would be required and how much could be earned to pay the remaining interest to the bondholders and to pay back the $1 million due in ten years. Such a plan is much more complex and is not illustrated here.

Summary

Long-term planning is often required in order to make major changes in the services of the library. This planning may involve purchases of large items that require funding beyond that available through the normal operating budget.

There are many special considerations in planning for the purchase of capital assets, and the library must be sure that the best available alternative is chosen. Rental agreements, leases, and purchases are all options available on many large items, and each should be analyzed in view of its long-term value and the effect on the annual operating budget. Whether or not an item is to be depreciated is one of many factors that will affect current and future budgets.

If large items cannot be purchased from one year's operating funds, a special capital budget may be needed. Funds must be sought, either through contributions, earnings, or long-term financing, and care must be taken in planning for repayment of any debt incurred. Contractors should be carefully chosen, with special attention to the bidding process and the final contract agreement. Funds that are acquired but are not to be used immediately should be invested for maximum return with minimum risk, and the earnings may be used to reduce the total amount of outside funding required. Through careful planning, the library may enhance its ability to achieve its long-term goals and objectives and maximize service to its patrons while making the best possible use of available funds.

Additional Reading

Bryce, Herrington J. *Financial & Strategic Management for Nonprofit Organizations.* Englewood Cliffs, N.J.: Prentice-Hall, 1987.

Collins, Stephen J. *Recognition of Depreciation by Not-for-Profit Institutions.* Washington, D.C.: National Association of College and University Business Officers, 1988.

Cummins, Thompson R. *Planning, Measuring, and Evaluating Library Services and Facilities.* New York: Neal-Schuman, 1991.

Hirshon, Arnold, and Barbara A. Winters. *Managing the Purchasing Process: A How-to-Do-It Manual for Librarians.* New York: Neal-Schuman, 1991.

Holt, Raymond M. *Planning Library Buildings and Facilities: From Concept to Completion.* Metuchen, N.J.: Scarecrow Press, 1989.

Prentice, Ann E. *Financial Planning for Libraries.* Metuchen, N.J.: Scarecrow Press, 1983.

Public Securities Association. *Fundamentals of Municipal Bonds.* 3d ed. New York: Public Securities Association, 1987.

Ramsey, Inez, and Jackson E. Ramsey. *Library Planning and Budgeting.* New York: Watts, 1986.

Smith, Lester K., ed. *Planning Library Buildings: From Decision to Design.* Chicago: American Library Association, 1986.

■7

Revenues and Sources of Support

Without adequate funding you cannot expand or even maintain the services of your library. During the budget process you have probably found that many worthwhile services must be limited due to financial constraints; it is helpful to understand why some of these constraints exist and what alternative funding sources may be available.

While the final responsibility for library funding usually lies with upper management, a library board, legislative body, or other funding agency, the successful library manager must understand the basic sources of library support and may need to provide innovative ideas in order to obtain support from nontraditional sources. By providing direction and expertise to obtain additional funding, you may ensure that the library has adequate resources to continue its programs and to provide your patrons with the best possible service.

Traditional Sources of Support

Sources of financial support for libraries vary depending on the type of library or parent organization. *Support* is a broad term that includes all resources used for the benefit of the library and its services to patrons. The library may earn revenues through library fines, book fairs, contracts to perform specific tasks, or interest and dividends on investments. Other customary sources of support for governmental and nonprofit libraries include property taxes, membership fees, gifts, and contributions. Volunteer services and cost reimbursements, while not direct sources of support, have a similar effect in that expenses may be reduced and less total support is required.

For many years business libraries have been supported by the earnings of the business, public libraries have been supported by taxes, academic libraries have received funding from tuition and fees, and many libraries have received some revenue from fines and charges for lost books. Understanding how this support originates may help you to understand some of the limitations of these sources.

Business Earnings

If the library is part of a for-profit enterprise, support for the library usually comes from the earnings of the business. In some businesses the costs of library operations may be charged directly to the customers; in others, library costs will be combined with other costs to become part of the cost of the final product or service that is sold.

Because for-profit enterprises do not use fund accounting but rather look at the revenues and expenses of the enterprise in its entirety, the exact sources of revenue that support the library are not likely to be of concern. However, the ability to identify any revenues attributed to the library, to trace expenditures directly related to client services, or to allocate library costs incurred to fulfill critical needs of other departments within the organization may be a significant factor in the library's ability to maintain or expand its level of service.

Taxes

In libraries that are part of governmental agencies, taxes usually make up the primary source of support. Some money is still provided to school and public libraries by the federal government, and most states provide some support for school and public libraries as well as libraries in public colleges and universities. Lobbying efforts of library supporters have proved to be worthwhile in maintaining some state and federal funding for libraries. Governments use property taxes, income taxes, sales taxes, and other miscellaneous taxes to produce revenues for support of government operations, including libraries. These funds are budgeted as estimated revenues; however, if actual revenues fall short during the fiscal year, governments are often forced to reduce expenditures below budgeted levels.

At the local level, the primary source of school and public library support is the *property tax*, also known as an *ad valorem tax*. Because the government has a claim on specific property if the taxes are not paid, the collection of revenues from property taxes is fairly certain, although an allowance must be made for some uncollectible taxes. Taxes are levied on the *tax base*, which is the assessed value of the property within the governmental unit minus property that may be exempt for various reasons. The *tax rate*, sometimes called *millage*, is applied to the total tax base except for any applicable exemptions.

In Chapter 6 we discussed bond issues as a source of funding for capital projects. When voters approve a request to issue bonds, they agree to pay taxes in future years to repay these bonds, and the repayment of the debt becomes a mandatory part of the taxing agency's budget. In addition to the mandatory repayment of debt, the taxing agency must use projected expenditure levels to estimate the amount of money needed to fund its operating programs for the next fiscal year. This is the total amount that must be raised through taxes. Allowing for the fact that some of these taxes are likely to be uncollectible, the actual tax levy must be higher than the amount to be collected. If it is estimated that 3 percent of taxes levied will not be collected, then the other 97 percent of the property must provide the required tax revenue.

The tax base is determined by first subtracting the value of nontaxable property (used by churches, schools, and other tax-exempt organizations) from the total assessed value of property in the taxing district. Next, an estimate of tax exemptions must be made, such as those given for old age, disability, veterans, or homestead exemptions. After deducting the value of all nontaxable property and exemptions, the net assessed value of the property in the district can be estimated. Finally, the total tax amount required is divided by the net assessed value of property to determine the tax rate required to fund the activities for the next fiscal year. The process is illustrated in Example 7.1.

Example 7.1 ▪ *Determination of Tax Base and Tax Rate*

Total amount of taxes required for funding	$ 100,000	
Allowance for uncollectible property taxes (collectible amount = 97%)	3%	
Required tax levy = $100,000/.97	$ 103,093	
Total assessed value of property	$ 9,000,000	
Less value of nontaxable property	(1,500,000)	
Net assessed value of taxable property		$ 7,500,000
Less exemptions:		
Homestead	$500,000	
Veterans	300,000	
Old age and disability	600,000	
Total exemptions:		(1,400,000)
Net assessed value of property (tax base)		$ 6,100,000

$$\text{Tax rate} = \frac{\text{Required tax levy}}{\text{Tax base}} = \frac{\$ 103,093}{\$6,100,000} = .0169$$

The tax rate is often expressed as a rate per $100 of net assessed valuation; the tax rate as shown would be $1.69 per $100. It may also be expressed in mills (thousandths of a dollar) as 16.90 mills. In the example shown, the owner of property with a net assessed value of $90,000 would be required to pay property taxes of (.0169 times $90,000) $1521.

Because the tax rate depends on both the tax base and the total tax levy required, it is necessary to have a reasonable estimate of the tax base before governmental budgets can be completed. If unacceptable tax increases appear necessary to finance proposed budgets, those budgets usually must be reduced. Recently, depressed real-estate values have resulted in a loss of total assessed valuation in many areas; this fact, combined with inflation, has forced many local governments to raise tax rates just to maintain existing services.

Local taxpayers usually have a certain amount of choice in the budgets passed by their elected officials and will not tolerate excessive increases. Good public relations that increase public awareness of the value of the library can result in expanded community support and may well translate into votes resulting in more tax money for the library. However, with competition for tax revenues soaring and taxpayers becoming increasingly unwilling to pay more, public libraries need to locate other sources of funding.

Tuition and Fees

Colleges, universities, and private schools receive funds through the tuition charged to students, and a portion of these funds is used to support the library. Occasionally, a specific fee may be charged for library services, or a fee may be charged to students registered for courses requiring library resources beyond those normally provided. When tuition and fees are the primary sources of revenue, the library's resources are heavily dependent on enrollment and on the governing body's willingness to increase the charges to students. Public schools and universities also receive funding from a variety of tax sources in addition to their tuition and fee revenues.

Many universities also have endowment funds that support all programs, including the library. However, there is a great deal of competition for any unrestricted income from these funds, which may also be used to keep student tuition rates at reasonable levels.

Fines and Lost-Book Charges

Most nonprofit and governmental libraries collect fines for overdue or damaged materials and include a certain amount of such revenue in their annual budgets. In determining charges for overdue materials, it is worthwhile to consider your administrative costs of assessing and collecting the fines as well as the possible effect on public relations.

Money from payments for lost or damaged materials may be available but at best serves only to replace a small portion of those items that are lost or damaged. There are various practices regarding lost and damaged materials; some libraries charge the full replacement cost of the lost item plus a processing charge, while other libraries charge a minimal amount, especially for an older item. In many cases funds collected for these purposes are not retained for the sole benefit of the library but instead must be passed through to the funding agency where they are deposited into the general fund.

Other Sources of Support

To expand and improve library services, it is often necessary to secure funds outside the normal sources of support. User fees and chargeback systems, grants and contracts, and a variety of fund-raising campaigns are some of the methods used successfully in libraries.

User Fees

Most libraries are intended to serve a specific clientele, and the basic support provided is expected to cover the cost of basic services to those patrons. When searching for extra sources of revenue, however, questions may arise: What are the basic services, and who is the basic clientele? Usually the basic clientele is defined by its inclusion in the funding base; for example, residents of the taxing area or students registered in a school would be part of the basic clientele, while non-residents or students from other schools would not be included. Outside the basic areas, user fees may be appropriate.

Many libraries provide services to some groups other than those for which they are primarily intended. Public libraries located near businesses often have a large number of patrons who are not part of the base of taxpaying support. Academic libraries provide services for many users who are not part of the school or university community. It may be feasible to require that those patrons who are not part of the library's primary user group pay a user fee, such as an annual fee for a library card or a per-item cost for borrowing. It must be decided whether all outside users should be charged or whether the library should continue to provide free services to certain groups. For example, a university may feel that free library services should be provided to local high school students but that adults in the community should pay a fee. Each decision must be weighed in terms of public relations and the cost to administer the program.

It is becoming increasingly common to charge users for certain types of library services. No longer only a book-lending body, the modern library may offer copying services; database searching; and loans of typewriters, artworks, and videocassettes and equipment. While the ethics of fees is not a topic for this book, the use of fees as a source of revenue or cost recovery is worthy of discussion.

Research and university libraries are more accustomed than public libraries to charging for specialized services, although the purpose of the fee is likely to be for the recovery of the expense rather than for the production of revenue. Preparation of research reports and bibliographies, translations, in-depth reference service, and indexing are only a few of the services often provided for a fee. Online search services, which are valuable but costly, provide information specifically tailored to the needs of the user, and libraries must often recover all or part of the cost of the service.

If a decision is made to charge for a service, a separate decision must be made about how much to charge. Should the library try to recover the full cost (including all direct and indirect costs) or only the direct cost attributable to the service? The cost of an interlibrary loan, for example, includes a portion of the loan department's time and expenses required to process the loan, but it may be desirable to charge the user only those costs for copying, postage, and other easily identified direct charges.

The most acceptable charges to patrons are for those services in which patron-specific costs are incurred and are charged to the patron using the service. Charges are usually based on the time period of the loan or the service. When charging for online services, the use of a client-specific password or number can ensure that the correct time and charges will be separated automatically and shown on the billing statement from the vendor. Through careful analysis of costs associated with a particular service, a reasonable decision may be made concerning the amount of fees required. However, the final decision concerning "fee or free" will depend on the mission of the library, its clientele, and the services it wishes to provide them.

Chargeback Systems

Libraries that exist to serve for-profit businesses find many benefits in a chargeback system to charge time and dollars to the appropriate areas of the business. Depending on the type of business, library services may be charged to specific projects, clients, or departments. Because a librarian may be able to do research much more efficiently than other professionals in the business, a client may receive better service while being charged less than he or she would pay for the services of a higher-paid professional. The billing may create an additional source of income for the business and may result indirectly in improved status and higher morale for the library and its staff. If the library can be recognized as a source of revenue rather than as an added expense, its value to the business will improve and the addition of staff and services may be justified.

Whether library charges include full costs or are limited to direct costs is only one of many decisions to be made before the final implementation of a chargeback system. Any chargeback system used in a business must be thoroughly discussed, supported, and understood by upper management, and the time to administer the system must be justified. Cost analysis and careful monitoring of time and services used for specific departments or projects are essential for a successful chargeback of library costs since management or clients who are billed are likely to require documentation to support the charges.

Fund-Raising Campaigns

Many programs that may be beneficial to the patrons of nonprofit and governmental libraries cannot be adequately funded through the customary funding sources. If support is not forthcoming elsewhere, it may be realistic for the library director and board to undertake their own fund-raising campaign. The campaign may be an operating campaign to raise funds for annual support, a capital campaign for special building needs, or a campaign to create an endowment for supplemental income in future years.

Setting Campaign Goals and Objectives

One of the first steps in a fund-raising campaign is the establishment of the financial goal the campaign will attempt to reach. The goal is an important part of campaign strategy, since too high a goal may discourage volunteers and contributors and result in failure and loss of credibility. Too low a goal may fail to challenge the library's constituency and miss the opportunity to advance new programs for the library.

Those individuals with input in the budget process should participate in the establishment of campaign goals, since they already have knowledge of the costs of desired programs and services and the amount of funding available from traditional sources. The individuals who will run the campaign also need to have input to determine what amounts they may realistically be challenged to achieve. This may require analysis of such factors as current economic conditions and other trends that may affect the campaign. If a similar campaign has been successful in the past, the new campaign should at least achieve a goal that is adjusted for inflation. The final compromise should present a challenging but not impossible task.

Community Resources

The community that benefits from the services of the library is one of the first sources that should be considered in a fund-raising effort. Individuals who support the library's programs, local service organizations, and businesses are some of the areas that may provide ongoing financial support for the library. Corporations with plants or offices in the community often make donations to local projects and are excellent potential sources of support. An effective fund-raising campaign will explore the desires of the donor community to ensure that the library is responding to their needs. It is also important to explore staff attitudes and enlist support within the library and the organization.

One of the fundamental requirements of a successful fund-raising campaign is competent leadership. An influential and well-liked campaign chairperson lends credibility to the campaign and provides support from the top. A chairperson obtained from the community rather than from within the organization helps to broaden the base of support for the campaign. A successful campaign also needs good leadership to secure equipment, develop jobs and committees, arrange for printed materials, keep records, and lead the staff. Some of this work may be done by paid staff within the organization.

Whether the campaign seeks direct contributions or sponsors a fund-raising event, the project should be carefully planned from beginning to end. A special event to kick off the campaign often provides valuable publicity. Records should be kept of donors, both for subsequent recognition and for possible later solicitation, and acknowledgment and appreciation should be provided to all supporters. A thank-you note, disclosure of donor names in a publication, or other public recognition is usually welcome. Memorial gifts and commemorative opportunities, such as bookplates, plaques, or even named rooms or buildings also provide an incentive for donations of varying magnitudes.

Potential contributors often require a great deal of information before committing funds. They may be particularly concerned about the fiscal responsibility of the library and the organization. They may desire evidence of a good track record in budgeting and accounting for the funds the library has already received and assurance that these funds have been used as intended to provide efficient, cost-effective service. It is appropriate to compile a financial data package to be used in fund-raising efforts, since you can improve your library's chances of receiving funding by demonstrating a good record in handling its financial affairs. Such a package should include financial statements, particularly comparative statements showing activities for two years or more; current and proposed budgets for revenues and expenses; and an explanation of how funds are to be obtained. Donors also need complete information on services that the library provides for its patrons, the programs for which funding is sought, how these programs will be implemented, and how they will contribute to the mission of the library or the organization.

Any campaign that involves many cash contributions must ensure that all contributions are received by the library and properly accounted for. One helpful method is the use of prenumbered acknowledgment forms to provide donors with a receipt for tax purposes, with a duplicate kept by the library for later reconciliation. Donor names might also be published on a regular basis, since donors whose names are absent from a published list are likely to complain.

Grants and Contracts

Grants and contracts may be obtained from numerous sources in addition to those in the local community. Most grant and contract funding is provided by government agencies, private foundations, and corporations. Foundations usually exist for the purpose of making grants subject to the guidelines prescribed when the foundation was established.

Prior to applying for outside funding, it is helpful to compile a needs assessment to determine exact goals and objectives that require funding, specific tasks needed to accomplish these objectives, and the cost of completing these tasks. It is important to determine specific needs for which outside funding might be appropriate and to select a funding source that is likely to support the request.

If it is determined that a program is worthwhile and that special funding is desirable, a source of funding must be found. State agencies and publications of the federal government and foundations provide detailed information to assist in the identification of funding agencies and the types of assistance they are likely to provide. The *Catalog of Federal Domestic Assistance* describes federal programs intended for libraries, and the *Foundation Grants Index* and *The Foundation Directory* give detailed information on several hundred large private foundations.

It is wise to take advantage of political and ideological trends and to look for organizations that support specific goals, emphasizing the objectives of the funding agency rather than the library. For example, library programs aimed at improving adult literacy, providing reading opportunities for children in poverty, or enhancing access to books for the elderly or homeless might be programs suitable for outside funding. Such programs could benefit a targeted group while also supplementing the basic goals of the library.

Before requesting funding, it is important to determine that the program has support within the organization and that the resources acquired would be beneficial in both the short term and the long term. It would not be wise to obtain a grant to install a computer system if no money would be available for maintenance or to obtain a special book collection if there would be no funds for preservation and storage. The impact of the program on the library's long-term plan is very important.

Grants may be requested for a variety of purposes. A new program establishing service for a particular group of users may be desired. If a grant is requested to establish the service, you should demonstrate how the library intends to continue the service when funding ends. A research proposal may be appropriate, in which a specific service or program is to be evaluated, or a problem or group is to be studied. You may have an idea for a pilot or demonstration program providing a new concept in service; in this case it is important to specify how the success of the program will be determined and how results will be distributed to others. Training grants are appropriate when specific training might be needed by the library staff or when training is to be offered to others. Grants may also be appropriate methods of obtaining technical support, equipment, or even construction of new library buildings.

Grants for general library capital improvements are increasingly difficult to obtain, but some awards for library construction or equipment purchases may be available from private foundations, government agencies, or corporations. Funding possibilities are greatest for capital improvements that reflect the special purposes of the granting agency, such as energy conservation measures or renovations that will assist the elderly or disabled. These may require that the library obtain a portion of the necessary funds to demonstrate that the project has additional support. Requirements and application procedures need to be determined prior to making a formal request; in some cases an informal request may be all that is necessary.

Prior to writing a proposal to request funding, it is necessary to develop a clear plan for the program and its future. When this has been accomplished, the program may be described in the proposal for funding. Because of the large numbers of organizations seeking grants, granting agencies have become increasingly discriminating and selective. It is a good idea to develop grants skills within your library, perhaps selecting a staff member to receive special training to serve as a grants coordinator.

The Proposal

The proposal is a written request for funding to accomplish a specific purpose. The quality and presentation of the proposal are critical to the success of the project. The proposal should be a positive statement that sets forth a program to the funder in a way that maximizes the chances of acceptance. The proposal should include the program plan, the request for funding, and sufficient information to persuade the funder that the program is needed and can be accomplished by the requester.

Proposals may be solicited or unsolicited. A solicited proposal responds to a formal *request for proposal (RFP)*. Such requests may be found in foundation and government publications; one that is particularly well known is *Commerce Business Daily*, a government publication covering federal funding. When responding to an RFP, it is especially important to ensure that the proposal meets the requirements of the funding agency. If these requirements are not clearly stated in the RFP, it would be wise to contact the funder for the required specifications. Because the proposal will be evaluated by the funding agency, it is important that it be clear and accurate. An organization may also seek support by initiating an unsolicited proposal; prior to submitting such a proposal it is very important to ascertain the requirements of the funding agency and its willingness to consider such a proposal.

The program plan demonstrates the organization's planning ability and should include complete guidelines for the program's implementation. Information concerning the number and type of staff required, the method of accomplishing the goal, equipment needed, completion time, and specific costs involved should all be a part of this plan. If funds are granted, the program plan provides an effective management tool during implementation.

The request for funds should include the exact amount of money needed and why, with justification for each item. In return for these funds, the library promises the funding agency that specific tasks will be completed within a specific time at a specific cost. If the request is granted, this may become a legal contract.

A successful proposal is likely to include most of the following components.

1. A letter of transmittal includes the name, address, and phone number of the organization; a summary of a proposal; why the request is being made of the specific funding agency; and a contact person and phone number.

2. The introduction establishes the basic reason for the request, including a general description of the nature of the problem and the methodology of the program.

3. The problem statement defines and documents the nature and extent of the problem and assesses a need for a solution.

4. Program objectives state the strategies and goals of the program, including specific measurable accomplishments. Presentation of objectives in list form may be helpful.

5. A description of program activities describes the methods to be used to accomplish the objectives and states why these methods have been selected. This section may be lengthy and should clearly show what will be done and how the activities will accomplish the objectives. Organizing the activities into groups may contribute to a clearer proposal.

6. The description of personnel describes the persons who will direct the project and how their credentials relate to the objectives of the program. Résumés should be provided noting individuals' relevant accomplishments, such as fiscal expertise or experience in similar projects.

7. A timetable shows the projected accomplishment of activities on a chart or a time line.

8. An evaluation plan provides a method to determine effectiveness of the program in accomplishing the objectives. The level of evaluation required by the funder should be determined prior to developing this plan.

9. The budget lists anticipated personnel and other direct costs. Personnel costs include wages and salaries, fringe benefits, consultants, and contract services. Other direct costs include travel, lease, purchase or rental of equipment, phone charges, rent, consumable supplies, and other related costs. Guidelines should be obtained from prospective funding agencies to determine allowable and nonallowable costs; indirect costs should be included if permitted. Budget information should be verified with the fiscal officer of your organization to determine that you are following any guidelines and restrictions your organization may have.

10. Future funding information presents a strategy for continuing the program after grant funding ceases.

An objective individual with expertise in grant requests should review the proposal prior to submission. Using a consultant for this purpose might well prove to be worthwhile.

Often the granting agency will require that the recipient match the grant in some way. This may be a *hard match*, or equal-dollar amount, that may require a special fund-raising effort if funds are not forthcoming from the governing agency. If regular employees are to work on the project, funds to pay for their salary and fringe benefits may be part of this contribution. An *in-kind,* or *soft,* match may be required, whereby the library must supply services equal in dollar value to the funds provided. A soft match usually is easier to accomplish, since the rental value of equipment, the contribution of staff time, and other services may be used to complete the match. Be sure to include indirect costs, such as fringe benefits and value of space utilized. Including these indirect costs may make your job of finding matching funds a great deal easier.

If a grant is awarded, the award is usually communicated by letter. There is usually some flexibility in the use of grant funds; while some general services may be specified, there is usually no requirement of a final product. A contract is usually more specific, requiring definite results, and often specifying certain forms to be used and reports to be submitted. The agreement between the funding source and the recipient is summarized after negotiations are completed; this written summary is often called a *letter of agreement.*

After a project is funded, it must be carefully monitored and evaluated. The funding agency usually requires a report that demonstrates that the project was completed for the funded purpose. Most grants, even for long-term projects, are provided for a one-year period and must be renewed if the program is not to be completed within one year. For this reason it is especially important to adhere to all requirements of the funding agency, maintain complete records on the project and its finances, submit timely and complete reports, cooperate with audits, and adhere to all regulations. Prior approval should be obtained for any changes that may be necessary during the project's implementation, and problem areas should be given careful attention so that they may be resolved.

Because the granting agency lends its name and prestige to the project, it has a commitment to its success. A good relationship with the funder, the parent organization, and the clientele are all important to the successful continuation and renewal of grants.

Minigrants

Small grants, or minigrants, occasionally may be obtained by a short proposal in the form of a letter to the potential funder. Such a letter should include the following:

1. A description of the need for the program, or a description of the problem that needs to be solved, including documentation showing the extent of the problem.
2. A description of the program, its overall purpose, and the major activities to be undertaken, including a listing of the major objectives and the time period during which these are to be accomplished.
3. An explanation of the reason that the proposal should be supported by the potential funder, including recognition of the funder's goals and history of related support.
4. The background and capability of the organization requesting the funding, including supporting documentation as appropriate.
5. A detailed budget request, including an outline of the staff to be paid from the grant, with position requirements or staff qualifications. (If the budget includes more than a few items, a separate page is recommended.)

The miniproposal may be more efficient than a lengthy proposal and often is more likely to be read than a thick proposal, which might be added to a large stack of such documents. However, there is the risk that a brief request will not fully convey the importance of the project to be undertaken or that a funder might be more impressed with a larger document. As with any proposal, it is wise to contact the potential funder prior to submission to determine if a brief form would be welcomed.

Capital Contributions

Capital contributions are donations that are not intended for operating purposes. For this reason they are not considered revenues and do not affect net income. Instead, they are direct additions to the equity or fund balance of the organization.

The two primary types of capital contributions are contributions for endowment and contributions for plant (capital assets). Large contributions of money are often designated for endowment purposes, and only the earnings from these funds may be used for operations. Income from operating activities will not be affected by such contributions;

therefore, separate funds are established for endowments and for contributed plant to keep them separate from current operating funds.

Contributions for plant include capital assets or funds specifically designated for the purchase of such assets. Contributed plant may include such items as land donated for the site of a new library building, sculpture or artwork for the lobby, a computer system, or a large donation to pay for a new building or annex. Funds may be contributed to acquire a specific building or other fixed asset. Although such contributions present no cost to the library, they are recorded on the accounting records at their fair market value at the time they are received. This is an exception to the usual accounting rule of recording items at their historical cost. In-depth discussion of plant and endowment funds is included in the section on fund accounting in Chapter 3.

Obtaining Endowment Funds

An endowment fund is intended to be nonexpendable, meaning that the principal of the fund is not to be spent but that the earnings of the fund may be used to finance activities. The existence of an endowment fund provides a library with a perpetual source of revenue for current and future programs.

Some donors place restrictions on the investment of their donations or the use of the earnings; these are legal restrictions and must be carefully followed. Prior to accepting such an endowment, you should carefully analyze any restrictions and ensure that the library will be able to use the earnings in a way that will enhance its programs. If it does not seem likely, you should attempt to renegotiate the gift or possibly reject it entirely.

If there are no restrictions, the earnings from the endowment fund may be used as library management sees fit, whether to finance the normal activities of the library or to fund special programs that might not otherwise receive support. It is to the library's advantage to obtain this type of endowment whenever possible.

Deferred Giving

One method of building an endowment fund is a deferred-giving program, which allows donors to transfer cash or property to the library at some date in the distant future. Wills, trusts, and life insurance are potential methods by which libraries may receive significant financial assistance at minimum cost to the donor. To be successful, a deferred-giving program should be established with professional legal and financial advice and should be carefully marketed to attract potential donors. If you feel that deferred giving has potential for your library, it is helpful to set up a committee to monitor the program and to begin in a simple manner with the development of bequests.

Libraries may be beneficiaries of bequests as specified in a valid *will*, which directs how an individual's estate is to be distributed after his or her death. Because the donor has the right to enjoy the property during his or her lifetime and has no use for it after death, a will provides an opportunity for an individual to make a meaningful gift to a library at no immediate cost to the donor. Wills must abide by state laws, which vary greatly, but must generally be written, signed, dated, and witnessed. Problems may arise if the will is contested or if the estate is not large enough to cover all bequests.

If your library is interested in soliciting bequests, it is helpful to provide potential donors with a statement that may be inserted in a will; for example, "I bequeath the sum of $ ____ to XYZ Public Library, located in XYZ, N.Y." A local attorney should be consulted to ensure that the language is correct for your state. Providing this information to your patrons is one of the simplest methods of developing a deferred giving program.

A bequest provides no benefit to the donor during his or her lifetime and provides no benefit to the library until after the donor's death. In comparison, a trust may be established that provides many current benefits for the donor, while the library usually receives benefits at a later time. The donor receives an immediate tax deduction for the allowable value of the trust but may continue to receive some benefits from the donated property.

A *trust* is a legal entity created for the purpose of managing funds on behalf of a beneficiary, which may be an individual or an institution such as a library. The trust requires a separate administrative board that is responsible for management of funds and reporting on its activities.

A trust has two basic parts. The first is the principal, or *corpus*, of the trust, and the second is the income from the principal. One of the most common types of trusts is the *charitable remainder trust*, where the donor transfers principal to the trust and the donor or other beneficiary receives annual payments; at some designated time the remainder of the principal is turned over to the named charity. Such an action provides the donor with an immediate tax deduction and may also reduce the taxable value of the estate. There are many types of trusts; because the laws governing them are quite complex, professional assistance is necessary.

Life insurance provides a method for individuals to make large gifts that might otherwise be well beyond their means. A donation of a paid-up insurance policy provides an immediate tax deduction for the donor without any transfer of cash and provides the library with the face value of the policy at the donor's death. Other attractive alternatives might be the payment of the premiums on a new or existing policy that names the library as beneficiary or the assignment of dividend payments to the library. In either case, the donor is entitled to a tax deduction for the contribution but pays out little or no cash for the future benefit to the library. Over time, the proceeds from life insurance policies can provide the library with a substantial endowment.

For the library to be assured of receiving the benefits of an insurance policy on a donor's life, it is preferable for the library to be the owner of the policy. If the policy is owned by the donor, it is subject to the donor's control; the beneficiary may be changed, the policy may be used for a loan or as collateral, and the proceeds of the policy must be included in the donor's estate, subject to estate taxes or claims of creditors or relatives who choose to contest the will. These difficulties may be avoided if the library owns the policy; the donor may take the tax deduction for the cash value of the donated policy and for payment of later premiums.

Friends of the Library

Libraries have been supported by private benefactors for hundreds of years, but recent years have seen more support from ordinary citizens through groups known as Friends of the Library. These groups are incorporated separately from the library and have their own bylaws, thus permitting them financial flexibility and independence in choosing the programs and services they wish to support. They often provide fund-raising support, volunteer services, and public relations assistance for libraries and may act as advocates when funding is threatened. Encouragement of a Friends group and a spirit of active cooperation may result in significant benefits to the library and to the community.

Friends of the Library usually collect membership dues and often sponsor book sales for the library. These sales are one of the most common revenue sources of Friends organizations, often including donated books as well as library discards. Active Friends groups may also sponsor other fund-raising events unique to the community, such as dinners, telethons, auctions, and social, cultural, or sporting events.

Friends groups are most common for academic and public libraries but occasionally may be appropriate for other types of libraries. To obtain information on establishing a Friends organization for your library, contact the Secretary of State for your state for instructions on the incorporation of a nonprofit organization, and consult current IRS publications for information on tax-exempt status.

Volunteer Services

The value of volunteer services should not be overlooked when seeking sources of support. Able and willing volunteers may provide many of the services otherwise required of paid staff, such as conducting story hours; checking out, repairing, or shelving books; or other clerical or semiprofessional services. It is obvious that funds freed from staff requirements may be used elsewhere, although too much reliance on volunteers certainly may be risky. To encourage volunteer participation, it is very important to provide recognition and to show appreciation to loyal volunteers.

Operation of an Unrelated Business

It may be opportune to raise funds on a regular basis through operation of a business unrelated to the regular program of the library. Examples would be rental of unused storage space to a local business or sale of binding services to for-profit advertisers. If the library is tax exempt but the business is not related to the tax-exempt purpose of the library, profits from the income may be taxable. Sale of products or services to other nonprofit organizations and sale of donated property are considered by the IRS to be related businesses and therefore are not taxable.

There are three items that determine whether an activity is an unrelated business.

1. The business is conducted to make a profit.
2. The business is a regular activity, not just an occasional one.
3. The business is not significantly related to the tax-exempt program of the library.

Careful planning may allow a business to be established so that it is not taxable, and up-to-date IRS regulations should be consulted for further guidelines. The possibility of a tax should not be the only factor in deciding whether or not to conduct a business for a profit, since after-tax profits from an unrelated business may be used as a source of support for the library.

The Library Development Office

When large amounts of funds are sought, it may be feasible to hire a development officer or consultant to direct and coordinate fund-raising activities. Such a position probably will be required to pay for itself through increased funding.

In selecting a development officer or fund-raising consultant, interpersonal skills are very important. The individual must have superior ability to work successfully with management and staff as well as volunteers and potential donors. The position also requires planning and administrative skills to guide and carry through successful fund-raising activities.

Investments

As discussed in Chapter 6, it is important to invest unused funds for maximum return with minimum risk. If the amount of funds to be invested is significant, an investment committee or professional management may be appropriate.

Summary

Librarians must be aware of traditional sources of funding and the ways in which increasing demand for critical services may have an impact upon the resources available to libraries. It may be beneficial to increase library support through consideration of new alternatives and active participation in the funding process. All types of libraries may find it appropriate to consider services to recover their costs or produce added revenues, while nonprofit and governmental libraries can also benefit from actively seeking grants and donations.

The benefits of donated services and assets should not be under-estimated nor should the importance of active participation of volunteers, Friends of the Library, or other local groups. By providing the donor community with the information and the incentive to provide additional support in a variety of ways, the library can increase its ability to provide expanded services while also enhancing community awareness of the many benefits it offers.

Additional Reading

Annual Register of Grant Support. 26th ed. New York: Bowker, 1993.

Association of Research Libraries. *Fee-based Services in ARL Libraries.* Kit #157, September 1989. Washington, D.C.: ARL, 1989.

Barber, Peggy, and Linda Crowe. *Getting Your Grant: A How-to-Do-It Manual for Librarians.* New York: Neal-Schuman, 1991.

Boss, Richard W. *Grant Money and How to Get it.* New York: Bowker, 1980.

Breivik, Patricia, and E. Burr Gibson, eds. *Funding Alternatives for Libraries.* Chicago: American Library Association, 1979.

Corry, Emmett. *Grants for Libraries: A Guide to Public and Private Funding Programs and Proposal-Writing Techniques.* 2d ed. Littleton, Colo.: Libraries Unlimited, 1986.

Dewey, Barbara I., ed. *Raising Money for Academic and Research Libraries: A How-to-Do-It Manual for Librarians.* New York: Neal-Schuman, 1991.

Drake, Miriam A. *User Fees: A Practical Perspective.* Littleton, Colo.: Libraries Unlimited, 1981.

Firstenberg, Paul B. *Managing for Profit in the Nonprofit World.* New York: The Foundation Center, 1986.

Herring, Mark Y. *Organizing Friends Groups: A How-to-Do-It Manual for Librarians.* New York: Neal-Schuman, 1991.

Lee, Sul H. *Library Fund-Raising: Vital Margin for Excellence.* Ann Arbor, Mich.: Pierian Press, 1984.

Lefferts, Robert. *Getting a Grant in the 1990s.* New York: Prentice-Hall, 1990.

Lord, James G. *The Raising of Money.* Cleveland, Ohio: Third Sector Press, 1986.

National Guide to Funding for Libraries and Information Services. New York: The Foundation Center, 1991.

Non-Tax Sources of Revenue for Public Libraries. ALA Survey Report, ALA Office for Research. Chicago: American Library Association, 1988.

Razek, Joseph R., and Gordon A. Hosch. *Introduction to Governmental and Not-for-Profit Accounting.* Englewood Cliffs, N.J.: Prentice-Hall, 1985.

Steele, Victoria, and Stephen D. Elder. *Becoming a Fundraiser: The Principles and Practice of Library Development.* Chicago: American Library Association, 1992.

Warner, Alice Sizer. *Making Money: Fees for Library Services.* New York: Neal-Schuman, 1989.

■ 8

Control of Library Operations

Through the planning and budgeting process you have carefully analyzed alternatives and made decisions concerning the future of your library. While the planning period establishes the guidelines for the operating period that follows, it is the activities of the operating period that determine the actual success or failure of the library's programs.

The budget is only one of the methods used to ensure that library operations are conducted in accordance with certain management guidelines. There are several other ways in which libraries must maintain control over their operations in order to ensure that funds are properly accounted for and used in the most productive way. Whether your library is part of a nonprofit, governmental, or for-profit organization, the procedures for controlling operations are essentially the same.

Internal Control

Leaders of any organization must recognize the importance of capable management and appreciate the need for adequate and consistent control of the organization's operations. Internal control is a broad concept that includes the means by which an organization safeguards its assets, promotes accuracy and reliability of records, encourages compliance with policies, and evaluates the efficiency of the operation. Just as librarians exercise bibliographic control over the library's contents, they must also exercise control over the library's operations. Libraries have practiced internal control for years; library cards ensure that materials are loaned only to authorized users, overdue notices help to ensure that materials will be returned, and controlled checkpoints prevent users from bypassing standard checkout procedures. Shelflists, regular inventories, and magnetic security systems are examples of some of the other internal controls commonly found in libraries. The budget is also an internal control mechanism because it documents management's approval for the goals and objectives of the library and for the specific ways in which these goals and objectives are to be funded. Internal control affects all activities of an organization, and includes both administrative controls and accounting controls.

Administrative controls encourage adherence to policies, promote efficiency, and help to provide reasonable assurance that the objectives of the organization will be achieved. Administrative controls extend beyond the accounting area but provide the basis for the decision making, authorization, and record-keeping procedures that affect the financial welfare of the organization. A procedures manual listing each task and how it should be done is a worthwhile administrative control that assists managers and others in reviewing the system. It is also helpful for training new employees and providing guidance for temporary replacements. Procedures for registering new borrowers, issuing library cards, and keeping circulation records are some administrative controls commonly used in libraries.

Accounting controls deal with safeguarding assets, maintaining reliable accounting data, and ensuring that expenditures are authorized and in accordance with appropriate regulations. These controls deal directly with items that affect the reliability of the financial records of the organization; lack of controls may result in confusion and difficulty in making wise financial decisions. Authorization for purchasing or disposing of library materials and equipment; regular inventories; and procedures for collecting, recording, and depositing fines are some examples of accounting controls used in libraries.

Internal control systems depend upon the size, structure, and objectives of the organization and vary greatly among different types of libraries. Essential features are a well-designed organizational plan, a logical accounting system, adequate control over assets and records, and well-trained, high-quality personnel.

The Organizational Plan

The organizational plan provides the framework for planning, directing, and controlling operations. It should include definite lines of responsibility, providing for the delegation of tasks while making it clear where final responsibility for each activity lies. Organization charts and position descriptions outlining the duties and constraints of specific positions are helpful in providing additional clarification. Each individual should know to whom he or she is accountable and should have a written job description, preferably with written standards of performance. It is also important to be able to identify who has authority to make decisions and to act in case of an emergency at any time, particularly in a library that is open during hours when the top administrator is not present.

One of the most basic concepts of internal control is the separation of duties, a system of checks and balances designed so that no individual or single department handles all aspects of a transaction from beginning to end. The organizational plan should be designed in a manner that separates incompatible activities and provides independent cross-checking of work. For example, record keeping should be separate from authorization for and custody of assets, and purchasing should be separate from receiving. This provides reasonable assurance that every transaction will be reviewed and recorded by more than one individual, thus reducing the opportunity for dishonesty as well as the chance of error. Separation of duties also promotes operational efficiency by making individuals and departments responsible to other areas. If there are not enough individuals in your library to separate all functions, the separation of consecutive functions provides some measure of control.

Depending on the size and staff of the library, the procedures to segregate authority and responsibility may vary a great deal. A large library may have an acquisitions staff or a variety of departments to deal with ordering, receiving, and processing books and materials. Small libraries may have only one professional to perform these tasks; in this case some of the duties inside the library may be completed by clerical staff or volunteers, while the final purchase orders and payment of invoices may be completed outside the library. At least two persons should participate in any transaction before it is completed, and there should be provision for the overall review of activities by higher levels of management.

The Accounting System

Sound accounting practices are very important to the well-being of the organization. The basic practice of double-entry accounting, which requires that debits equal credits, will reveal many errors if items are out of balance. The accounting system should be designed to accommodate the unique features of the organization, and the organization's accounting procedures should be clearly defined in the procedures manual. A chart of accounts listing each account, its number (or name), and its use should be available to all personnel who make decisions concerning the classification of transactions. Information concerning the major accounts and the object codes to be used must be available. Authorization to spend money from specific accounts should be restricted to the individuals who have been approved to make decisions concerning the use of those accounts. For example, the librarian should have authorization to spend money from accounts assigned to the library but should not be able to spend money that belongs to another department. If fund accounting is used, each fund should have a separate account and employees should be made aware of any restrictions on the use of various funds. For example, if your library has been given a donation to purchase large-print books, funds from the donation should be assigned a separate account number, and you must be sure that you do not purchase a new office computer or add to the library's cassette collection with funds from that account.

Forms and documents should be simple and designed to ensure proper completion, with instructions as necessary and designated spaces for numbers, authorizations, dates, and so forth. Forms are often used for data entry into a computer; if this is the case, information on the form should be organized in the order in which it will be entered on the computer screen and should be limited to the number of spaces that may be entered. When a form is used to record financial information, the data-entry form may later be needed to trace the transaction. For this reason it is helpful to have additional space to write an explanation of any unusual circumstances surrounding a particular transaction even if this information is not entered into the computer system.

Important transactions, such as purchase orders, invoices, checks, payroll, and any unusual entries, should be reviewed and approved by a responsible and knowledgeable individual. Transactions should be recorded as soon as they take place. Payments should be made by check with two signatures required on checks for large amounts. Prenumbered checks, receipts, and purchase orders should be used, and all documents should be accounted for. Documents that must be voided for any reason should be recorded, and duplicate copies of those documents that leave the library should be maintained for later audit purposes. In computerized accounting systems, paper copies are often not necessary, but complete backup copies of the system should be saved at regular intervals to ensure that all transaction records are on file.

Purchasing

Because most libraries purchase a large number of materials each year, it is particularly important for librarians to understand how the purchasing process works—from the initial order to the final payment. Because the principle of separation of duties is so important in the overall purchasing process, several individuals are likely to be involved, and communication is extremely important.

The purchasing process usually begins with a *purchase requisition*, which is a request for authorization to purchase. Purchase requisitions usually are sent from the requester to the department authorized to make purchases. This may be the library's own acquisitions department or the organization's purchasing department, which can verify the availability of budgeted funds and the acceptability of the vendor.

Following proper authorization, a *purchase order* is created. These are usually multipart forms so that one copy may be sent to the vendor or jobber while one is retained by the library; the department responsible for paying invoices also may require a copy to prove that purchases were properly authorized. Purchase orders should be numbered and controlled to prevent the possibility of unauthorized purchases being made. Orders should clearly show the name of the vendor and the quantities and prices of goods ordered. Individual purchase orders should be approved by a responsible person who first must verify that funds are available to make the purchase. If it is necessary to telephone a rush order to a vendor, it is important to follow up with the regular purchasing procedures, confirming the order in writing and providing a purchase order number for the request.

Most organizations have strict purchasing rules; it is wise to learn these and follow them carefully. Many of these rules exist for legal reasons, and there may be strict penalties for breaking them. In some cases it may be a requirement to obtain a bid or quotation from more than one vendor. This is true when federal funds are involved or when goods or services over a certain dollar limit are purchased. Procedures for obtaining these bids should be carefully followed.

Governmental bodies follow the practice of encumbering funds when a purchase order is issued. The *encumbrance* signifies an obligation that has been created by the purchase order; since a limited amount of funds is budgeted, it is important that the total amount ordered be less than or equal to the budgeted amount available. With each order, the available balance of budgeted funds is reduced by the amount of the encumbrance; this practice serves to prevent departments from ordering items they later will be unable to pay for. After the item is received and paid for, the encumbrance is removed and the balance available is reduced by the amount actually spent. The encumbrance process is simply a method of keeping track of what has been ordered but not yet received; the technique can prevent embarrassing and detrimental cost overruns in all types of libraries. While the practice of encumbering funds is used formally in governmental units, it is a helpful practice for any librarian to follow.

Outstanding purchase orders should be reviewed periodically so that orders that are not completed on a timely basis may be canceled if necessary. If funds are fully encumbered, further orders may not be placed; if the original purchase orders are not filled, the fiscal year may end with money encumbered but not spent. In many cases, these orders will then be filled from the new year's budget, and the prior-year funds will be lost. For this reason, it is critical to keep track of outstanding purchase orders and to contact vendors prior to the end of the budget year if problems arise. A record should be maintained of canceled orders so that there is no doubt concerning a missing purchase order number.

When items are received, it is necessary to carefully compare the packing slips with the actual items to be sure that all items listed are actually received. It is also important to compare these with the original purchase orders to ensure that unwanted items have not been shipped. The record of information received is called a *receiving report;* this may be the packing slip or some other document. Usually, it is necessary for someone in the receiving department to verify in writing that all items listed on the receiving report actually have been received and to note missing or damaged items. This information then is conveyed to the department that pays the invoices; receiving reports must later be compared with the invoices to be sure that the library is not being billed for materials it did not receive. Receiving reports that have not been matched with purchase orders and/or invoices need to be reviewed periodically, since a problem may be indicated. Procedures need to be in place to determine which department will work with the vendor to resolve problems related to the various stages of the purchasing process.

It is important to understand that a purchase order or encumbrance does *not* create an immediate liability. When any organization orders goods or services, it incurs an obligation to accept and pay for these items, but the order usually may be canceled prior to shipping or delivery. (An exception exists when the order is customized, such as printed stationery or other products that are specially produced and cannot be used by others. In such a case the liability is incurred at the time the vendor begins the customizing process.) You usually do not have a liability to pay for an item until you have received it in good condition, although some vendor terms may state that you are responsible for the item at the time and place of shipping. The actual liability usually is incurred on the date of receipt, not the date of the order or the date of the invoice. This ordinarily is not an issue except at the end of each fiscal year; at that time it is helpful to understand just what your outstanding liabilities, or accounts payable, really are. If you receive a $900 shipment of books on June 29 and your fiscal year ends on June 30, you have a current liability to pay for those books even though the invoice may not arrive until July 8. Your accounting department will need to know that you received the books prior to June 30 so that the $900 liability may be shown on the financial statements for the fiscal year being completed. If you ordered (and encumbered) the books in June and did not receive them until July 2, you do not have a liability for the fiscal year that ended on June 30.

Accounts payable is the term used for the outstanding current liabilities of an organization; the term may also be used for the section of the accounting department that handles the payment of bills. This operation may be handled within the library or another department in the organization, but it is important that it be separated from the purchasing and receiving functions. It is particularly important for the library to notify the accounts payable area that materials have been received so that the receiving report may be compared with the invoice before payment is approved. If invoices are paid by another department in your organization, be sure that any invoices vendors send directly to your library are forwarded immediately. There must be continual communication between the library and the department responsible for payment to ensure that only approved invoices are paid but that payments are not delayed because of a lack of verification by the library.

Invoices should be recorded as soon as received, and careful attention should be paid to the due date of the invoice. Some vendors provide discounts for payments within ten days (or other specified period); it is sometimes possible to save substantial amounts by ensuring that payments are made within the discount period. If there is no discount or if the time limit cannot be met, the full amount of the bill must be paid when due. Usually this is a twenty-five- to thirty-day period from the date of the invoice. If the library's funds are invested in interest-bearing accounts, it is wise cash management to delay the payment of these bills until they are due (unless you can obtain a discount greater than your investment earnings) so that the library, and not the vendor, will obtain the benefit of the funds for as long as possible.

Prior to final payment of an invoice, a voucher usually is prepared. A *voucher* is a document that authorizes payment; vouchers should be consecutively numbered and should indicate the vendor name and address, invoice number and date, amount to be paid, account to be charged, and authorization signature or initials. In computerized systems, only authorized individuals should be allowed access to the part of the system that creates a voucher. Vouchers provide an extra safe-guard in separating the authorization and payment functions. It is often standard practice to require a copy of the purchase order and the receiving report before preparing the voucher authorizing payment. This provides added assurance that correct procedures were followed throughout the purchasing process.

The voucher provides authorization for payment and is followed by the production of a check. Checks should be prenumbered and care-fully controlled; checks that for some reason are not used should be voided and recorded. As previously stated, there should be separation of the functions of invoice approval, check writing, and check signing.

The purchasing cycle follows an established pattern, which varies slightly according to the structure of the organization. The pattern illustrated in Figure 2 is one of the most common for organizations that have separate purchasing and accounting departments. Some organizations also may have a separate receiving department where items are checked in prior to delivery to the library.

In Figure 2 the library sends a requisition (1) to the purchasing department, which creates a purchase order (2) and sends a copy to the vendor, as well as a copy to the library and the accounting department. The vendor ships the requested materials (3) to the library and sends

Figure 2 ▪ *The Purchasing Cycle*

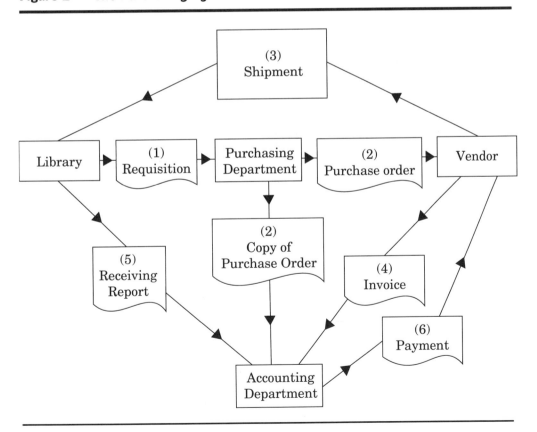

the invoice (4) to the accounting department. The library receives the materials and verifies that the order is correct, then sends a copy of the receiving report (5) to the accounting department. When the accounting department has the purchase order (showing authorization for purchase) and the receiving report (showing receipt of the items) it authorizes payment and sends the payment (6) to the vendor.

Credit Memos

It is sometimes necessary to return items that have been received from a vendor or jobber. An incorrect item may have been shipped, or an item may be damaged or simply inappropriate for the library's needs. It is important to obtain proper credit for these materials. Usually it is necessary to contact the vendor for return instructions and the method of obtaining credit; in most cases a credit memo will be issued. If the invoice has already been paid, this credit will need to be applied to a later invoice. If possible, it is wise to obtain approval for the credit prior to paying the invoice, since it may be difficult to use the credit at a later time. Carrying over credits from one fiscal year to the next also may create difficulties and should be avoided if possible. It is a good idea to maintain a record of all credits due the library from vendors to verify that they are deducted from later invoices. These decisions also may be affected by the payment policies of the organization, the reliability of and relationship with the vendor, and the time in the fiscal year that the problem arises.

Identifying Assets

Items that are received and are satisfactory should be immediately identified as library property and added to the library's shelflist or inventory as soon as possible. Numbered labels should be attached to all equipment immediately after delivery, and a periodic inventory should be taken to ensure that all equipment is present. Books may be stamped, bar coded, or tagged; equipment that does not need to be moved should be bolted in place, and portable equipment should be kept in a locked place when not in use. Missing items should be investigated immediately and steps taken to prevent further loss.

Tracking Encumbrances and Expenses

Libraries are likely to send many purchase orders during the budget year, and a system is needed for tracking those purchase orders that have been filled, those that have been canceled, and those that are outstanding. Because a purchase order creates a commitment to pay for the items ordered after they are received, orders must not exceed the amount of the budgeted funds. Inability to keep track of these commitments may result in an overexpenditure or a failure to spend badly needed budgeted funds. Not all items ordered are usually available; because of discounts, taxes, and shipping charges, the amount finally expended for any item is not often the exact amount of the original purchase order. For this reason encumbrances often must be estimated, and adjustments must be made when orders have been completed and the exact amount of the purchase is known.

A computerized accounting system may be available that shows outstanding purchase orders, encumbered amounts, and unencumbered balances available. If these reports are received on a regular basis, they may provide a method of tracking funds. Even if such a system is available, reports are often received a few weeks after transactions are completed, and the library needs its own internal system to keep track of its purchasing records.

If you have a computer, you will probably find it helpful to set up a system to keep your encumbrances and expenses up to date. Otherwise, columnar books and analysis pads may be purchased through local business supply houses; a looseleaf notebook provides added flexibility and room for expansion. Prior to purchasing books or pads it would be a good idea to sketch the format to be used so that the forms selected will have sufficient columns. A page probably will be needed for each line item in the budget (or, if broad expense groupings are allowed, a page for each group may be preferable). If the library has prepared a program budget, it may be advisable to use a record book or a section for each program. The system used to record purchases needs to be relevant to the actual purchasing system; otherwise, too much time will be needed to convert the purchasing information to the form used by the library.

It is important to remember that the purpose of your system is to assist in tracking expenses; if the system is too cumbersome or time-consuming, it will not serve its purpose well. A balance must be found between the value of the records and the amount of effort required to maintain them. If any new system is being developed, it is wise to try using it for a small portion of the library's expenses prior to making a firm decision on its use, since good ideas often come up while a system is being established. Be prepared to experiment with any new system for a few months so that improvements may be made as new ideas evolve.

Example 8.1 illustrates a form that may be used to track outstanding purchase orders for a specific account. If you work in a for-profit business, one page for each expense group probably will be adequate, whereas libraries in nonprofit or governmental organizations will need to keep a separate page for each fund.

At any time,

Budget balance available =
Total budget − Total encumbrances − Total expenses

Example 8.1 illustrates how a columnar format may be used to track encumbrances, expenses, and available balance for supplies expenses in the operating fund. Column headings are entered for date, vendor name, type of document, voucher number, purchase order number, expense amount, total expenses, encumbrance amount, total encumbrances, and available balance along with a space for comments. The beginning budget balance of $1,000 is entered on the first line on July 1, the beginning of the fiscal year. Also on July 1 purchase order #1 for $100 is sent to a vendor, Miller, and the encumbrance is entered in the encumbered and total encumbrance columns. On July 2

Example 8.1 ■ Tracking Purchase Orders, Encumbrances, and Expenses

Fund ___Operating___   Expense Object or Group ___Supplies___

Budgeted Amount ___$1,000___

(1)	(2)	(3)	(4)	(5)	(6)	(7)	(8)	(9)	(10)	(11)
Date	Vendor	Document	Voucher Number	PO Number	Expense Amount	Expended YTD	Encum-bered	Total Enc.	Balance Available	Comments
7/1									$1,000	Begin balance
7/1	Miller	PO #1		1			$ 100	$100	900	
7/2	Smith	PO #2		2			200	300	700	
7/9	Smith	Voucher	1	2	$ 75	$ 75	(75)	225	700	Partial order
7/11	Miller	Voucher	2	1	95	170	(100)	125	705	PO #1 complete
7/14	Smith	CredMemo		2	(15)	155		125	720	Defective item

purchase order #2 for $200 is sent to another vendor, Smith. The new encumbrance of $200 is entered, and the total encumbrance amount is increased to $300, leaving an available balance of $700.

A partial order arrives from Smith, followed by an invoice for $75. After verifying that all items listed on the invoice have been received, voucher 1 is prepared on July 9 to authorize payment. The expense of $75 is recorded in the current and year-to-date expense columns, and the encumbrances are reduced by $75 as shown by the (75) in the encumbered column. Note that the total budget balance available does not change at this time, since $75 of the encumbrance amount has simply been replaced by the $75 expense, and a partial order for Smith is still outstanding.

Next the complete order from Miller arrives, followed by an invoice for $95. In this case the order cost slightly less than estimated. After verifying that the invoice includes only those items that were ordered and received, voucher 2 is prepared to authorize payment of the $95, and an expense of $95 is recorded. The $95 is added to the previous expense of $75 for a year-to-date expense total of $170. Since the purchase order is complete, the encumbrance amount is reduced by $100 at this time. Notice that these two transactions have the net effect of increasing the balance available by $5, the amount by which the purchase order was overestimated. (Placing a check mark or other indication next to the purchase order number will help you remember that this purchase order is no longer active.)

Soon it is discovered that one of the items in Smith's order is defective, and Smith is contacted for instructions. Smith sends a credit memo for $15, which then reduces the total expenses and increases the budget balance available.

You may wish to use a variation of this form to track your outstanding purchase orders for specific areas of your budget. Depending on the information available to you, it may be more appropriate to record checks, check numbers, and check dates rather than voucher information, or you may find it helpful to increase the number of columns and include both check and voucher information. Receiving information might be of additional value. You probably will also want to adapt the terminology to match that used in your particular organization.

If a microcomputer is available for library use, this same format may be used with software programs that will automatically update totals as new entries are made. Procedures should be in place for the system—whether manual or computerized—to be updated each time a transaction takes place. Since it is important to maintain such a system even if the individual responsible is absent, someone on the staff should be able to handle the duties in the absence of the regular employee. If the system is not maintained properly, it may be useless.

Control over Grants

The library has a legal obligation to monitor the expenditure of grant funds in accordance with the requirements of the funding agreement. Each grant should be identified with a separate account number that can be easily incorporated into the organization's accounting system, and attention should be paid to project control, reporting requirements, and expiration dates. There should be regular internal reports on the status of all grants so that the responsible person can ensure that all funds are being spent as agreed. Often grant funds have a limited time period during which they may be spent; failure to spend these funds within the required time period may result in loss of funds.

Control over Assets and Records

A library has a large investment in books, audiovisual equipment, hardware, software, and other noncash assets; the security of these items is of primary concern to librarians. The library's assets need to be protected against theft, fire, and weather-related damage, yet there must be balance among the controls used, the cost of these controls, and their effect on service. While permanently locking all items in a fireproof, weather-controlled environment might provide the best control over the assets, it would severely limit service. In some libraries all materials must be requested from a staff member who retrieves them from a controlled environment; no browsing is permitted. Many libraries restrict access to and circulation of certain valuable materials; decisions such as these must be made in view of the unique operating environment of each library and the desired balance between service and control.

There should be established procedures for borrowing and checking out library materials and equipment by library patrons and library staff. Periodic inventories should be taken of library books, furniture, materials, and equipment to ensure that items listed in the library records are actually in the library's possession. This provides a means to identify missing materials and judge the scope of any problem. In accordance with the principle of separation of duties, the inventory should be taken by someone other than the individual responsible for maintaining the records. The records should contain price information and should be updated whenever additions and deletions are made to the library's assets.

Clear procedures should be in place for the discarding of library materials and equipment. Disposal procedures often are governed by organizational policy and may be subject to legal restrictions. Before final disposition is made of any item, it is important to verify that proper authorization has been obtained.

In addition to control over the public areas of the library, it is also important to maintain limited access to supply areas, cash, and library records and to the keys that access these areas. Only authorized persons should have access to these materials, and records should be kept of all keys distributed. Limiting exit points and monitoring those that exist help to guard against theft of materials. It is helpful to have only one exit point for patrons, with other exits restricted to emergencies. Care should be taken to confirm that the exits are properly maintained so that safety is ensured.

Losses should be investigated as to cause and possible future prevention. If large numbers of books are missing from one subject area, perhaps moving that particular area to a more conspicuous location will alleviate the problem. Very large losses may indicate the need for a security system. There are numerous security systems designed for libraries, although even these usually can be circumvented by determined individuals.

Many controls, such as monitored checkpoints and limited circulation of high-risk materials, can be instituted at very little cost. Other controls, such as security systems, total separation of duties, or secured access to materials, may be expensive to institute and may be deemed not cost-effective. Before deciding to institute a new control, a cost-benefit analysis should be performed to determine if the benefit (amount of loss prevented) is greater than the cost of the control. For example, a library that judged its annual theft losses to be $500 would not be wise to spend several thousand dollars on a security system; but such a system might be a wise purchase for a library that faced several thousand dollars of such losses annually. If the amount of loss is greater than the cost of acquiring, installing, and maintaining a security system, the system is worthy of serious consideration.

Because a library cannot totally measure its service in terms of dollars and cents, it often is necessary to use subjective judgment in library cost-benefit analyses. Some materials that are lost cannot be replaced and therefore cannot easily be assigned a monetary value. When it is possible to assess the actual dollar value of a specific action, its effect on service also must be determined and taken into consideration. Although a certain decision may result in savings to the library, if it would be detrimental to overall service it may not be the best alternative.

Library records also must be protected against loss and should be maintained in duplicate at a separate location. Computerized records should be frequently backed up on disks or tapes, while other records may be microfilmed on a regular basis. If a record is lost and a duplicate exists, only information since the last date of duplication needs to be reproduced. Because the shelflist contains the library's purchasing records and its current inventory, it is particularly important to ensure that a duplicate copy exists, perhaps on microfiche.

Control of Cash

Cash (in the form of bills or change) always requires particular care, since it is much more difficult to label and trace than library books or equipment. Cash should be handled by as few people as possible, with separate control over the receipting, depositing, and reconciling of cash. Cash due to the library for fines or other purposes should be recorded as soon as it is received; a numbered receipt should be given and a duplicate kept in the library. The total amount of cash should be verified with the total of the receipts. If money is received from copy machines, sale of used books, or other library services, this income should be recorded promptly and reconciled periodically (preferably daily).

Coin-operated copiers, bill-changers, and vending machines all should be secured and the keys to these machines kept to a minimum. Money boxes should be emptied regularly and frequently, and all cash should be kept in a safe place and deposited on a regular basis. It is not wise to keep large amounts of cash on hand. All cash and checks should be recorded prior to being deposited, and the deposit slip then should be verified by another individual. Although the timing depends on amounts collected, daily deposits are preferable. A third employee should reconcile the bank statement each month, verifying deposit records with bank statements to ensure that all funds actually were deposited and credited to the proper account.

Petty cash is the cash that usually is permitted in an organization for the purchase of small items without following formal purchasing procedures. Dollar limits, authorization methods, and reimbursement procedures for petty cash all should be clearly stated so that it is not used as an improper means to bypass the purchasing system. Each use of petty cash should be accompanied by a voucher signed by a responsible person and a receipt that supports the use of the money for an appropriate purpose. Any payments made with cash should be recorded immediately in the petty cash account and the expenses should be charged later to their appropriate expense accounts, such as Books or Office Supplies, *not* to Petty Cash.

With an established amount in the petty cash fund, the petty cash box or drawer should always contain that total amount in cash plus receipts. In other words, a petty cash fund of $50 might at some time have $32 in cash plus $18 in receipts or $10 in cash plus $40 in receipts. Periodically the expenditures are recorded in the accounting system, and the petty cash fund is reimbursed.

Example 8.2 illustrates an example of a petty cash log for a petty cash fund of $25. Purchases are made for coffee, staples, and file folders. An authorization voucher (shown in Example 8.3) is completed for each purchase, and each receipt is saved. These documents are placed in the petty cash drawer along with the remaining cash.

Example 8.2 ▪ *Petty Cash Log*

Date	Paid to	Item	Amount	Authorization	Balance
7/1					$25.00
7/1	ABC Grocer	Coffee	$2.49	M.L.	22.51
7/13	XYZ Supplies	Staples	1.99	M.L.	20.52
7/27	XYZ Supplies	File folders	7.19	R.Z.	13.33

To replenish the petty cash fund, the vouchers and receipts are turned in to the accounting department, which enters the transactions into the accounting records as a debit of $11.67 to Supplies Expense and credit of $11.67 to Cash. Then, the cash is used to replenish the petty cash drawer.

Management Reports

Library managers should receive reports on a regular basis so that the status of operations is evaluated, errors are caught in a timely manner,

Example 8.3 ▪ *Petty Cash Voucher*

```
┌─────────────────────────────────────────────────────────────┐
│                                                               │
│     (Attach Receipt)                                          │
│   Number ___1___              Date __7/1_____               │
│   Paid to __ABC Grocer_____                │
│   For __coffee_____               │
│   Amount __2.49_____                                          │
│   Received by __Joan d.___    Approved __M.L.___             │
│                                                               │
└─────────────────────────────────────────────────────────────┘
```

and necessary changes are implemented as soon as possible. To maintain control over the library's finances, the individual responsible must have access to the budget information for each fund, documentation of each transaction affecting the library's accounts, and a regular report that allows reconciliation of the library's records with the accounting system. Responsibility for checking and correcting errors must be clearly assigned and carefully monitored. There should be ongoing comparisons of budgeted and actual expenditures with explanations of any significant variances. (A further discussion of management reports is presented in Chapter 9.)

Insurance

While good internal controls can greatly reduce the risk of losses in the library, some assets should be covered by insurance. It also may be necessary to insure against certain types of liability. Property may be insured against various types of risks, such as fire, theft, vandalism, flooding, etc., whereas such causes as wear and tear, warfare, and other specific risks usually are excluded. Liability insurance should be considered, since negligence on the part of the board or a library employee may result in damage or injury to an outside party. Employees who have access to library funds should be *bonded*, which insures the library against dishonesty on the part of those employees.

Decisions concerning what types and amounts of insurance to purchase usually are made using the principles of *risk management*. Through this concept, it is recognized that some types of losses may be absorbed while others should be insured against, and the cost of insurance must be balanced against the value of the property and the risk of loss. Considering the library's financial condition and its responsibilities to its patrons, the librarian and board need to develop a policy concerning what risks must be covered. A reputable insurance agent should be able to provide specific advice concerning the type of policies that might best serve the needs of the library within the framework of the available funds.

Insurance costs may be reduced somewhat through the use of a deductible clause, whereby the library absorbs the risk for the initial losses up to a specified dollar amount. Many large organizations, especially the government, choose to be self-insured, since their size allows them to spread the risk of loss across several agencies. The assumption used in self-insurance is that losses would be less than the cost of the insurance that would be required to cover these losses.

The property of the library, including the building and its contents, should be evaluated to determine its actual worth. Buildings and improvements may be valued by appraisal or by adjusting the original cost for inflation and improvements. If the building is leased, any improvements that the library has added should be valued in the same way. The inventory of library furniture and equipment should contain original cost information; replacement cost may be determined from current library catalogs. The shelflist should provide historical cost information on books and library materials; missing information may be supplied through use of the *Bowker Annual* or through pricing information determined by the library's own records.

Property is most often insured for actual cash value (which may be determined through an appraisal), comparable market value, or an analysis of replacement cost minus depreciation. It usually is possible to provide replacement-cost insurance through the payment of an added premium; this may be a better choice when the item (particularly the building) is critical to the library's operations and replacement would be cost-prohibitive.

Selection and Training of Personnel

Internal control is highly dependent on the capability and honesty of the organization's personnel. Carelessness, poor judgment, and inability to understand instructions can result in errors, and collusion between employees can circumvent many control procedures. Prior to hiring, potential employees should be screened to ensure that they are qualified and that their integrity is not questionable. New employees should be adequately trained; cross training, regular vacations, and job rotation all help to reduce the likelihood of fraudulent activity and therefore serve as control mechanisms.

Policies and procedures related to hiring, evaluation, compensation, training, and promotion are essential to the continued employment of honest and capable personnel and will greatly contribute to the efficient operation of the library. Terminations should be reported promptly to the payroll and personnel offices, and steps should be taken to remove privileged access to records or systems as soon as employment is terminated. Access to employment records should be limited to authorized individuals, with procedures in place to ensure that these records remain confidential.

Payroll

It is important to carefully monitor all personnel records relating to payroll. Such records may have long-term significance, such as payment due for accumulated vacation when an employee leaves or retires, credit toward a pension, accurate tax payments, or even legal ramifications. Precise records should be kept of time used for vacation and sick leave, and time should be carefully recorded for all employees who are paid on an hourly basis. Overtime should be approved in advance and carefully regulated, and hours recorded on timesheets should be verified. Timesheets should be collected, authorized, and delivered to the payroll department by someone other than an employee whose time is recorded on the timesheet. Disbursement procedures for payroll checks should be subject to the same controls as disbursements for other goods and services with prenumbered checks, authorized check signers, and separation of the duties of authorization, time-keeping, payroll preparation, and check distribution.

Year-End Planning

The end of the fiscal year requires some advance planning so that budgeted funds are expended to the maximum extent possible and sufficient money is available to pay necessary expenses of the final months. It is important to ascertain whether unexpended funds may be carried forward from one fiscal year to the next. Because funds often may not be carried forward, it usually is wise to place large orders at the beginning of the fiscal year to allow time for arrival and resolution of any problems. Many items take several months to arrive; if orders are not placed until late in the fiscal year, there is a risk that they will not arrive and that the opportunity to fully utilize budgeted funds will be lost.

In nonprofit and governmental libraries, it usually is important to spend all funds that have been authorized through the budget process; losing funds because of unfilled orders demonstrates a lack of proficiency. When the remaining amount of funds is known, it may be possible to send a purchase order for a large quantity of books or library materials with instructions to send only a specified dollar amount prior to the end of the fiscal year and the remaining materials at the beginning of the next fiscal year. This depends heavily on vendor cooperation and clear instructions on the purchase order. Another method of using all available funds is canceling all outstanding purchase orders on a specified date and purchasing materials locally where prompt delivery is assured. Working closely with vendors and jobbers helps to ensure good service.

At the end of the year extra care must be taken to verify the date of receipt of library materials and to accumulate original cost information for any assets that have been discarded. If the collection has been capitalized or included on the organization's list of capital assets, the cost of missing or discarded items should be totaled (by adding the original cost as noted on the shelflist card or computerized inventory) and relayed to the accounting department so that the cost of the assets may be removed from the financial records. If original cost information is not available, it is acceptable to use cost data from the *Bowker Annual* for the approximate year of purchase for discarded books. This process also should be followed for all other disposals and deaccessions regardless of the reason for disposal. If your organization is depreciating library materials, this procedure may vary. By learning in advance what information the accounting department expects at the end of the year, you can ensure that you will be able to provide it.

The Internal Audit Function

Most organizations employ one or more individuals, reporting to top management, to review the internal control system of the organization and to make recommendations to correct weaknesses and improve deficiencies. These employees, known as *internal auditors*, are intended to assist management in achieving the most efficient administration possible; for this purpose they review both administrative and accounting controls. They should analyze the operations of the library as well as other components of the organization. The internal auditor should be familiar with the overall operation of the organization and may be a valuable source of assistance in improving problem areas.

An internal auditor is likely to conduct an *operational audit*, which evaluates the library's performance as measured by its stated objectives. Information contained in operating reports is reviewed for accuracy, consistency, relevance, and timeliness to determine its usefulness to management. Work is analyzed to ensure that approved procedures are being followed. The internal auditor is likely to make suggestions for improving the efficiency and effectiveness of library operations.

The internal auditor may also conduct a brief *financial audit* in the library to ensure that the library's financial records are in satisfactory condition. The internal auditor is especially concerned with the library's internal control system and may verify a sample of inventory, examine purchase order authorizations, match receiving reports with invoices, and perform other tests on library activity and records to ensure that the library is operating on a sound financial basis. For example, the auditor might take a sample of the shelflist and verify that every book on the list is either on the shelf or checked out to a user. A shelflist with numerous missing books indicates many potential problems—perhaps books are being stolen due to poor supervision or are being discarded without being recorded. The results of these investigations have an impact on the library's financial records and its service to its users. A review by an internal auditor can be very beneficial and can prevent serious problems from being discovered later by an independent auditor.

Summary

Control of daily operations is essential for the financial well-being of the library. Administrative controls promote overall efficiency and adherence to procedures, while accounting controls ensure that assets are protected and that financial information is reliable. Personnel should be selected carefully, trained well, and given work assignments that separate incompatible functions.

Librarians must carefully monitor the purchasing process, ensuring that the areas responsible for payment are informed as items are received, that encumbrances are removed as purchase orders are completed, and that orders that cannot be filled are canceled in time to use available funds before the end of the fiscal year. Assets and records must be protected from various hazards, with particular care given to the handling of cash. For practical advice concerning procedures and controls that may improve the efficiency of library operations, the organization's internal auditor may be a valuable resource.

Additional Reading

Anthony, Robert N., and David W. Young. *Management Control in Nonprofit Organizations*. 4th ed. Homewood, Ill.: Irwin, 1988.

Brand, Marvine, ed. *Security for Libraries*. Chicago: American Library Association, 1984.

Coffey, James R., ed. *Operational Costs in Acquisitions*. Binghamton, N.Y.: Haworth Press, 1991.

Fennelly, L. J. *Museum, Archive, and Library Security*. Boston: Butterworth, 1983.

Herbert, Leo, et al. *Accounting and Control for Governmental and Other Non-business Organizations*. New York: John Wiley & Sons, 1987.

Hirshon, Arnold, and Barbara A. Winters. *Managing the Purchasing Process: A How-to-Do-It Manual for Librarians*. New York: Neal-Schuman, 1991.

Hoffman, Herbert H. *Simple Library Bookkeeping*. Newport Beach, Calif.: Headway Publications, 1977.

Hughes, Carol A., and Robert H. Patterson. *Library Disaster Planning: A How-to-Do-It Manual for Librarians*. New York: Neal-Schuman, 1991.

Kurth, William H., and David S. Zubatsky. *Recommended Procedures for the Internal Financial Auditing of University Libraries*. St. Louis, Mo.: Washington University Libraries, 1977.

Myers, Gerald E. *Insurance Manual for Libraries*. Chicago: American Library Association, 1977.

Pitkin, Gary M., ed. *Cost-Effective Technical Services: How to Track, Manage, and Justify Internal Operations*. New York: Neal-Schuman, 1989.

Prentice, Ann E. *Financial Planning for Libraries*. Metuchen, N.J.: Scarecrow Press, 1983.

Ramsey, Inez, and Jackson E. Ramsey. *Library Planning and Budgeting*. New York: Watts, 1986.

Razek, Joseph R., and Gordon A. Hosch. *Introduction to Governmental and Not-for-Profit Accounting*. Englewood Cliffs, N.J.: Prentice-Hall, 1985.

Smith, G. Stevenson. *Accounting for Librarians and Other Not-for-Profit Managers*. Chicago: American Library Association, 1983.

———. *Managerial Accounting for Librarians and Other Not-for-Profit Managers*. Chicago: American Library Association, 1991.

■ 9

Reporting and Evaluation

To monitor the activity of the library and to evaluate its success in achieving its objectives, librarians and upper management must have access to timely, reliable, and relevant information. During the operating period, management reports are an important control mechanism coordinating the activities of the library and the organization and measuring the library's ongoing success in achieving its financial objectives. At the end of the operating period, financial statements are needed to evaluate the organization's overall operating performance and its financial status. These reports form a basis for program evaluation and revision, so that plans may be modified as needed for the future.

In addition to library managers, many other groups are interested in the financial affairs of the library or its parent organization. Employees, trustees, taxpayers, grantors, donors, and volunteers, as well as those who may provide future resources, have reason to be informed about the financial condition of the library or of the organization to which it belongs. External funding agencies often require regular reports as a condition of continued funding. Stockholders, owners, and creditors are particularly interested in the financial statements of for-profit organizations as a means to assess the financial health and future prospects of the company.

Management Reports

As discussed in Chapter 8, timely, complete, and accurate information for management is one of the most important features of financial control. Through the use of regular well-designed reports, errors can be found and problem areas pinpointed in time to take corrective action. Regular reports also provide a basis for continuing appraisal of the programs and planned activities as well as for evaluation of library management performance. These reports demonstrate how resources were used to carry out the objectives of the organization, identify important programs and their costs, and compare the actual results with the original plan. Effective reports should be related to specific areas of responsibility, focus on significant information, and provide a comparison of actual performance with some expected level of performance.

Both financial and nonfinancial data are likely to be of interest in displaying the library's success in achieving its stated objectives. Administrative reports showing acquisitions, circulation or reference statistics, or attendance at special programs all provide information relevant to the success of the library. Numbers of volunteer hours and employee hours are also appropriate.

Because a library's primary function is to provide service, financial reports that compare the quantity and quality of service provided with the amount of money spent are of significant value. For example, a report might show total monthly expenses for the Reference Department, along with the number and percentage of reference questions answered and the number of new reference books purchased. Comparisons with prior-year data may be useful as well as comparisons with any stated objectives of the department.

Areas of Responsibility

Areas used for budgeting and control usually correspond to the levels of authority on an organizational chart, and management reports should be categorized in the same way. Each report should be distributed to a specific person, such as the manager of the area, who has both the responsibility and the authority to make decisions based on the information given in the report.

It often is helpful to have reports that roll up to higher levels of responsibility. Through this process lower-level supervisors are provided with information specific to their departments, and their supervisors in turn are provided with information for the entire area for which they are accountable. For example, if reports are distributed to the managers of Technical Services, User Services, and Administration, the library director (who may also be the manager of Administration) also should receive a summary report for the entire library. This practice allows higher-level supervisors to be informed of problems in areas for which they are indirectly responsible so that small problems are not allowed to get out of hand because a lower-level supervisor has failed to act in time. Because problem areas are subject to review at more than one level of management, different levels of reporting provide an added control mechanism.

Examples 9.1 and 9.2 display typical monthly reports that may be distributed to two levels of management. The library receives a report summarizing its monthly and year-to-date activity, while the Educational Services department, of which the library is a part, receives a similar report that includes all areas within the department. Each report shows information on the total budget, current month and year-to-date expenditure totals, amount of outstanding encumbrances, amount of budgeted funds available, the percent expended, and the percent available (uncommitted). The percent expended plus the percent

Example 9.1 ▪ *Lower-Level Report (Library)*

Monthly Budget Report
Library
12/31/94

Expenditures	Budget	Actual Current Month	Year-to-Date	Encum-bered	Balance Available	Percent Expended	Percent Available
1100 Salaries FT	$250,600	$20,294	$121,368	$ 0	$129,232	48	52
1200 Salaries PT	35,300	2,906	17,654	0	17,646	50	50
1300 Wages Temp.	12,200	900	6,912	0	5,288	57	43
1400 Wages OT	8,000	692	4,216	0	3,784	53	47
1800 Benefits	81,200	7,468	40,619	0	40,581	50	50
1xxx Total personnel	387,300	32,260	190,769	0	196,531	49	51
2300 Educ. supplies	5,000	542	2,789	599	1,612	56	32
2400 Repair supplies	1,100	65	465	13	622	42	57
2500 Postage	2,100	150	1,032	0	1,068	49	51
2600 Office supplies	3,300	632	2,204	54	1,042	67	32
2700 Periodicals	14,000	954	10,954	2,744	302	78	2
2xxx Total supp. & mat.	25,500	2,343	17,444	3,410	4,646	68	18
3100 Travel	4,600	420	1,657	0	2,943	36	64
3200 Communication	2,500	208	1,316	116	1,068	53	43
3400 Printing & binding	6,300	1,400	3,557	1,503	1,240	56	20
3800 Data processing	10,700	991	5,430	4,402	868	51	8
3xxx Total services	24,100	3,019	11,960	6,021	6,119	50	25
4100 Library books	88,000	12,122	54,368	14,512	19,120	62	22
4200 Office equipment	5,300	852	3,778	1,267	255	71	5
4400 EDP equipment	12,400	1,400	8,540	3,144	716	69	6
4xxx Total capital	105,700	14,374	66,686	18,923	20,091	63	19
Total controllable costs	542,600	51,996	286,859	28,354	227,387	53	42
5100 Rent	15,700	1,308	7,848	0	7,852	50	50
5200 Insurance	4,300	0	3,912	0	388	91	9
5300 Maintenance	12,300	640	6,104	321	5,875	50	48
5500 Utilities	4,600	503	1,965	0	2,635	43	57
5xxx Total operations	36,900	2,451	19,829	321	16,750	54	45
Total expenditures	$579,500	$54,447	$306,688	$28,675	$244,137	53	42

Example 9.2 ▪ *Higher-Level Report (Educational Services)*

Monthly Budget Report
Educational Services
12/31/94

		Actual					
Expenditures	Budget	Current Month	Year-to-Date	Encum-bered	Balance Available	Percent Expended	Percent Available
1100 Salaries FT	$ 933,000	$ 78,124	$ 460,054	$ 0	$472,946	49	51
1200 Salaries PT	125,000	15,620	61,149	0	63,851	49	51
1300 Wages Temp	69,730	15,438	30,226	0	39,504	43	57
1400 Wages OT	41,000	3,110	19,688	0	24,312	41	59
1800 Benefits	301,000	25,006	149,084	0	151,916	50	50
1xxx Total personnel	1,469,730	137,298	717,201	0	752,529	49	51
2300 Educ. supplies	54,000	5,680	36,551	4,360	13,089	68	24
2400 Repair supplies	5,600	1,147	2,755	116	2,729	49	49
2500 Postage	5,200	600	2,752	0	2,448	53	47
2600 Office supplies	15,000	2,010	8,231	623	6,146	55	41
2700 Periodicals	18,000	1,122	12,669	2,744	2,587	70	14
2xxx Total supp. & mat.	97,800	10,559	62,958	7,843	26,999	64	28
3100 Travel	26,000	1,154	10,622	0	15,378	41	59
3200 Communication	16,000	1,255	7,995	681	7,324	50	46
3400 Printing & binding	7,500	1,600	4,166	1,503	1,831	56	24
3800 Data processing	26,000	1,981	14,650	6,402	4,948	56	19
3xxx Total services	75,500	5,990	37,433	8,586	29,481	50	39
4100 Library books	88,000	12,122	54,368	14,512	19,120	62	22
4200 Office equipment	16,800	1,744	12,364	3,625	811	74	5
4400 EDP equipment	44,000	5,119	34,200	6,288	3,512	78	8
4xxx Total capital	148,800	18,985	100,932	24,425	23,443	68	16
Total controllable costs	1,791,830	172,832	918,524	40,854	832,452	51	46
5100 Rent	63,000	5,248	31,488	0	31,512	50	50
5200 Insurance	18,000	1,200	14,598	0	3,402	81	19
5300 Maintenance	55,000	4,400	35,447	1,663	17,890	64	33
5500 Utilities	14,000	1,500	6,237	0	7,763	45	55
5xxx Total operations	150,000	12,348	87,770	1,663	60,567	59	40
Total expenditures	$1,941,830	$185,180	$1,006,294	$42,517	$893,019	52	46

available will be less than 100 percent whenever there is an outstanding encumbrance. The report is for the month of December, halfway through the fiscal year ending June 30. Because large book and equipment orders were placed at the beginning of the year, most of these items have already arrived and been paid for, so the fact that limited funds remain is not necessarily a problem. When the summary reports indicate that problems exist, they should be investigated by checking more-detailed reports such as listings of individual transactions. By verifying that no areas are overexpended and by reviewing areas with limited funds remaining, a manager may prevent problems. Any unexpected expense should be investigated to determine if it is due to a one-time error that must be corrected or if it is the first sign of a larger problem, such as unauthorized overtime, waste or pilferage of supplies, or rapidly increasing use of data services.

Significant Information

Reports may include a variety of analytical information for the manager. Because modern computer systems often provide enormous amounts of information, it is difficult to decide exactly what information, in what quantity, will be useful to a particular manager. A manager should be provided with as much information as can be worthwhile but not more. When too much information is given, it is all likely to be disregarded, making the whole process useless. If information provided is insufficient to make a decision concerning necessary action, it is likewise of little value.

A management control report may include two types of financial information. *Controllable costs* are those for which the manager is directly responsible and permitted to make decisions that may affect the amounts expended. These would include expenditures for books, supplies, travel, personnel, and fringe benefit costs for the area. *Noncontrollable costs*, such as overhead or utilities, often are included for informational purposes but have no effect on the decision-making process.

Controllable costs should be shown in sufficient detail to provide a basis for analysis and action. Relevant information that might be shown on a management control report is budgeted and actual expense data for the current period and for the year-to-date, and detailed information concerning purchase orders, encumbrances, payments, or any other transactions that have taken place since the last report was distributed. Such reports enable the manager to verify any internal records kept in the library with the financial records of the organization. A brief summary report followed by detailed information allows for a quick overview prior to a careful analysis of the supporting documentation.

The inclusion of noncontrollable cost information in reports aids management in understanding the full cost of operations but has little relevance in the day-to-day decision-making process. However, inclusion of this information on a regular report makes it readily available if some cost analysis is desired for long-term planning, budgeting, or cost recovery. If information on noncontrollable costs is desired, it should be shown separately.

Specially designed reports can be particularly helpful in monitoring restricted funds, since any unusual situation with these funds may be a symptom of a potential problem. If a budgeted area in an unrestricted fund is overspent, management has the right to allocate money from another unrestricted area to make up the deficit. Restricted funds do not have this flexibility, and any overexpenditures may indicate serious problems. Deficits may need to be made up from unrestricted funds or may even result in legal action. Grant funds often must be spent by a certain date; showing the expiration date on the regular grant report helps to remind the library manager that funds must be spent. Funds may be restricted for certain uses; a report that flags disallowed expenditures can be very useful.

Example 9.3 shows a portion of a report for a grant that is to be used exclusively for the purchase of computer software, for which the organization uses the detail code 6100. The report is designed to show any other expenditure with asterisks so that the error can be observed immediately. Any overbudget situations are also shown with asterisks to gain the attention of the reader.

Example 9.3 ▪ *Budget Report (Grant)*

Monthly Budget Report
12/31/94

Account 25001: Library Software Grant
Expiration Date: 06/30/95

			Actual			
Expenditures	*Budget*	*Current Month*	*Year-to-Date*	*Project-to-Date*	*Encumbered*	*Balance Available*
6100 Software	$5,000	$2,500	$2,800	$3,200	$500	$1,300
***6500 Books	0	500	500	500	0	(500)**

Reports of the type shown in Example 9.3 enhance control by drawing attention to possible problem areas. The book expenditure shown on the report is marked by asterisks to identify an unbudgeted item. It might have been a software purchase assigned the incorrect object code or a book purchase assigned to the wrong account. The error might be due to a data-entry error or an incorrect authorization of a book purchase order. The situation should be investigated and corrected and may require further action to prevent its recurrence.

A common method of identifying problem areas is the use of *exception reports*, which draw attention to only those areas or items that differ significantly from some standard. Worthwhile examples might be reports listing encumbrances that have been outstanding for a specified time or over-budget items of more than a certain dollar or percentage amount. Internal reports showing such items as book fines more than one month past due also might prove useful. In using such reports, management first must identify what items and amounts are significant. Exception reports greatly diminish the quantity of information needed to identify obvious problems but may also result in some less obvious problems being overlooked.

Comparison of Actual Performance with a Standard

By comparing actual data with some predetermined measure of performance, differences can be analyzed and acted upon if necessary. The usual standard against which expense data are compared is the authorized budget, since a carefully prepared budget that has been approved by the governing body is considered to be the best available guideline by which to operate during the fiscal year. With costs that are evenly distributed throughout the year (personnel and fringe benefits), it may be most helpful for a report to show the percent used or available. Where costs are uneven (books or travel) information may be more useful if differences are shown in dollar amounts. Depending on the space available on the report, it may be possible to show information in both forms.

Since the budget usually is shown on an annual basis, it is important to continually monitor the amount of budgeted funds remaining. Upper management may wish to require managers to provide written reports explaining variances over a specified percent or dollar amount, since these variances from the approved budget may indicate problems that should be acted upon. The requirement of a written report forces a manager to observe and investigate any variances.

Report Design

Since the purpose of the management report is to communicate information, it is important that it be clear and easily understandable to the manager who will receive it. Reports should contain only relevant information at a level of sophistication appropriate to the individual manager, and the most important information should be the easiest to locate on the report. If there is any doubt about various library managers' ability to understand their reports, a training session might be appropriate. Such a session also offers the opportunity to consider suggestions for added information that might be useful if included on a regular report.

When reports are distributed to different levels of management, there should be consistency in format so that lower-level reports can be easily related to those at higher levels, as shown in Examples 9.1 and 9.2. Detailed reports often are distributed to areas of direct responsibility, while summary reports are distributed to higher-level management.

The Reporting Period

There must be a balance between the cost of producing and distributing management control reports and the resulting benefits. It costs money to produce and distribute reports, and time is required to analyze them. If reports are produced more frequently than needed, time, paper, and money are wasted. Usually, a monthly report is satisfactory for a manager with direct responsibility for operations; the board or higher levels of administration may be adequately served by quarterly reports.

There also should be a balance between timeliness and accuracy; a report should be accurate enough to reveal problems but must be available soon enough to take action. Reports should be produced and distributed very soon after the end of the period covered so that problems can be investigated and acted upon before it is too late. Monthly reports should be distributed within a few days after the close of the month; quarterly reports should be distributed within a few weeks at the latest. By carefully checking and correcting problems throughout the operating period, there should be few errors remaining at the end of the period when final reports must be prepared.

Investigation and Action

Management reports must be checked carefully, and problem areas should be investigated promptly. Each manager should have a process for reviewing reports on a regular basis, verifying the information provided, and taking corrective action as required. If a problem is indicated, its cause must be found. An unusual expense may be due to an accounting error or a random occurrence indicating a problem that has already passed. Perhaps your library account has been charged for another department's purchases, or an invoice has been paid but the corresponding encumbrance has not been removed. If they are not corrected, errors such as these will reduce the amount of funds available to your library; but you must notify your accounting department immediately so that the situation can be investigated. Some problems may be due to one-time errors; others may indicate a need to take corrective action to prevent a problem from recurring or becoming greater.

A good manager will anticipate some problems; for example, if a great deal of overtime is needed temporarily, it will not come as a surprise to see an overexpenditure in that area on the next report. However, if unbudgeted overtime seems to be a regular occurrence, some action may have to be taken to reduce the need for overtime as well as to ensure that all overtime is properly authorized.

Using Microcomputers for Management Reporting

Using a microcomputer, reports may be tailored to the needs of individual library managers rather than to the needs of others in the organization. Information can be processed rapidly, with data entry followed immediately by report preparation so that information can be analyzed swiftly and decisions made.

We have previously discussed the use of spreadsheets, with a format of columns and rows, in the analysis of accounting and budgeting information. Spreadsheet software has provided managers with the ability to design customized reports that rapidly can produce updated financial information. A valuable feature of spreadsheet software is its ability to calculate new information by using new data with previously entered formulas. Because formulas are entered in the computer's memory, new data can be entered and new reports produced with very little effort. Information or formulas entered in one area also can be copied to another area, reducing effort and the risk of error.

In designing a spreadsheet report, it is advisable to sketch the desired information on paper first so that headings, spaces, column widths, and other items may be determined prior to entry in the computer. This will help to provide an overview of the finished report, which may very likely be wider and longer than the size of the computer screen. When you set up your initial report on the computer, you will need to enter the formulas for performing calculations and carefully verify them so that you are sure your reports are correct. Once formulas have been entered and verified, the report format may be used over and over by only changing a few items. Drafts can be printed and reviewed prior to running final copies for distribution; if an error is found, the correction can be made and checked on the screen without having to retype the entire report.

Spreadsheet software is particularly helpful in producing management reports such as comparative budget-to-actual reports as shown in Examples 9.1, 9.2, and 9.3. Budget information should be entered only once (unless a revision is made); formulas may be used to subtract amounts expended from budgeted amounts to show the remainder available at any time. By entering a new expenditure or encumbrance amount, information on total expenses and available funds may be updated instantly. Because the computer program allows for recalculation of totals throughout the spreadsheet, changing a single number may produce entirely different results. These programs also are very helpful in budgeting and planning, since you can perform what-if analyses to predict the results of many different scenarios.

Financial Statements

At the end of the fiscal year, most organizations prepare financial statements, which are the primary means of communicating accounting information to external users as well as to internal parties. Financial statements are prepared to show the financial status of the entire organization; unless a library is an independent entity, it does not ordinarily have its own set of financial statements. Instead, its revenues, expenses, assets, and liabilities are included in the statements of the organization of which it is a part. (As we have previously noted, however, separate financial statements *could* be prepared for any funds that are restricted for library use; however, most organizations combine similar types of funds for financial reporting purposes.)

The information of interest to users of financial statements varies with the type of organization. Readers of statements of a for-profit business will be primarily concerned with the net income of the business, its financial stability, and the promise of future growth. Financial statements of for-profit businesses should be prepared according to generally accepted accounting principles so that their meaning can be consistently interpreted by all users. As noted in Chapter 1, other organizations should follow these generally accepted standards as closely as possible in preparing their financial statements. The financial statements of a nonprofit organization should also provide information about the services the organization provides, how effectively and efficiently it provides its services, and how likely it is to be able to continue to provide those services.

If your library is independent, its financial statements will display its overall financial condition. If your library is part of a larger organization, it is important that you, as a librarian, have a reasonable understanding of that organization's financial position. You will find it very informative to read the financial statements and annual reports of your organization, since these reports usually provide a great deal of information about the whole organization, its purpose, progress, and problems.

Although the preparation and analysis of different types of financial statements are subjects that accountants cover in detail, this chapter will present only an overview and brief explanation of some of the most common financial statements. The two most basic financial statements are the balance sheet and the statement of activity; other statements may present additional information if needed. The format and exact names of the statements vary according to the type of organization for which they are prepared.

The Balance Sheet

While there may be slight variations in balance sheet format, it is the most consistent of the financial statements for the multitude of organizations that exist. The balance sheet shows the organization's financial situation at one point in time, usually the end of its fiscal year. It also is customary to provide comparative information displaying the organization's status at the end of the previous year.

As noted in Chapter 3, the balance sheet receives its name because it has two main parts that are equal, or balanced. The left-hand, or assets, side shows the resources of the organization as of the balance sheet date. These assets usually are classified into current and long-term categories. The right-hand side of the report displays liabilities, the obligations to outside parties, which are also classified as current or long-term. The right side also reports the equity or fund balance, which is the difference between the assets and the liabilities. In the earlier discussion of the accounting equation (or balance sheet equation), it was noted that the left side of the equation must equal the right side.

$$\text{Assets} = \text{Liabilities} + \text{Equity}$$

Because of space limitations, the balance sheet often is shown with assets at the top of the page and liabilities and equity at the bottom. This is true particularly when fund accounting is used and several funds need to be shown on the balance sheet. Examples 9.4 and 9.5 show some of the similarities and differences that may be found in the balance sheets of nonprofit and for-profit organizations.

Example 9.4 ▪ Nonprofit Organization Balance Sheet

Nonprofit Library
Balance Sheet
June 30, 1995
(With Comparative Totals for 1994)

	June 30, 1995					June 30, 1994
	Current Funds					
	Unrestricted	Restricted	Endowment	Plant	Total	Total
Assets						
Current assets						
Cash and temporary investments	$300,000	$200,000	$ 25,000	$ 17,000	$ 542,000	$ 532,000
Grants receivable (Note 1)	50,000	125,000	–	–	175,000	177,000
Prepaid expenses	40,000	25,000	–	–	65,000	64,000
Total current assets	390,000	350,000	25,000	17,000	782,000	773,000
Investments (Note 2)	–	–	350,000	135,000	485,000	478,000
Books and collections	–	–	–	375,000	375,000	357,000
Land, buildings, and equipment	–	–	–	1,624,000	1,624,000	1,571,000
(less accumulated depreciation)				(300,000)	(300,000)	(250,000)
Total assets	$390,000	$350,000	$375,000	$1,851,000	$2,966,000	$2,929,000
Liabilities and Fund Balance						
Current liabilities						
Accounts payable	$ 75,000	$ 35,000	$ 20,000	$ 34,000	$ 164,000	$ 161,000
Current portion of long-term debt	50,000	–	–	45,000	95,000	96,000
Total current liabilities	125,000	35,000	20,000	79,000	259,000	257,000
Long-term debt (Note 3)	–	–	–	420,000	420,000	440,000
Total liabilities	125,000	35,000	20,000	499,000	679,000	697,000
Fund balance	265,000	315,000	355,000	1,352,000	2,287,000	2,232,000
Total liabilities and fund balance	$390,000	$350,000	$375,000	$1,851,000	$2,966,000	$2,929,000

Example 9.5 ▪ *For-Profit Organization Balance Sheet*

For-Profit Company
Balance Sheet
December 31, 1995
(With Comparative Totals for 1994)

Assets

	December 31, 1995	December 31, 1994
Current Assets		
Cash and temporary investments	$ 542,000	$ 532,000
Accounts receivable (net) (Note 1)	175,000	177,000
Prepaid expenses	65,000	64,000
Total current assets	782,000	773,000
Investments	485,000	478,000
Land, buildings and equipment	1,999,000	1,928,000
Less accumulated depreciation	(300,000)	(250,000)
Total assets	$2,966,000	$2,929,000

Liabilities

	December 31, 1995	December 31, 1994
Current liabilities		
Accounts payable	$ 134,000	$ 131,000
Income tax payable	30,000	30,000
Current portion of long-term debt	95,000	96,000
Total current liabilities	259,000	257,000
Long-term liabilities		
Bonds payable	420,000	440,000
Total liabilities	$ 679,000	$ 697,000

Stockholder's Equity

	December 31, 1995	December 31, 1994
Common stock—$5 par value 200,000 shares authorized and issued	$1,000,000	$1,000,000
Retained earnings	1,287,000	1,232,000
Total stockholder's equity	2,287,000	2,232,000
Total liabilities and stockholder's equity	$2,966,000	$2,929,000

Example 9.4 shows a balance sheet for a nonprofit library and displays information for each of the various funds. Example 9.5 shows a balance sheet for a for-profit organization and displays only totals for the whole organization. Each balance sheet shows current assets and liabilities as well as long-term assets and liabilities; in each case it is important to note that current assets are greater than current liabilities, which means that each organization should be able to pay its current obligations without difficulty. It is also important to note that each organization (and in the case of the nonprofit library, each fund) has more assets than liabilities. These are important indicators of the financial health of the organization, since if current liabilities are greater than current assets or if total liabilities are greater than total assets, the organization may have difficulty in meeting its obligations. The equity of the nonprofit is shown as the fund balance; in the for-profit company, equity is represented by the stockholders' investment in the company plus *retained earnings*, which represent earnings that have remained with the business since its inception.

Notes to Financial Statements

You will notice that Examples 9.4 and 9.5 mention notes; this refers the user to additional information that would be too cumbersome to include in the body of the statement but that is important for the full disclosure required in financial statements. Typical notes found in financial statements are summaries of accounting policies, information concerning receivables due to the organization, additional information on investments, analysis of fixed assets and long-term liabilities, information about pension plans, outstanding commitments or potential liabilities that the organization reasonably expects to incur, and any other circumstances that may affect the organization's financial well-being.

Statement of Activity

While the balance sheet shows the financial position of the organization at a specific time, the statement of activity shows how the organization acquired and used funds during the year. The statement is known by a variety of names, some of which are *income statement, operating statement,* or *statement of revenues and expenses.* This statement identifies sources of revenue and support, expenses for the time period, and the net income or change in fund balance resulting from operations.

Example 9.6 illustrates an income statement for a for-profit company; the statement displays summary revenues and expenses and the resulting net income. This statement is valuable because it indicates the status of the company's operations for the past fiscal year. If a company's balance sheet shows that assets are greater than liabilities but its most recent income statement shows that expenses are greater than

Example 9.6 ▪ *Income Statement of For-Profit Company*

For-Profit Company
Income Statement
For Year Ended December 31, 1995
(With Comparative Totals for 1994)

	Year Ended December 31, 1995	*Year Ended December 31, 1994*
Revenues:		
Net sales	$103,000	$114,000
Rental income	43,000	40,000
Investment income	12,000	14,000
Total revenue	158,000	168,000
Expenses:		
Cost of merchandise sold	51,000	57,000
Selling expenses	15,000	16,000
General expenses	23,000	22,000
Interest expense	10,000	10,000
Income taxes	5,000	6,000
Total expenses	104,000	112,000
Net income	$ 54,000	$ 56,000

revenues, the company may be in danger of eventually depleting its assets and diminishing its equity.

The financial statements of a for-profit company are generally intended to show if and how the company is making a profit. Because users of a nonprofit organization's financial statements are likely to be more interested in how the organization is achieving its mission, financial statements of these organizations often show the information by function or program. Administrative and fund-raising expenses are shown separately from expenses that support the services or programs for which the organization is chartered.

Example 9.7 illustrates a statement of support, revenues, expenses, and changes in fund balance for the current funds of a nonprofit library. Support and revenue are shown by source, and expenses are shown by function.

In addition to the balance sheet and statement of activity, other financial reports often are prepared at the end of the fiscal year. The *statement of changes in financial position*, also called the *cash flows statement*, summarizes available resources and their use during the fiscal year. It provides information about operating activities as well as about other sources of support, such as loans or investment income, and about the use of funds for purposes other than daily operations. The *statement of changes in fund balance* may be a separate statement or

Example 9.7 ▪ *Nonprofit Statement of Support and Revenue, Expenses, and Changes in Fund Balance*

Nonprofit Library
Statement of Support and Revenue,
Expenses, and Changes in Fund Balance
Current Funds
For Year Ended June 30, 1995
(With Comparative Totals for 1994)

	June 30, 1995			June 30, 1994
	Unrestricted	*Restricted*	*Total*	*Total*
Support and Revenue				
Grants				
Government	$100,000	—	$100,000	$ 90,000
Other	—	$ 50,000	50,000	45,000
Contributions and bequests	40,000	90,000	130,000	150,000
Service fees	12,000	—	12,000	20,000
Fines	6,000	—	6,000	6,000
Annual fundraiser	15,000	—	15,000	16,000
Investment income	25,000	10,000	35,000	40,000
Total support and revenue	198,000	150,000	348,000	367,000
Expenses				
Program services				
Research library	49,000	68,000	117,000	125,000
Circulating library	93,000	31,000	124,000	133,000
Educational services	8,000	24,000	32,000	35,000
Community services	4,000	12,000	16,000	15,000
Total program services	154,000	135,000	289,000	308,000
Supporting services				
Administration	34,000	15,000	49,000	47,000
Fund-raising	5,000	—	5,000	6,000
Total supporting services	39,000	15,000	54,000	53,000
Total expenses	193,000	150,000	343,000	361,000
Excess (deficit) of support and revenue over expenses	5,000	—	5,000	6,000
Fund balance at beginning of year	219,000	101,000	320,000	314,000
Fund balance at end of year	$224,000	$101,000	$325,000	$320,000

may be combined with the operating statement of a nonprofit, and a *statement of owners' equity* or a *retained earnings statement* may be prepared separately or combined with the income statement of a for-profit business.

Accrual Reporting

Although management control reports often are prepared on a cash basis, financial statements usually are prepared on an accrual basis in order to correctly measure the activity of the period. As discussed in Chapter 3, accrual accounting includes all revenue actually earned during the period (whether or not the cash has been received) and all expenses actually incurred during the period (whether or not the item has been paid for). Because budget reports are usually on a cash basis, you may observe that the revenue and expense amounts shown on your budget reports at the end of the year are not the same as those shown on the financial statements. This is because adjustments have been made to include revenue that has been earned but not received (for example, investment interest) and expenses that have been incurred but not paid (such as books and equipment received but not yet paid for).

Many organizations operate on a cash basis during the year but prepare adjusting entries at the end of the year so that the financial statements will be in accordance with generally accepted accounting principles. In addition to adjusting entries for revenues and expenses, information concerning disposal of assets (discarded library books, missing equipment, etc.) also should be relayed to the accounting department at this time so that the necessary adjustments may be made to the financial records. The library usually must compile this information for the accounting department and must be particularly careful to note what items are received or due at the last day of the fiscal year. Since accounting practices differ from one organization to another, it is advisable to determine well in advance exactly what information will be required. Otherwise the information is likely to be requested after the date when it can be easily determined, resulting in aggravation and inaccuracy.

The Audit

As previously noted there are variations in the accounting standards applied by different kinds of organizations. To determine if the accounting practices of the organization are objective, fair, complete, and accurate, an audit may be performed. An *audit* is an independent review of an organization's financial statements for the purpose of evaluating and expressing an opinion on their fairness. While an internal auditor is concerned with the overall operations of an organization, an external auditor (one who is not an employee of the organization) is expected to apply objective criteria in deciding if the organization is financially sound and if it is presenting a reliable financial picture to its public. To carry out their function, auditors are likely to focus on financial statements such as the balance sheet (which lists the assets and liabilities of the organization) and the revenue and expense statements (which explain the sources of revenues and the purposes for which expenditures were made).

If a library is an independent organization, it is probable that an audit may be necessary at some time, perhaps even yearly. If the library is part of a larger organization, the library records may be only a portion of the many records examined by the auditors. The value of a library's holdings may be a significant part of the assets of the organization; if this is the case, it is likely that the auditors will need to examine library records carefully.

State and local governments, colleges and universities, libraries, and other nonprofit organizations that receive federal assistance are required by law to be audited to ensure that grantees are administering federal funds properly. Through the single-audit process, the auditor is required to audit both federal and nonfederal funds to verify compliance with standards and guidelines. The federal Office of Management and Budget issues periodic circulars describing these requirements as well as defining the allowable and prohibited costs that may be charged to federal awards.

One of the first concerns of the auditor is the system of internal control that exists in the library. If the library has a well-trained staff with distinct separation of responsibilities and well-defined procedures with clear control measures, the auditor may feel that only limited auditing procedures are necessary. The auditor will review existing accounting and procedures manuals and will test to determine whether the written procedures actually are being followed. A comparison of actual expenditures with the approved budget may provide the auditor with an indication of how well the library has followed its authorized plan. Auditors check for evidence that expenses were authorized and approved by a responsible member of the management team, that they were correctly classified by function and time period, and that they are supported by documents, such as invoices, timesheets, and so forth. Auditors also verify that there is control over the receipt, recording, and depositing of revenues and that they are properly accounted for, especially if there are any restrictions on their use. Auditors also carefully check the control over cash and securities. There may be an analysis of direct and indirect costs in order to ensure that overhead has been correctly charged when necessary.

The plan by which an audit is performed is called an *audit program* and lists the functions that the auditor will perform to carefully test the library records. Often, a team of auditors will work together, each taking responsibility for a part of the audit, such as purchasing, cash receipts, disbursements, payroll, and other functions. Areas that are found to have problems may require further work on the part of the auditor.

During the audit process, the auditor attempts to document the correctness of each transaction from its origin all the way to the financial statements or to trace the summary totals in the statements back to their original sources. The evidence linking these transactions is known as an *audit trail*, and the trail should enable the auditor to follow all the way from the original transaction to the financial statements or vice versa. For example, if you show a total of $961 as fine revenue, you should be able to produce documentation that this was the total amount of fines collected and that the amount was correctly assessed, collected, recorded, and deposited. Such documentation might include overdue lists, notification procedures, copies of receipts to patrons for fines paid, daily totals, and deposit slips.

A group of transactions is likely to be tested to confirm the adequacy of the procedures and controls; from this initial review an auditor may determine the effectiveness of the internal control and the resulting necessary extent of the audit. Because auditors do not have time to check every item or transaction in the library, they are likely to work with samples selected in a variety of ways. A *judgment sample* may be used in which items to be examined are selected based solely on the auditor's judgment. A *block sample* tests all items in one period, such as one month's accounts payable transactions or one week's payroll. A *random sample* is drawn completely at random from the entire group of possible items that may be tested; this technique is widely used and computer programs that quickly select the desired number of statistical samples are available.

The Audit Opinion

At the end of an audit, auditors may render a written opinion that describes the scope of the audit, a paragraph explaining any departures from standard accounting procedures, and an opinion that states the auditors' judgment as to the organization's conformity with generally accepted accounting principles. Auditors also check for consistency in accounting methods from year to year.

The most desirable result of an audit is an *unqualified opinion*, in which the auditor expresses confidence that the financial statements fairly express the financial position of the organization. If there is concern about some of the practices of the organization, the auditor may issue a *qualified opinion,* and if the records are very incomplete or erroneous a *disclaimer* may be issued stating that the auditor cannot vouch for the correctness of the organization's financial statements. If the auditor feels that the statements are an unfair presentation of the financial position, an *adverse opinion* may be issued.

Evaluation

The audit process is concerned primarily with evaluating the financial well-being of the library or of the organization, and the audit report provides one measure of evaluation. In a nonprofit organization, the amount of resources spent for programs in comparison with the amount spent for administration and fund-raising is an important part of the financial evaluation. It is likely to be of concern to the auditor and possibly to the IRS, particularly when the organization is a 501(c)(3) organization to which contributions are tax deductible. The methods by which expenses are allocated to programs and to supporting services are also of concern and should be supportable.

At regular intervals it is important to compare the library's accomplishments with its stated goals and objectives. If specific objectives are incorporated in the operating budget, the method of evaluating the success of achieving these objectives should be determined at that time. The budgeting period for the new fiscal year provides an appropriate period for review and evaluation; the end of one fiscal year and the beginning of the new year provides another. If the objectives were not met, it is important to ascertain why not. Were they desirable *and* attainable? What objectives should be deleted, and which should be added? What can be done to ensure that the desired objectives are met during the next operating period?

User surveys often reveal valuable information concerning the success of a library's programs. Because the library's primary function is to provide service to its patrons, their opinions reflect the perceived success of this function. By requesting patron opinions on the quality of the collection, convenience of hours of operation, and suitability of other services, the library can evaluate its success in satisfying its patrons.

In some circumstances it may be appropriate to measure performance against external standards provided for similar circumstances. Possible standards might be the state-mandated number of books per student, the turnover rate of the collection in libraries of similar size, or guidelines provided by national, state, or local associations. Several outside organizations provide quantitative standards for the evaluation of library resources and services. State libraries or departments of education, accrediting agencies, or divisions of the American Library Association provide standards by which an individual library may be measured.

The evaluation process should be ongoing throughout the operating period but should be emphasized when long-term planning and budgeting for the new fiscal year are taking place. By analyzing the successes and failures of the past, the library may best plan for the future.

Summary

Reports during and after the library's operating period provide a basis for ongoing review and evaluation of the library's programs. Management reports can provide early warning of problem areas so that these areas may be investigated and corrected before a situation is out of control. At the end of the operating period, financial statements are prepared on an accrual basis, displaying the organization's financial position for interested external parties. To ensure that these statements are prepared with consistency and in accordance with generally accepted accounting principles, an audit may be performed to verify that the information on the statements presents a fair picture of the organization's financial position. Auditors are likely to check internal control and trace a sample of transactions to ensure that the statements are reasonably correct and at the end of the audit will issue an opinion as to the fairness of the statements.

Throughout the operating period and at its end, the library may use various methods of evaluating its success in achieving its goals and objectives. The audit report, patron surveys, and comparison of actual performance with the plan and with external standards are methods that may be used to evaluate the performance of the library in order to improve its service in the future.

Additional Reading

Anthony, Robert N., and James S. Reece. *Accounting Principles*. Homewood, Ill.: Irwin, 1988.

Anthony, Robert N., and David W. Young. *Management Control in Nonprofit Organizations*. 4th ed. Homewood, Ill.: Irwin, 1988.

Bryce, Herrington J. *Financial & Strategic Management for Nonprofit Organizations*. Englewood Cliffs, N.J.: Prentice-Hall, 1987.

Clark, Philip M. *Microcomputer Spreadsheet Models for Libraries*. Chicago: American Library Association, 1985.

Cummins, Thompson R. *Planning, Measuring, and Evaluating Library Services and Facilities*. New York: Neal-Schuman, 1991.

Horngren, Charles T., and Gary L. Sundem. *Introduction to Management Accounting*. Englewood Cliffs, N.J.: Prentice-Hall, 1987.

Machalow, Robert. *Using Lotus 1-2-3: A How-to-Do-It Manual for Library Applications*. New York: Neal-Schuman, 1989.

Razek, Joseph R., and Gordon A. Hosch. *Introduction to Governmental and Not-for-Profit Accounting*. Englewood Cliffs, N.J.: Prentice-Hall, 1985.

Smith, G. Stevenson. *Accounting for Librarians and Other Not-for-Profit Managers*. Chicago: American Library Association, 1983.

———. *Managerial Accounting for Librarians and Other Not-for-Profit Managers*. Chicago: American Library Association, 1991.

10

Automation in Libraries

While the functions of budgeting, controlling, and reporting on operations can be performed effectively with manual systems, the rapid development of computerized information systems has had a significant impact on the management of library operations, and a book on financial management for libraries would not be complete without some discussion of automation. Automation has enabled libraries to provide new and sophisticated services to users but has also presented library managers with new problems in planning for and financing the implementation and ongoing support of the systems and related services.

Modern electronic data-processing systems can store, process, and retrieve large amounts of data, and computers have the ability to collect, organize, and communicate information with great speed. Libraries are turning to computers for word processing, scheduling, budgeting, tracking acquisitions and encumbrances, estimating shelving capacity, computing fines, monitoring payroll information, recording expenditures, and handling numerous other applications. Many libraries today also have automated systems for cataloging, circulation, patron access, and other standard services. These systems provide libraries with greatly improved control over their collections because the status and location of items can be instantly determined. Combining the technologies of computers and telecommunications, libraries can retrieve information from other locations, providing opportunities to share information and resources.

To make decisions concerning any aspect of library automation, it is necessary to have a basic understanding of computers and some of the services that the new technology provides. A brief review of some computer terminology follows; for a more thorough explanation, consult an introductory book on computers and computer systems.

Basics of Computerization

A computer system consists of *hardware*, which includes the computer and any peripheral equipment, and *software*, which includes the instructions for operating the computer. The principal component of the computer is the *central processing unit (CPU)*, which consists of a control unit to process the instructions for manipulating data, a storage unit to store the instructions and the data to be manipulated, and an arithmetic unit to perform high-speed calculation and comparison of the data. Storage often is described in terms of memory, with the most common type of memory being *random-access memory (RAM)*, which can be revised as well as read. Another common type is *read-only memory (ROM)*, which can be read but cannot easily be altered. The CD-ROMs that have become so popular in libraries are simply compact discs with read-only memory.

In addition to the CPU, there are hardware devices for recording input, storing data, output, and communications. Examples of these are keyboards for input, tapes and disks for storage, printers for output, and modems for communications. Devices in direct communication with the CPU are *online* (keyboards, printers, and modems), while those not in direct communication are *offline* (tapes and disks).

The most important part of the software is the *program*, which has the instructions for the computer written in a language that may be used by the computer. Programs determine what functions the computer will perform, and the accuracy of the results is dependent both on the accuracy of the data and the correctness of the program. Most computers require an *operating system*, a set of master programs that control the way in which other software can be used in the computer.

Mainframe computers are large central computers that can store and process large quantities of information. They usually serve several departments in an organization and are accessed by telecommunications lines linked to video display terminals and keyboards, which have no computing power on their own but are linked to the main computer and provide the means for a user to send or receive information. *Minicomputers* have less power, speed, and storage capability than mainframes but are smaller and less expensive and are often suitable for the applications required by small organizations or by departments within a larger organization. *Microcomputers* are run by a *microprocessor*, which is a single microcomputer chip with sufficient capabilities to function independently when linked with a terminal and keyboard. There are a wide range of microcomputers available, and many are capable of performing functions recently reserved for minicomputers and mainframes. Increasing power, decreasing prices, and a vast array of software have placed microcomputers within reach of large numbers of people, and many libraries today offer their patrons ready access to microcomputers for personal use.

The smallest unit of information to be processed by a computer is a *bit*; these are grouped into larger units called *bytes*. Computer information is stored in *files*, which consist of a number of *records* made up of individual *fields*. For example, the catalog file for all the books in the library would consist of a record for each book, and each record would contain the fields for the author, title, publisher, date, and classification number. A patron file would consist of a record for each patron, and each record would have fields for the patron's name, mailing address, city, state, zip code, and phone number. When designing or implementing a system, it is important to know which files, records, and fields will be needed as well as the amount and type of data to be stored in each.

An entire collection of stored data is referred to as a *database*. The database may be used by various programs, managed by special software known as *database management systems (DBMS)*, or accessed through information retrieval systems. Since many of an organization's files contain interrelated information—for example, the acquisitions, cataloging, and circulation files all contain information on the library's collection—it is becoming appropriate for many of these systems to share a common database in an integrated system.

Telecommunications

Communication between a terminal and a computer at another location requires some telecommunications capability. Data may be transmitted over telephone lines through the use of a *modem* (*mo*dulator-*dem*odulator), which converts the information used by the computer system to sound waves that are then transmitted over telephone wires. By connecting with systems owned by other users, the library may have access to resources far beyond those it could maintain alone. The speed of data transmission is measured in *baud* units, which is the number of bits transmitted per second. Because information retrieval charges and telephone charges are usually based on time, the baud speed of the modem is a very important factor in the cost of information transmitted or retrieved over telephone lines.

It is possible to connect several microcomputers with a *local area network (LAN)* so that they can be used independently or as part of the system. This type of system is especially useful if any of your library staff wishes to use the computers for word processing or spreadsheets. Such a network requires a *fileserver* (a dedicated microcomputer), as well as additional microcomputers that are supplied with the necessary LAN equipment. Software to run the network is also needed, as is cabling between the computers. Successful management of the network may require a significant amount of staff time and is a factor to be considered before selecting a LAN.

Types of Information Systems

Many types of information systems may be used in libraries. *Transaction processing systems* substitute computer-based processing for manual procedures, deal with structured routine processes, and are especially useful for repetitive functions. This type of system often is used for routine activities and record-keeping applications, such as purchasing, circulation of books and materials, and payroll functions.

Management information systems often use data that result from transaction processing but add specific information that can be used in making management decisions. These systems deal with recurring issues and are developed to produce regular reports containing the information required to make certain decisions. Because the information and the format are predictable, the system can be designed to produce the needed reports at regular intervals. Management information systems are particularly useful in reporting and analyzing accounting information to be used in financial decision making, such as comparisons of budgeted and actual expenses. Several of the management reports discussed in Chapter 9 demonstrated how the computer can be used to provide managers with specific information that can be analyzed rapidly and acted upon.

Decision support systems may be useful to managers in making decisions without clear procedures or identifiable factors and must have greater flexibility than other information systems. The key factor in using such a system is determining what information is needed to make a decision. The user must define certain needs and request specific information to produce custom reports containing the information needed to make a unique decision. This type of system requires ongoing user involvement and a fairly high level of user sophistication and is less common than transaction processing or management information systems. Many excellent systems provide managers the ability to obtain selective information by creating their own reports from data already in the system. For example, by creating a report that shows how many materials were checked out at different times during the month, you might decide to change the library's hours of operation or increase the tasks that are handled at the circulation desk during certain hours.

Most libraries require some combination of information systems and must find the best alternatives using the resources available. In some cases it may be most reasonable to design and produce a system specifically tailored to the needs of an individual library, while in other cases it may be possible to purchase and install a system that already has been designed to perform a broad range of tasks common among libraries. In making a decision about the selection and implementation of any kind of information system, there are certain basic procedures that should be followed.

The Feasibility Study

Once it is determined that some type of information system is needed (in addition to or in place of what is already available), it is necessary to clarify exactly what is needed and to determine the reasonableness of the request. A feasibility study should be done to determine what technology is required, what the costs and resulting benefits would be, and whether or not a new system would be accepted and used.

The feasibility study provides for a thorough investigation of a potential system before resources are committed. The study should be conducted by a project team, whose membership depends on the size of the library and the organization. If there is limited expertise within the library, the librarian and other staff members may choose to join with the systems staff of the organization or with members of the library board. Designation of a project team consisting of both users and systems staff helps to ensure a flow of communication throughout the project. Care must be taken to ensure that library users are well represented and that the benefit of the library staff and patrons takes priority over any individual interests.

Several steps are necessary in arriving at a decision concerning a new automated system. First and most important is a *needs analysis*, where the team decides which functions should be automated—which are necessary and which are optional. Part of this analysis should be based on a review of the existing system and the functions performed, such as acquisitions, reference, patron registration, circulation, and reporting for management and administration. A survey of tasks, collection of documents, and review of procedures used in the current system are techniques that can be used successfully to gather information about the various functional areas. Questionnaires and interviews with personnel who perform various tasks are also useful.

When information on the current system has been gathered, it should be analyzed to determine which tasks should be automated, what additional information is desired by the staff, and what changes in forms and procedures may be needed. Good candidates for automation are repetitive tasks that require large amounts of staff time; clerical staff members who perform these tasks should be involved in the planning process. Systems that will be used by library patrons should be very easy to use, and each system should have sufficient power to allow a user to accomplish a task rapidly.

If you are planning for a management information system, you must decide what information you need and what types of reports you require. A satisfactory system should be able to accept the information you have, process it, and produce reports that will be useful to you. A report writer that allows you to design and produce your own reports is a valuable option and will provide you with a useful decision support system.

There should be a determination of the volume of data to be processed and stored. In planning for any type of automation, the long-range needs of the library must be carefully analyzed. Growth of the collection, changes in the service area, conversion of current records, staff training and support, and capital and operating costs are all important factors to consider. If growth is anticipated, the selection of software and hardware should include plans for such growth so that purchases will not immediately become obsolete and need to be replaced. It is possible to select products that allow for expansion and updating, although these may be more expensive initially than a system that must remain static.

Any limitations on your selection of hardware or software should be determined carefully since there are often constraints that eliminate the consideration of certain products. If your library or organization already has computers, you probably will need to restrict your choices to software that can be used with existing computers or compatible ones. External factors, such as the opportunity to obtain local support or expertise on a certain product, may also be worthy of consideration.

It is often difficult to prove that an automated system can save money for an organization; instead, the system is usually intended to provide better service and more timely information for patrons and managers of the library. A cost-benefit analysis may be appropriate if benefits can be quantified in terms of dollars and cents. Examples might be a comparison between the cost of an online search and a typical manual search to obtain information or a savings in current periodical costs due to availability of certain online information.

When a recommendation is ready and it has been determined that a new system is feasible, a written report should be prepared for presentation to management. The report should include a brief description of the present system, current problems, the recommended solution and at least one alternative method, costs and benefits of the proposed system in comparison with the present one, a description of the work required for a successful implementation, and the changes and benefits that will result.

In addition to providing funds for the installation of a new system, senior administrators must provide support and active involvement when necessary. They also must make a commitment to the future to ensure that sufficient funds will be available to maintain the system, since maintenance charges for hardware, software, and necessary supplies must be included in the operating budget each year.

Selection of an Automated System

Whether to design and implement a system internally or to purchase packaged software (which may need some customizing to fulfill the needs of a particular library) is a decision that should be made carefully. Factors to be considered are the cost of the various options, the time required to write customized software, the availability of programmers to write and document the system, and the ability to maintain and update the system after implementation. Much of this information should be accumulated during the feasibility study, and the recommendation may be included in the report for senior management.

If very little money is available for automation, an inexpensive microcomputer and some off-the-shelf software may be a worthwhile starting point. If an inexpensive software option is selected, it is helpful to acquire one that can be *exported*, or transferred, to a higher level of software; this will prevent the need to reenter data if the library decides at a later date to upgrade. In other words, you may select a simple and inexpensive package to use this year but decide you need (and can afford) a more complex and expensive package next year. If your old software can export data and your new software can import it, you will not need to reenter all the data from your current files.

Most software programs today have the ability to export and import to ASCII files. ASCII stands for American Standard Code for

Information Interchange, which is a common format for storing information in a computer. Because of this standard, it usually is possible to convert information from the format needed for one software program into a format that may be used by a different software program.

In an organization with a strong systems staff, the design of the new system may be completed internally. Large organizations often have a staff that may be qualified to develop a customized system, while smaller organizations usually retain consultants or purchase software that has been produced for a similar purpose. If an organization has the ability and desire to design and implement the software, systems analysts who design the system need to work closely with those managers and librarians who will eventually use the system so that the needs of the library will be adequately met when the project is completed. It is becoming increasingly more practical to purchase systems that have been designed for common uses.

Whether selecting or designing an automated system, it is important that adequate internal control be present to ensure the security of the system. The physical security of the hardware and software is only one aspect to be considered since controls must also be adequate to maintain the day-to-day integrity of the system, particularly a system that will be accessible to library patrons. If financial records are maintained in the system, it must be capable of creating an audit trail and maintaining records for audit purposes. If such controls are not present in the system, they may be very expensive or even impossible to add.

Cost Factors in Selecting an Information System

There are many costs to consider when planning for an automated information system. Because of the continuing advances in computer technology, the average level of costs for both hardware and software has been decreasing. Although you probably will be consulting with experts before you make your final decisions, your knowledge of the basics can help to protect you from errors and omissions.

Because an information system includes both hardware and software, both should be chosen before a final decision is made. Your automation needs will probably determine what type of software you choose, and the choice of software then determines what type of computer is required. The combined costs of purchase and maintenance likely will be a determining factor in your selection.

If a microcomputer is selected, its cost should include the CPU, monitor, disk drives, and keyboard. A mainframe or minicomputer should also include a budget for the purchase of terminals that will share the power of the computer. The computer will require operating system software as well as the specific software that you have selected for your system. At least one printer is essential; usually more are needed for efficient operation. Whether printers are to be available for patrons or only for library staff must be decided. For library circulation systems, a bar-code reader is usually needed.

Prior to installation of a new computer system, some site preparation is usually required so that equipment may be installed and operated soon after it arrives. Space is needed for the computer as well as tables or workstations for the terminals, printers, and work areas. Additional wiring is usually required for the system to function properly, and cabling, electrical connections, and surge protectors (to protect from sudden electrical overload) should be part of the plan. The computer must function in a temperature-controlled environment; therefore, reliable heating and air conditioning are essential. Telecommunications facilities may need to be updated; a modem may be required as well as a dedicated phone line for which both installation and monthly charges must be budgeted.

The computer system likely will require some type of database; how this database is created is an important cost factor. New machine-readable bibliographic records usually conform to a national library standard developed by the Library of Congress. These records are called *MARC (MAchine-Readable Cataloging)* records and are supplied by database-processing vendors, bibliographic utilities, book jobbers, or vendors of CD-ROM products. Most academic and public libraries will find it preferable to select a system that will use this MARC record format; otherwise, the addition of bibliographic records or the future sharing of resources will be extremely limited. Libraries sharing equipment in a corporate environment may find it preferable to use a format consistent with the reporting requirements of their business. You should analyze the value of using MARC-record format in your library prior to designing your system or requesting vendor proposals.

The process of creating a bibliographic database for current materials in the library's collection is called *retrospective conversion*; the method and cost of accomplishing this should be estimated. Because retrospective conversion is a significant cost factor in the implementation of an automated library system, it is vital to thoroughly weed the library's holdings prior to automation. It is important to analyze methods by which existing information may be incorporated in the new system, since the use of information that is already available will usually reduce the cost and time needed for implementation.

Many other costs for system startup and maintenance should not be overlooked. Bar-code labeling of materials may be required; it is generally more economical for libraries to use commercially printed bar-code labels than to print their own. Funds must be available for initial staff training, including travel expenses. Maintenance contracts are usually required on software to pay for user support costs as well as system updates. Continuing funds for obtaining MARC records, if desired, should be anticipated in the operating budgets for future years. Maintenance contracts for hardware ensure that the system will remain functional and that service will be available promptly when needed. When analyzing vendor proposals, be sure that all initial costs as well as amounts for annual maintenance are clearly stated.

If you decide to purchase software from an outside source, it may be appropriate to prepare a *request for proposal (RFP)*, which will include the functional specifications of the desired system and the instructions for vendors to prepare and submit bids. In searching for a vendor to provide an information system for your library, you should consult other libraries in your area in addition to current journals specializing in library technology. By reading reviews and asking a few questions you soon will have an idea which vendors offer systems appropriate for your library.

Specifications should define just what functions the system is required to perform, and what additional functions are desired. Vendors should also be asked to supply the names of other libraries using their systems. To assist the library in its evaluation process, vendors should be required to follow a standard format that includes contract terms and conditions along with financial information. Technical considerations should be kept separate from cost data so that each proposal may first be evaluated on its technical merit without being prejudiced by the financial aspects.

Because of the high costs of some information systems, the difficulties faced by libraries in obtaining capital funding, and the rapid changes in computer technology, you should also explore the possibilities of leasing an automated system and should request vendor proposals for this option as well as the purchase option. Considering the lost interest on the capital or the interest that may need to be paid on borrowed funds, the total cost over a five- to seven-year period may be lower with a lease than with a purchase. This often depends on the current rate of interest at the time the decision is made; leasing is often more attractive when interest rates are high. In comparing a purchase with a lease option, the salvage value of the equipment and the time value of money must be taken into consideration, as discussed in Chapter 6.

Evaluation of Proposals

Vendors who do not satisfy the library's requirements may be eliminated, while those who offer only part of the desired features must be compared by analyzing the importance of those features and the costs of obtaining them elsewhere. In addition to the initial costs, the cost of maintenance and staff support over a five- to seven-year period should be considered to arrive at a total long-term cost.

Example 10.1 shows a five-year cost comparison of the proposals offered by three vendors. All offer the required features and some of the desired options. In the example shown, the costs of the most desired options are added to the original vendor bid so that each system would offer the features most preferred by the library. By doing this we are comparing the costs of relatively equal systems.

First the total startup costs are calculated by adding the cost of the desired options to the original vendor bids. Then annual costs are compared using stated maintenance charges and estimates for communications, personnel, and supplies. A total five-year cost is obtained by multiplying the annual cost by five, then adding that cost to the startup cost. In the example shown, the total five-year cost is lowest for Vendor B, even though the original bid is lowest from Vendor A.

Although cost is an important consideration, it should not be the only factor. Before final selection of an automated system, it should be determined that the vendor is reliable, financially responsible, and competently staffed. Good customer support should be available, and

Example 10.1 ▪ *Five-Year Cost Comparison of Vendor Proposals*

	Vendor A	*Vendor B*	*Vendor C*
Startup costs			
Computer hardware	$100,000	$125,000	$120,000
Communications equipment	6,000	4,000	5,000
Software	32,000	29,000	30,000
Conversion cost	13,000	10,000	22,000
Site preparation	9,000	11,000	12,000
Personnel	32,000	24,000	30,000
Training and travel	8,000	8,000	9,000
Total vendor bid	200,000	211,000	238,000
Additional cost of desired features	16,000	12,000	10,000
Total startup costs	$216,000	$223,000	$248,000
Annual costs			
Hardware maintenance	10,000	9,000	9,000
Software maintenance	9,000	8,000	8,000
Communications	7,000	7,000	7,000
Personnel	19,000	16,000	16,000
Supplies	10,000	9,000	10,000
Total annual costs	55,000	49,000	50,000
times five years	$275,000	$245,000	$250,000
Total five-year cost	$491,000	$468,000	$498,000
Average annual cost	$ 98,200	$ 93,600	$ 99,600

an active users' group can be a good source of new ideas and assistance. Because the vendor's record of quality and service is crucial, other libraries that have used its services should be contacted. If possible, it is desirable to visit some of these libraries to obtain opinions from their staff and to observe their system at work. It may be worthwhile to select a slightly more expensive system that is used by a neighboring library, since you may be able to obtain local assistance, form a users' group, or consider sharing resources in the future.

When the decision has been made to select a vendor's proposal, careful contract negotiation is important. Be sure that the contract contains written reference to all unique items relating to your particular system and that you fully understand the contract before it is signed. You should review it with the leader of your systems staff as well as the attorney who represents your organization and maintain a written file of all correspondence and agreements with the chosen vendor. A further discussion of contracts is included in Chapter 6.

Implementation of a New System

A great deal of teamwork and cooperation are needed to implement an automated system. When the decision has been made concerning vendor selection or internal system design, the project team should develop an overall plan to be approved by senior management. This plan should establish deadlines, identify resources, and assign responsibilities for each part of the project and should be revised and updated as necessary throughout the implementation. A project leader with an understanding of the project and its goals should lead the group and should have administrative support to ensure that the various members perform as required.

The first step in the implementation process is likely to be the installation of the new computer followed by the acceptance test for the hardware and software. Acceptance testing ensures that the basic system functions as intended and that it meets the specifications stated in the proposal and required in the contract. The initial testing should be done by the systems staff and followed by testing by the library users on the project team. Involving the users in the testing phase provides a useful training tool and ensures that the system actually does work.

Training is often provided by the software vendor; in addition to travel costs, there usually is a fee for this service. If a small number of employees is to be trained, it may be more economical to send them to the vendor site for intensive training; it may be cheaper to pay the instructor to come to your library if a large number of personnel is to be trained. If you decide to have training at your site, be sure your staff is scheduled for uninterrupted time and has sufficient preliminary training. (You do not want to use expensive training time to teach employees how to turn on the computer or how to type!) Training for all users should include an overview of the system, how it works, and what functions it can perform. A system shared by many users also requires basic understanding of how different parts of the system interact with each other, since an error made by one user may result in problems for another.

When you have completed the vendor's training materials, you should have a fairly good understanding of the basic workings of the software. The next, and more important, phase is to test the system using your own library data, forms, and situations. The completeness of this phase will be critical to the overall success of your project. Just because the basic system works for "the sample library" does not mean that it will work for you. Adequate training of all system users is a critical factor in the successful implementation of any new system and should be viewed as a wise investment. Library managers and clerks, data-entry operators, and data-processing staff must all be able to perform their functions satisfactorily with the new system prior to the final implementation date. User training involves the use of both the equipment (hardware) and the software and must include sufficient instruction so that users can determine whether a problem that arises is caused by the equipment, the software, or some action of the user. The ability to make this decision helps the user to determine the first steps toward correcting a problem and where to look for assistance.

Before final implementation, all operations to be performed by the new system should be tested by the users. By testing the system in the part of the library where it is to be used, the staff can ensure that the system is functional in a real situation. Re-creating a controlled situation using duplicate data is a useful testing tool. For example, a week's transactions from Circulation or Acquisitions may be entered and results analyzed to ensure that the information provided is both accurate and clear. An excellent way to complete staff training is to have the users perform a sample of their normal assignments using the new system. This permits them to relate the system to their regular work, provides an opportunity to raise questions on how problems may be resolved, and reduces the possibility that the system will be unable to perform certain regular job functions. This hands-on experience, particularly when mistakes are made and corrected, is one of the best ways to learn to use a new system.

One error commonly made during testing of a computer system is to simply erase mistakes and start over; since this cannot usually be done in a real-world situation, it is far more advisable to determine how the mistake can be corrected within the limits of the system. Such a practice can help users develop confidence in the system and often leads to the formation of valuable procedures for preventing errors as well as correcting them.

If some information, such as your patron file or shelflist, is already on a computer, it may be possible for a programmer to convert it to a format used by the new system. If conversions are necessary, be sure that the programs are in place long before your scheduled conversion date and that sufficient data are converted to provide your new system with the capabilities you expect. You should thoroughly test the system using a sample of converted data. Be sure that the system has the reporting capabilities you need and that you can obtain all necessary information from the system reports. If you need to design or customize some reports, do it during this phase of the implementation. Decisions and compromises made at this point are very important to the long-term success of your project.

Documentation of both operating procedures and computer programs is very important in the implementation of a new system. While the original users and system designers may understand all the intricacies of the system, future users and programmers must have sufficient information to operate the system and modify it if necessary. Without documentation, the system may be dangerously dependent on its original designers and programmers. Complete documentation should be provided at the time of purchase of any software package, and any new versions of the software should be accompanied by updated documentation.

Forms and Procedures

During the period of training and testing there should be an explanation of any work changes that will result from the new system. Implementation of a new system provides an excellent opportunity to review and improve procedures. If you have clear procedures with your current system, only simple revisions may be necessary. If you have no procedures at all, this is an excellent time to develop them. Good procedures can prevent many errors, especially if a substitute temporarily needs to perform the work.

Modifying software to fit your library's unique situation may be expensive and can cause problems with vendor support; a simpler and less costly technique is to modify some of your library practices to fit the software. Your old forms may not work; you probably will need to design and order (or print) new ones. Operating instructions, security, backup scheduling, and error correction are only a few of the areas that need to be reviewed and clarified; this should be done during the testing period.

System Security

Before final implementation, it is important to analyze the new user functions and to ensure that each user has access to only those parts of the system that he or she is authorized to use. Programmers should have access only to a test system and not the actual system, and other users should be restricted according to their job functions and the confidentiality of information in the system. For example, several staff members may be authorized to *view* information in the system, but only one or two staff members may be selected to *change* information. It is important to determine and test these levels of security prior to final implementation.

Systems that are available to library patrons should be carefully controlled so that patrons cannot change records or access inappropriate information. Although most libraries respect the confidentiality of borrower records, integrated systems that combine the cataloging, acquisitions, and circulation functions are vulnerable to breaches of information security. Restricting public-access terminals to precise functions controlled by the computer software helps to safeguard patron-specific information.

Passwords, or individual code words, may be used to restrict access to computer systems. A password may be assigned for certain operations, or each authorized staff member may have a unique password. It is important that all users recognize the importance of password security so that they do not inadvertently divulge passwords and allow unauthorized users to access the system.

It is important to have backup copies of the software that drives the systems as well as backup copies of the data in the files. Daily backup procedures should be in place so that if problems arise, only one day's data would need to be replaced or re-created. These copies should be stored separately from the original records to avoid their loss in case of theft or disaster. A disaster-recovery plan should be in place detailing procedures for emergency notification, protection, or removal of critical information or equipment (if time allows) and availability of a backup facility.

Final Implementation

When both the systems staff and library staff are satisfied that the new system will function properly, the final implementation process can begin. Various methods can be used.

A *pilot system*, which is a working version of the system, may be implemented in one area of the library before all areas begin to use the new system. For example, it might be appropriate for the main library to implement the system prior to installing it in branch libraries. The initial experience with the pilot system is often used as a basis for making changes before final installation in all areas. Users of the pilot system may be able to provide valuable training for other users; they will have operated the system in similar work situations.

A *phased installation* allows for the implementation to be done in stages and allows users to become accustomed to using one part of the system before progressing to the next. By beginning with the simplest basics of the system, users have an opportunity to become comfortable with the system before more complex features are used. This also provides an opportunity to further define procedures and resolve problems that may arise. For example, you might wish to add your book collection to the system before coping with the many variables involved with nonprint media. Or you might begin using the acquisitions and cataloging parts of the system before using the circulation system, reserving patron use of the system until your staff is more familiar with it.

One common but complex method of implementation is the *operation of parallel systems*. Using this method, information is processed in both the old and the new systems and compared for accuracy. This requires a great deal of effort and often displays problems that are due to human error instead of the computer system. It is an excellent technique for testing but may be expensive and impractical as a final implementation method. It does, however, provide added security; the old system may take over if there are problems with the new system.

The *direct conversion* method simply replaces the old system with the new one, perhaps over a weekend or even overnight. There are no parallel activities and no old system to fall back on; it forces users to make the new system work. This method requires the most careful planning, testing, and training prior to implementation, since there is less opportunity to correct errors in the system at a later time. It is often most appropriate for financial applications where the conversion is planned for the beginning of a new fiscal year or accounting period.

Ongoing Evaluation

Following the implementation of any system, it is important to review and evaluate it to ensure that it is performing as expected. Provisions should be in place to correct errors as they occur and to revise problem areas as they are recognized. It is helpful for the project team to meet on a regular basis following an implementation so that problems may be addressed and resolved.

Few automated systems are at their most effective during the initial months of operation. Several months after implementation, a thorough review and evaluation of the system is appropriate. Patrons and staff should be surveyed as to areas of dissatisfaction or suggestions for improvement. System performance and vendor service should be reviewed to ensure that it is both satisfactory and in keeping with the contract agreement. Procedures should be reviewed to ensure that policies that were in place at the time of implementation are still valid and are being followed; those that are not relevant may need to be changed. Security should be analyzed and updated if necessary.

When the staff and patrons are comfortable with the new system, there is usually enthusiasm to explore further possibilities in library automation. Technology has opened doors to vast amounts of information, and choosing the best options for library staff and patrons presents a continuing challenge to librarians and library managers.

Summary

Advances in technology have presented many new possibilities in the management of library operations and in the services that are available to library staff and patrons. The speed with which information can be available makes automation a valuable tool for providing standard library services as well as for planning, budgeting, controlling operations, and reporting. Because automation has both short-term and long-term financial impact on the library, any automation project should be carefully reviewed for its overall effect on library costs.

To communicate with systems staff and vendors to select the most appropriate automated system, librarians require a basic knowledge of hardware, software, and telecommunications. The automation process should begin with a feasibility study to explore the available options, their costs, and potential benefits to the library. Following management approval of the study's recommendations, a system can be selected and a plan must be developed for its successful implementation. Testing, training, documentation, and security concerns should be addressed prior to the final implementation, and the project should be carefully evaluated after completion.

Additional Reading

Auld, Lawrence W. S. *Computer Spreadsheets for Library Applications*. 2d ed. Phoenix, Ariz.: Oryx Press, 1993.

Cibbarelli, Pamela, comp. and ed. *Directory of Library Automation Software, Systems, and Services*. Medford, N.J.: Learned Information, Inc., 1992.

Clark, Philip M. *Microcomputer Spreadsheet Models for Libraries*. Chicago: American Library Association, 1985.

Cortez, Edwin M., and Edward J. Kazlauskas. *Managing Information Systems and Technologies: A Basic Guide for Design, Selection, Evaluation, and Use*. Applications in Information Management and Technology Series. New York: Neal-Schuman, 1985.

Dowlin, Kenneth E. *The Electronic Library*. Applications in Information Management and Technology Series. New York: Neal-Schuman, 1984.

Genaway, David C. *Integrated Online Library System: Principles, Planning and Implementation*. White Plains, N.Y.: Knowledge Industry Publications, 1984.

Hobrock, Brice G., ed. *Library Management in the Information Technology Environment*. Binghamton, N.Y.: Haworth Press, 1992.

Matthews, Joseph R. *Choosing an Automated Library System*. Chicago: American Library Association, 1980.

Pacqualini, Bernard F., ed. *Dollars and Sense: Implications of the New On-Line Technology for Managing the Library*. Chicago: American Library Association, 1987.

Plate, Kenneth H. *Cost Justification of Information Services*. Studio City, Calif.: Pacific Information, Inc., 1983.

Rowley, J. E. *Computers for Libraries*. 2d ed. London: Clive Bingley, 1980.

Saffady, William. *Introduction to Automation for Librarians*. 2d ed. Chicago: American Library Association, 1989.

Schuyler, Michael, and Jake Hoffman. *PC Management: A How-to-Do-It Manual for Librarians*. New York: Neal-Schuman, 1990.

Senn, James A. *Analysis and Design of Information Systems*. New York: McGraw-Hill, 1989.

Tedd, Lucy A. *An Introduction to Computer-Based Library Systems*. 2d ed. Chichester, Eng.: John Wiley & Sons, 1984.

Walton, Robert A. *Microcomputers: A Planning and Implementation Guide for Librarians and Information Professionals*. Phoenix, Ariz.: Oryx Press, 1983.

Index

Note: Boldface type indicates an example or figure.

Madeline Daubert began her professional career as a school librarian, media specialist, and library director in upstate New York. Following a move to North Carolina, she obtained CPA certification and held several financial management positions; she was listed in *Who's Who in American Accounting, 1990*. She has conducted workshops, seminars, and a telecourse on library financial management and has taught in library schools in North Carolina, Texas, and Florida.